A COU

THERE IS A REASON

by

JOYCE M KIDMAN

1990

First published 1990 in the UK as A Country Girl's Diary There is a Reason by Joyce M. Kidman.

Published by Nichola Dickinson 2017

Bristol, United Kingdom

ISBN 9781520880006

CONTENTS

FORWARD

My mum was called Joyce Kidman, she was a lovely woman so kind, caring and full of love. When my son Neil was born my mum and dad were wonderful, then we found out that he was disabled so they came every day to help us out.

Then one day she went to pick up my dad from work, a bus hit her (she was never the same again). Always in a lot of pain, one day she read a newspaper cutting about a healer, called Harry Harrison. They drove to Wales to see him when he gave her a healing and told her that the bang (accident) had awakened the poet she had been in a past life.

When she came home she wrote 200 poems, she stood up to write them all. Because of the pain in her back, resting the pad on a large cake tin, then my dad bought her a typewriter as she typed all of the poems with just one finger.

In 1990 I said why don't you write your life story, then as she wrote the book the poems went with every story. She also wrote proverbs as well .

I am sure it was planned that way by God, she was a good healer, she had been given wonderful gifts better than money. She also had lots of astral travels which are in the book.

My mother was a quiet lady and she never knew how wonderful she was to me.
I always called her the mother of mothers.

It has been my quest to get this book out into the world which will help a lot of people.

I am her daughter, Nichola Dickinson.

PREFACE

I started writing this book as my daughter Nichola thought that I should as she used to enjoy all the stories I told her about my past life, and she thought that it would be great if I put them all in a book.

Also my friend Harry Harrison always said to me, "Joyce, you sit and listen to all my stories, but I don't know anything about you," and I replied, "There is nothing to tell." So I thought I would write my story, and when I next went to see Harry I would say, "Here you are! The story of my life up to now," throwing the book in his lap.

So I persevered and it was a struggle to write as I had to stand up, resting my pad on a large cake box because my back was so painful, and I could not bend over, so I had to stand as straight as I could and write a little each day.

But what started as an ordinary story turned into something far greater with me adding poems I had written before I was ill, and yet each one falling into place with each story I wrote, and also before I became ill I had a great feeling of urgency to type all the poems I had written. So Arnold, my husband, bought me a portable typewriter and I typed them all with one finger.

And then my friend Harry passed away and I felt that I did not want to finish the book as it did not seem to matter any more. But each day found me writing a few more lines, and I suddenly felt it was all meant to be, not just a story for my family and friends, but for everyone to read and perhaps to make them think that although I was just an ordinary country girl, I had been given gifts far beyond my imagination, and I only hope that all who read my story will find lessons in love, kindness, understanding and humility.

I also wish to acknowledge with gratitude Mrs Beatrice Watkins of Almondsbury who very kindly typed my story for me.

Joyce M. Kidman, 1990

ACKNOWLEDGEMENTS

I would like to express my thanks and appreciation to all those that helped bring this book to life, were a constant support, never gave up on my dream in publishing my mums book.

Thank you Kate Cymbalista, the elegant copywriter, you so kindly helped to bring this book to peoples attention through the beautiful words used within the book description along with the added tips.

Thank you Stephen Musson, the talented illustrator, for the wonderful cornfield that melts my heart every time I see the cover of the book and my mother on the back reminds me of such beautiful memories. I simply just love what you have done in capturing the emotion through your design, along with your patience of getting the right cornfield and for being a part of this journey within your busy life.

Thank you Rebecca Jordon in particular, for being the inspiring editor, because with out you my mums book would have never been created. You have spent many evening and weekends while working in your day-to-day job to bring this book to reality, especially in going the extra mile. Along the way, you have been patience, have opened my world to digital and have given me the confidence to never stop dreaming. I appreciate all that you have done and for being a catalyst for change in my life, where I am experiencing new things I never thought were possible.

Once again, to you all, thank you, for making my life complete.

With love to you all, Nichola.

Nichola Dickinson, Daughter, 2017

CHAPTER 1

INGLESTONE COMMON

I remember when I was four years of age looking at my mother and thinking how lovely she looked. She was wearing a green velvet dress with a white lace collar. Her hair was dressed softly round her face and drawn back to the nape of the neck into a bun. And myself, dressed in a short skirt and top with a little apron to keep me clean, my hair short with a fringe. My name is Joyce and I have four sisters, the eldest being Winifred, then Bess, Milly and Dorothy. Dorothy and I were the only ones left as my three other sisters were married.

We went to school at Wickwar. It was a very long way to walk - two miles - and when it was cold and raining it was a struggle to keep walking, and in the warm days we used to linger by the streams and play ships with the pieces of wood we threw in.

Dorothy was always a bit of a tomboy. There was a Mr Bleaken who always cut down the thistles on the Common with a long scythe. My sister for a bit of fun ran and jumped on his back, but what a shock she had - it was not Mr Bleaken but a Mr Carter who was helping that day, and was he mad! After picking himself up off the grass he chased her threatening all sorts of trouble for her. She never did it again.

We used to skate on the frozen ice just outside the door. What fun we had! We all looked like a lot of ragamuffins as in those days money was very short, but it was the companionship that counted, and we always shared with each other in our games.

Dorothy used to take another little girl to school to look after her, but she always had half of her banana for doing so. She was a little bit of a bossy boots.

Sunday mornings you could hear the church bell from Hillesley calling people to worship. It was a single DONG, and the chickens strutting around in the sunshine picking at this and that, clucking all the while, made it sound very dreamy.

Dorothy and I went to the little Chapel at the top of the Common, and every year a lovely party was prepared for all the children. I used to love the bread and butter. It tasted so sweet and the fresh cakes and sponges, with lemonade and tea. Also, when we went to school Mum would give us money to buy broken biscuits and crisps from the shop on the hill opposite the school. The packet only cost a halfpenny, but what a treat it was!

I went to visit my brother-in-law's mother with my sister. I had not met her before and I was very curious. The cottage was low-lying. You had to go down steep steps to reach the door. Standing outside was a very small woman with her back to me. She was bending over picking up something. As I stood watching, she straightened up and turned to look at me. I don't know who was the more surprised. Her hair was flowing almost to her knees, and I realised she had difficulty standing up straight, but up she came very slowly, and as her eyes met mine, well, I just stared and stared. It seemed like hours, but of course it must have been just seconds. Her eyes were a very light brown, but they seemed to look right through me. I did not stay very long, but the picture of that lady will stay with me forever.

Mum used to sing to us all the old songs she knew, every word, such as Dolly Gray, Roses in Piccardy, Tipperary and many others, but her favourite was Two Little Girls in Blueland which she sang on every occasion. I loved to hear her sing, and just before bedtime I would always say, "Oh please, just one more".

Christmas time was always a delight. Dorothy and I would go carol singing. One old lady we sang to was very lonely and she would open her door and say, "Come in, my dears". After singing all the carols right through she would give us an orange each and a drink, and were we thirsty! In those days the carols consisted of many verses so that night we only went to one house.

On Christmas Eve we always went to bed early, but not to sleep. We lay awake listening for that quiet footstep on the stairs. As soon as the bedroom door opened we pretended to be asleep. We would hear all the sounds of paper and movement at the bottom of the bed. Then the door would close quietly and the footsteps descend the stairs. My sister would jump out of bed and fetch the goodies, and we would have a midnight feast because, you see, we already knew who Father Christmas was.

My sister and I slept together and we would tell each other stories tickling each other's backs at the same time, but every time it was my turn I was always asleep and Dorothy would wake me up to tell mine with a few digs in the back.

CHAPTER 2

CHARFIELD

Owing to financial difficulties my mother decided we would go to live with my eldest sister, Winifred, and her husband, Alf, who lived at Charfield. Dorothy and I did not want to leave Inglestone Common as we would miss our friends and the lovely woods we played in. But my mother needed someone to look after us while she went out to work.

My brother-in-law had a little black and white dog which I think was a Jack Russell, and his name was Tiger. We soon became great pals, roaming the fields together. We had great adventures, and he understood everything I said. When my brother-in-law played his melodeon he would sit on his back legs and sing with the music. Alf used to like Tiger to catch rabbits, and he always carried ferrets in his pockets which sometimes gave me a fright when they popped their heads out. But one day, on arriving home from school, my Mum said to me, "I have some bad news for you." Some rats had made a nest underneath the chicken coop, and on trying to get them out Tiger was bitten badly on the throat, and he had to be put down. I cannot describe the despair I felt on learning that my friend was dead. I ran out across the fields sobbing and calling his name. It was a long time before I felt happy again, but even then the sadness remained.

My mother worked at the farm doing their washing. In those days she only earned two shillings and sixpence, half a crown, for a whole day's work.

We walked one mile to school. It took quite a time to settle in as I was a very shy girl and I did not make friends easily. I used to sit in the classrooms during playtimes. The teacher was very nice to me. Many times she gave me her own pudding her mother had packed for her. But one day a little boy who always had plenty of money and sweets accused me of stealing one penny as he said I was the only one in the classroom who could have taken it. It was my word against his, but as no-one could find the penny on me, or in my desk, I was given the benefit of the doubt. I did not take it and the penny was never found.

It was the school's Sports Day and we all submitted our work of art and school work for the judges to give prizes. How thrilled I was to find I had a first prize for the neatest sewing. The ticket was pinned to the nightdress I had been working on. So with great joy I waited for my name to be called on the loudspeaker so that my Mum could be proud of me. But no name did I hear. I just could not understand it so I chased back to the classroom where it was in black and white - my name on the nightdress. I asked the teacher what had happened. She looked very upset and told me she would find out what had happened. Later I was called into the classroom and I was told they were very sorry but a mistake had been made and would I accept the prize money instead. But it wasn't quite the same.

We used to have flower shows at Charfield, and all the children would find as many wild flowers as they could - all different species. I would walk miles round the fields and lanes searching for them, but I never won. Someone always had more.

And then the school was busy preparing for a play and when it was ready we would all be going to a hospital at Stonehouse to act in front of children who were ill. I was chosen as the fairy. I could hardly believe my ears. Of course I was very slim and in the dress I looked perfect, or so I thought, and when at the last minute things were changed, instead I was to be the court jester, I was very disappointed, and I did not look forward to the play so much. But on the day I was dressed in a red jester suit with hat to match with bells on and a bugle in my hand. The first time I ran on stage blowing my bugle and yelling, "Make way, make way for the King and Queen", I thought I would die - there was such a commotion in the audience, clapping and banging. I thought they did not like me. I was glad to leave the stage. For the fairy it was a quiet reception which still made me think I was awful, and I just did not want to do it all again. The teacher said, "Don't be silly. They love you - that is why they are making such a noise", so on I went to the same reception. I found myself looking down on the children, and I suddenly knew the teacher was right. Their little faces were all smiles. There were lots of bandages on them, and some could hardly sit up. Every time I yelled, jingled my bells or blew my bugle the children yelled, "More, more", so in the end I was glad I was the jester to bring such joy to little children.

We lived in a cottage at Little Bristol Lane, and we could look across the fields to Church End at the top of Charfield. Just a little way down the road lived a neighbour who had a donkey and cart. He used to fetch coal from the wharf, but one day his son waiting for him in the cart could not get the donkey to move, so his father came and gave the donkey a good slap on the bottom which gave the animal a fright. It chased off with the boy hanging on to the reins and it did not stop until it had run itself out of breath. The little boy did not return until late afternoon very distressed. I felt very sorry for him and for the donkey.

My sister Winifred, who we now call Win for short, went visiting a friend at Charfield, and she told me she would take the short cut home from Church End to Little Bristol Lane. Well it was very late and getting dark and she still had not arrived home so my mother decided to go and meet her. The short cut was a very narrow path with high hedges each side, and it looked very spooky in the dark. Anyway, my Mum came back home without her and we were all very worried. It was nearly midnight when she arrived very upset and shaking. She said she had started down the path and had seen a ghost walking towards her. She just turned and fled, and decided to return another way. Well, on talking about it and the time it happened, we realized Mum was the ghost because she did not wear a coat as the evening was warm and as she always wore an apron which she had not removed. The apron was white and she hadn't thought how much it would show up in the dark, so of course Win thought it was a ghost. She never went up the path again. Although we joked about it after, the fear still stayed with her.

I joined the Brownies and Dorothy joined the Girl Guides. We used to have picnics by the streams and learnt all kinds of things about how to look after ourselves. About this time the children gave us nicknames - Dorothy was called Pop and I was called Pip. I still don't know why.

We used to walk home from school. In front of us were two boys from the farm at the end of the lane. They went to the Grammar School at Wotton-under-Edge. Every day they were fighting, bashing one another with their satchels, and we weren't much better. Dorothy was always bossing me like elder sisters do. In fact, one day, going to school, my Mum had bought me a fluffy mauve beret. I thought it was wonderful, but during an argument with my sister suddenly it was whipped off my head and thrown over the hedge into the field. I had to go all the way back until I reached the gate and then walk through very wet long grass to find my beret which also was wet through. By then my sister had already gone to school and I had to follow on my own.

We used to go paddling, and some who could swim swam in the deeper water of the streams. It was all great fun.

It was about this time my sister Win lost her first child. It was stillborn. She was very unhappy and I remember her packing away all the baby clothes out of sight. I also had been looking forward to taking the baby for walks. I recall I was about seven years old then. My sister Dorothy was eleven.

Dorothy used to give me rides on the back of an old bicycle. One day I caught my foot in the back wheel, and I nearly ripped off my big toe. It was very painful for a long time, and the nail never grew properly again.

We didn't like the boys stealing birds' eggs so we used to tell them off, but one day my sister

Dorothy was shot in the face with a catapult by one of the boys, nearly losing her left eye.

One Sunday morning Dorothy lost the paper money and my brother-in-law, Alf, was very angry. He chased her down the lane. She very quickly climbed an ash tree and she would not come down. He said, "Alright! You wait until you come home! You can't stay there forever!" I was very worried because I knew money was so short that to lose any was a crime. Dorothy crept back into the house when she thought it was safe, but Alf was waiting. Dorothy was halfway up the stairs and I had joined her, picking up the poker from the fireplace so that I was standing between them menacingly. I brandished the poker shouting, "Don't you dare touch her!" One look at my face and he decided to leave it, warning Dorothy not to let it happen again.

Alf used to work at the clay pits at Charfield. It was very hard work and very thirsty work, so on the lunch time he used to call at the local pub for a pint of rough cider to have with his sandwiches, and sometimes more than one.

Summer evenings, when we were sent to bed and it was still light, Dorothy used to jump out of the bedroom window into the field at the back of the cottage and walk round to the front door when she felt like coming back.

I used to love curling up in a half-open doorway wrapped up in coats, listening to the wind. It always made me feel dreamy and so glad that I was in the warm. The door was a faded pink colour with a latch to open it. It was never locked as there was never any fear of anyone breaking in.

The lane we walked from school was lined with lovely old oak trees with branches that interlocked across the road. On warm days it was nice and cool from the sun, and wet days shelter from the rain. A friendly little tawny owl sat in the centre branches. One day, as I looked up, we both stared at each other inquisitively. I passed underneath and then looked quickly back, but the owl was a bit faster. In fact it looked exactly the same as it did from the front view. It was as though we were playing a little game backwards and forwards. Of course I learnt later that an owl can turn its head right round without moving its body.

My mother had not been feeling very well and had to take to her bed leaving us all very worried. She became very weak and my sister Win called the doctor to see her. He told her that Mum had pernicious anaemia and that she should have a blood transfusion which she refused. The doctor said there was no chance of her living without it and she was given the last rites. What an up setting time that was with lots of tears for us all and sadness. I could not imagine our lives without her. But like a miracle she did not die. She was a very strong-minded woman and I think that is what pulled her through. She was very weak for a long time, and she lost all her lovely long hair.

Mum used to sit and talk to me about the past, how she had been an orphan. She remembered that she had sisters and brothers and something about living in a jeweller's shop. Her memory was not very good. She must have been very young. She did a little nursing as she grew up, and when she worked at Windsor Castle as a maid her maiden name was Amelia Nicholls. There she met and married a sergeant in the Grenadier Guards when she was twenty-one whose name was William Dowsell who later died from war wounds in the 1914 to 1918 war.

While Mum had been ill we had been very short of money as there was no extra money from her work coming in. We were offered help from a charity to buy Dorothy and me new shoes which Mum was pleased to accept. But when the time came to fetch them we found out they were boots. We were very upset as we knew if we wore boots to school we would be the laughing stock of the children. After lots of tears Mum decided not to accept them. We would wait a little longer for new shoes.

About this time Win and Alf decided to move to Hillesley. What a day that was! It was alright until we came to move the wardrobe down the stairs which were very steep, narrow and crooked. Alf could not move it easily and it got stuck on the stairs. He pushed and pulled for ages. With all the bangs and swear words it was like a comedy script. In the end he gave up and said, "I am going out for a drink". Later he came back happier and he had another go with all of us helping. Finally we got it down the stairs to the waiting lorry. Then we were off to our new abode.

CHAPTER 3

HILLESLEY

We arrived late, but we all settled in quite amiably. It was a big three-storey house with a very large walled garden. Alf was a very good worker in the garden and Win took in washing to help the funds. Every Monday she would work all day, washing and boiling the clothes in the old fashioned boiler with the little fire underneath. You could not see her for the steam sometimes. I am sure she loved it. The clothes lines in the garden were full of beautiful white sheets billowing in the wind and sunshine. My mother still worked at Charfield once a week doing the washing at the farm. She walked roughly five miles still for half a crown, ten miles there and back. It was always late when she arrived home. My sister Win would keep a meal for her.

In fact Win was a mother as well as a sister to Dorothy and me. She was a lovely girl, never lost her temper and was always trying new things to help. She used to make lovely spotted dicks and treacle puddings which she put in a big saucepan in greaseproof paper and a cloth. When she dished it out our mouths would water. They were very filling and tasty. Her garden in the front of the house was full of lovely chrysanthemums of all colours and sizes. On the ground floor there was a long passage and she had a long bench with barrels of homemade wines. I used to collect all the cowslips, dandelions and other flowers and berries for her.

Dorothy and I settled into the new school. In fact Dorothy had passed all her exams at Charfield for the grammar school at Wotton-under-Edge, but unfortunately Mum could not afford the uniform or a bicycle to ride there so she finished her school days at Hillesley School.

I used to join the children playing on the corner as we stood chatting together. We used to play fox and hounds chasing each other through the fields and lanes. All good fun. I met my first badger while I was out looking for flowers. It was just getting dusk and just as I rounded a corner I nearly ran into it. I don't know who was the most surprised. We just stood and looked at each other. I was a little afraid, but I need not have worried as the badger just turned and walked away, and I hurried home.

The gypsies had been camping in a clearing in the wood, on the top of the hill just outside the village. We had already seen them about and sitting outside their caravans, round the camp fire busy cooking, or making pegs, but we only passed by as their dogs would always be on guard to keep us away. The women would knock on our doors to sell us the pegs or any other wares they had. They would also say "Cross my hand with silver, lady, and I will tell your fortune". But our Mums did not always believe that they could and would say "No thank you, I don't want to see the future", but I think they were really afraid to know. It would take a long time to get rid of them unless you bought something. They were very good at selling their wares, and if you didn't buy anything they would walk away muttering under their breath very annoyed.

You would see the men walking about with shot guns in the crook of their arms and a pair of rabbits hanging, tied to a long piece of string, from their waists. They were blamed for a lot of stealing that went on. Perhaps they did have a rabbit or swedes out of the farmers' fields, or maybe a chicken, but I suspect it wasn't always the gypsies that did the stealing.

Then we heard the gypsies were on the move. Someone had passed them coming down the hill. All of us children gathered at the bottom of the hill to watch them pass by, and what a glorious procession it was! First came the head caravan pulled by a small horse that looked hardly strong enough to pull the caravan, the gypsy sitting upright in the front on a small seat giving the horse encouragement, and then there followed about six caravans all very brightly coloured, each one with horse and driver. There were buckets that clattered and banged, hung underneath the caravans, and on every hook they had something was tied. Behind the last caravan all the young children walked, and all the dogs were tied on long pieces of string or rope so that they could not run away, but did they bark! What a noise! They did not trust all us children watching. They dared us to go too near. It was the children I remember, all very solemn, just looking back at us as they passed by. Not a word or a smile we gave each other - all very suspicious and wary. It was just like a scene in a pantomime, all the colours and noise, you would almost expect a jester to appear on the scene to break the tension. Last of all came the spare horses, all tied to each other in a little group. They were very nervous as they passed the cottages. We followed them through the village just watching every move. Every now and then the little children would look back to see if we were still there, with such wondering expressions on their faces. What a lot of stories they could have told us about their travels if only we had said "Hello".

It was the chapel anniversary. I was very excited as Mum said I could have a new dress made for me. It was green with a half tie belt and a white collar. The night before my hair was washed and I had, or so it seemed, about one hundred curling rags in my hair. The next day with my hair all curls, a big white ribbon, new dress, white socks, and polished black shoes, I was frightened to move in case I spoilt something. When I stood up to say my piece, I thought I was a rich girl.

All the boys and girls had a trip to Weston stopping at Cheddar. It was an open top charabanc. We were all very excited, singing as we drove along waving to the people we passed. At Cheddar I lost the heel on my shoe, and all day I had to limp around. It made my leg ache a lot. When we arrived at Weston we saw our first glimpse of the sea. Well it was wonderful! We all shouted and sang, "We can see the sea! like a little ditty over and over. It was a nice dry day and the tide was in. After eating our sandwiches we looked around the shops and the arcade for presents and rock to take home. I bought my Mum a brooch with 'Mother' written on it, and some rock for Win. I bought myself a white beret, but when I wore it, on returning home everybody yelled "Who stole the donkey?" I still don't know why or the connection it made. I always used to admire Dorothy. She used to wear a beret, or should I say almost, because it was so much on one side of her head it was a wonder it stayed on. She had beautiful auburn curls hanging the other side, and she looked a picture. Of course she was working then, and could afford different fashions and she had plenty of boy friends.

About this time Mum said I should l give away my pram and dolls to my sister Milly's girls, Freda and Esme. It was a big decision as although I didn't play with them any more, I did not want to give them away, but in the end I did, but a week later I heard that the pram had been broken and the dolls smashed, but as my Mum said I was too old to play with them anyway.

Once a year there was a big flower show at Hawkesbury Upton and people would gather from miles around. We would have our hands marked to go through the gate into the field. There was a large carnival which paraded through the streets and we all followed a band playing at the front. I loved to hear the music and to have a ride on the Noah's Ark roundabout. It was heaven and to hear all the show people calling everyone to play shove-a-penny or throw a coconut was like a scene in a pantomime. On the Monday following the show people offered the children a free ride on the Noah's Ark roundabout. I could hardly wait. I would rush home from school and walk up the hill to Hawkesbury Upton and wait for the ride to begin. There were so many children trying to get on that it was a struggle to find something to sit on so most of us stood up wishing the ride would never end, and all laughing and singing with the music. We were always sorry when the show people left to go to another village.

I had my first boy friend. We used to write each other little notes, but my sister Dorothy found them and she tormented me. She used to read them out with her now steady boy friend, William Chappell, but to me they were very innocent and personal. Bill, as he was called for short, used to ride a powerful motorbike and he wore a big leather coat, but he was very nice to me.

One day my sister Win, who was expecting a baby, started her labour pains. Mum called the doctor and I was very worried because I could hear her crying. I sat on the stairs just outside the bedroom door. I wasn't going to let anyone hurt her. The doctor arrived. He was very smart and young. He patted my head as he passed. "It will be alright", he said. I waited and waited, listening to all the different sounds beyond the bedroom door, and when all was quiet the doctor and Mum came out looking very sad. "What has happened" I cried, "is she alright?". Mum sat down beside me, putting her arm round me. "I am afraid the baby is stillborn," she said, "and Win is very unhappy". I dashed into the bedroom to see for myself. Win gave me a gentle little smile and said, "Perhaps next time". So that was the second stillborn child for my dear sister Win.

One day I and some other children decided to climb the farm shed to look at the bull that was kept there. It was very dangerous and slippery. At the top of the shed was a little window which we could just reach. On looking in for a moment I could not see anything, and then a sudden movement and I found myself gazing into a pair of melancholy eyes. The bull was tied with a ring through its nose and did not seem to have enough room to move. It just stood there. When I got down on to the ground, I thought how lucky I was to be free and to feel the wind and the sun on my face. I would like to have set it free.

Every Sunday morning a crowd would gather outside the house as the paper man would arrive on his bicycle and he used our wall to lean it on. He also sold chocolates and cigarettes. He rode all the way from Inglestone Common. In the summer a man came round on a motorbike with a side-car, and sold ice-cream which was delicious. Everybody had one, and we would stand around licking and talking as it was a big occasion.

I remember one time when my girl friends and I used to sit on the outside lavatory and smoke paper cigarettes with the door shut so that no one could see us, but after one mishap I decided not to smoke any more as I drew in so hard to light up the paper that I set fire to my eye lashes, eyebrows and hair. My Mum tried everything to find out what I had done to be in such a mess, but it was a case of `on my honour' with my friends not to tell.

Near Bonfire night all the children would gather together paper, rags, wood and anything that would burn, and carry it about half a mile up to a hill called the Mears. It was a very big Bonfire and on the night, when it was lit, it could be seen for miles around. What fun we had letting off all the fireworks and hearing the loud bangs.

I remember a little old lady who lived on the end of the row. She had a very bad birthmark on her face, but she always loved talking to us all and would always be seen leaning on the gate waiting for someone to pass by.

At school it was time for me to move up a class and I was rather worried as I knew the headmistress was very strict. The first day, on looking up from writing, I looked right into her eyes watching me, and as I have always had a born insight about people I knew I was in for trouble. I was not a clever pupil, in fact I was a bit of a dreamer which did not suit the headmistress. I cannot remember the many times I held my hand out for the cane, but I never cried. I think she wanted to break me, as each time it was a little harder. In the end I could not sleep and I did not want to eat as the worry of going to school became too much for me. It came to a head one day. I was kept in for something quite trivial. One of the children told my Mum and sister Win about it. Suddenly the door opened. In came Mum, and behind her my sister Win with her sleeves still rolled up to her elbows from washing. They took me home and called up the doctor explaining my worries and not eating or sleeping. He said, "You must take her away from the school or you are going to have an ill child on your hands", which they did.

I was accepted as a pupil at Wickwar School, the school I had attended all those years ago. Mum bought me a second-hand bicycle, and I had to ride four miles every day, but I was a lot happier. The first day, riding through Inglestone Common it was like returning home. The little cottage where I used to live was still there, and I felt I wanted to linger about. I did not have the time to see more of the familiar places - the woods, the lanes, the bridge over the little stream which I had thought about so many times.

The first week at school was very hard with so many hills to walk, too steep to ride all the way. I don't know which hurt the most - my feet, my legs or my bottom from sitting on the hard saddle. Playtimes at school I just rested, but I soon became used to it, and my energy returned. Then Win and Alf decided to move again.

CHAPTER 4

KILCOT

Kilcot was another mile for me to ride, so now it was five miles a day. Kilcot was very low lying, with hills and woods surrounding it with lots of little streams, farms and cottages scattered here and there. Our cottage was big enough for two families. The garden was also large with a stream running through it. We had to cross the bridge just outside the back door. We had lots of gooseberry bushes, and when the fruit was ripe I used to fill the basket for my sister Win to make jam, helping myself at the same time. The lovely ripe fruit was just too delicious to leave alone.

Win became a barmaid at the Portcullis pub at Hillesley, and Alf used to play his melodeon and entertain the customers. One night on returning home he missed the corner in the dark and rode his bicycle straight into the farm pool. That was the end of his music. I am afraid he came home a very sorry sight, wet through and swearing.

Weekends I did all the shopping, riding to Hillesley for lovely fresh bread. The baker's name was Mr Coates. I was always loaded with shopping bags, and sometimes oil containers. Many times I fell off my bicycle and broke bottles which I had to return for. I used to buy fresh jam doughnuts, and for a treat I was given one to eat on the way home, the jam oozing through my fingers.

Dorothy married Bill at Hillesley Church - a lovely day. She had four bridesmaids - Bill's sister, Dorothy Chappell, my sister Milly's two girls and myself. Dorothy wore a long lemon dress with big puff sleeves and a picture hat. Bill's sister, Dorothy, and I wore long pale green dresses with puff sleeves and picture hats. Milly's girls, Freda and Esme, wore pink dresses and a circle of flowers round their heads. My sister Win was maid of honour and Mum, Bess and Milly looked very smart. It was so nice to have all the family together. Dorothy and Bill lived with us until they could find a nice house.

I bought myself a mouth organ to keep me company to and from school. I would whizz down the hills on my bicycle playing my favourite tune, "When it's springtime in the Rockies", and evenings I would play records. Win and Alf had an old gramophone like `His Master's Voice'. There was a tin full of old needles which I changed every now and then, but they had been used so many times that the scratching was terrible. The records weren't much better. My favourite was Sandy Powell singing "What's the price of swedes Sammy".

I made friends with another girl. Her name was Vera Bull who lived at Kilcot. She tried to teach me how to tickle and catch trout which abounded in the streams. We lay on our tummies with our hands searching underneath the banks, but I did not like the feel of the slippery trout, and I was always afraid of what else was lurking under the stones. We also used to pick the fresh watercress for sandwiches, and would walk to Upper Kilcot as far as the main road which travelled from Bath to Stroud, and there we would wait to see if any cars passed by. It was quite an event if we saw any. Then on the way back, which was about one mile, we would pick wild strawberries. It would be a day out for us as we were in no hurry.

There was a big mill pool where the trout were leaping up and down. The herons could be seen waiting on the edges to catch their meal, also a pair of swans who nested there and would become very agitated as we passed by, half flying across the pool with their necks stretched out and hissing a warning to us to keep away.

When the rains were very heavy and there were floods, the sluice gates would be opened to lower the level of the water, and when that happened the little bridge in our garden was dangerous to walk over. I used to collect lighting wood for the fire where the bluebells grew, and when in flower they made a beautiful carpet underneath the trees looking so cool and serene. I would meet the children at Hillesley and we would all walk to Alderley village and in the fields we would climb the lovely big chestnut trees and pick the chestnuts, eating as many as we could and taking some home for the family.

Mum gave me a fright one day. She was busy chopping firewood when a big stick flew up and hit her between the eyes. She passed out and all the while she was calling out, "I am coming Will, I am coming Will", the name she always called her husband. I was so afraid I would lose her. She sounded so far away, but like the strong woman she was she returned to us, but she was very giddy for a few days.

On Easter Monday I decided to walk to Hawkesbury Upton to see the fox and hounds meet at the farm pool. It was a very gay sight. The Duke of Beaufort was Master of the hunt and in the centre he rode cracking his whip and calling the hounds by name. The ladies and gentlemen all wore riding habits, the men making a splash of colour in their red jackets and the ladies looking very elegant with veils on their faces and long black skirts riding side saddle, and they were all sipping a glass of wine and enjoying the general conversation before setting off on the chase. Then the Duke blew his hunting horn and they were off, the hounds baying excitedly, knowing exactly what it was all about. The people followed on foot as best as they could, but soon they were left far behind, so I set off once more to return home.

This time I took a short cut through the woods and fields. Just as I was reaching home, and walking down a narrow lane and cart track I heard the huntsman's horn. Suddenly, flying past me, was a fox, followed by the baying hounds. I had to leap on to the bank to get out of the way, and they were followed by the riders galloping as though their lives depended on it. When I reached the end of the track I discovered that the fox had hidden in an old drain just outside my home. One of the huntsmen had sent a fox terrier down the hole after it to drive it out. I stood and watched thinking about my game of fox and hounds. I had played and enjoyed with other children. I still did not realize what it was all about until suddenly the fox came out. I have never seen such terror on an animal's face. Suddenly I knew this was no game like I used to play. The hounds rushed at it pulling this way and that, tearing it to pieces, and I heard someone say, "Quick, get the brush". That was enough for me. I fled home feeling very sick and upset. Never would I play that game again. That scene will stay in my mind forever.

As I grew more used to my long journeys to school, I started to linger as I reached Inglestone Common, riding very slowly, taking everything in and remembering. I would park my bicycle against the gate, enter the wood, and I would watch the squirrels dashing up and down the trees. They were not afraid of me. They were a lovely red colour, or so it seemed in the morning sunshine. I would climb up trees to pick the honeysuckle which rambled from tree to tree, the perfume delicious on the fresh morning air. I would have liked to have stayed in the woods instead of going to school, but in the end I knew that I must go.

The headmaster would look at me when I arrived with the flowers in my hand, shaking his head, and when it was time to leave school in the afternoon, I was left in the classroom alone, writing one hundred lines - `I must not be late for school'. But the call of nature was too strong for me and I wrote those lines so many times and my fingers became very stiff. In the end I gave up and I would stop on the way home instead.

My sister Dorothy was expecting her first baby and one afternoon she started her labour pains. She was resting on the sofa underneath the window crying out every now and then when the pains were hard. Mum started to build a nice fire for comfort for her and also so that we would have lots of hot water in the kettles which was already steaming on the hob. Mum must have overdone the fire because suddenly the chimney was on fire. Then it was panic stations. Burning soot was dropping everywhere. The fire was too far gone to stop. Mum said, "It will have to burn itself out". But that was not the end. It caught the neighbour's shed on fire, the farmer's hay rick and a man's little three-wheeler van that sold wireless sets caught fire outside the window where my sister was resting. The heat was terrific. Everybody was running around with buckets of water to put it out. But I'm afraid that was the end of the van as with the acid in the batteries it didn't stand a chance. I am afraid that our neighbours were not very happy about it all. My sister forgot her pains in the excitement, and in the evening she had a little girl who was beautiful, and she said, "I am going to call her Shirley".

Well it was my dream come true at last - a little baby to take for walks which I did many times.

CHAPTER 5

INGLESTONE COMMON

Mum decided that she and I would go and live with my sister Bess and her husband, Ernest Crew, and their little daughter, Greta. They lived at the top end of Inglestone Common called Orange End, so now I had three miles to ride to school which was a lot better for me.

I used to look after Greta, picking primroses round the fields. She had a lovely laugh, and I would do all kinds of funny things just to hear it. We would also sit by the common gate which divided the common from Hawkesbury Upton, and also it stopped the cattle which roamed on the common from straying. I used to give her swings on the gate which she loved, and also opened it for the cars passing by. The people would throw me pennies for doing so, and it was a great help for my pocket money.

One day I rode with my sister Bess to Wotton-under-Edge to do some shopping and I accidentally ran into her new bicycle knocking out four spokes. She was very upset and angry with me.

Bess had a very bad tempered cockerel who would jump on peoples' backs, pecking their necks. I used to listen to the wireless at night to some spooky plays, but then Mum stopped me because I was sleep-walking, and she had to put something at the top of the stairs in case I fell down. Then I had a very bad attack of measles, and I had to stay in bed. My sister Dorothy and her husband Bill came to see me bringing me a big basket of fruit which I could not eat so Dorothy enjoyed herself.

Then Mum found a little cottage on Hawkesbury common, just for the two of us, but she had to find other work to keep us going.

CHAPTER 6

HAWKESBURY COMMON

So now it was four miles to school for me. It was nice to have our own home, but I did miss the company. I was now enjoying my school days playing hockey on games days, and every Friday Mum gave me pocket money to buy something at the shop on Inglestone Common. I always bought a fresh pork pie and a Turkish delight bar which I would eat sitting by the side of the wood, and I would enjoy every morsel.

I started to linger longer on Inglestone Common, walking home with the other children, and my young niece, Freda. I sometimes gave her a lift on the back of my bicycle until one day, coming down a steep hill, I fell off, dragging my knee all down the hill, holding on to the handlebars, too frightened to let go as I knew Freda might get badly hurt. She had lots of bruises and cuts and I tore the skin from my knee. Freda's father forbade me to give her any more rides.

My sister Milly used to give me some tea and I would stay until quite late. Her husband, Stanley Bowen, was rather strict, and everything had to be done by the rule.

We would all play cricket, making our own teams, everyone joining in. One day, on trying to catch the hard ball, it landed on my head. Well, I didn't know what to do for the awful pain. I didn't like to complain and to be thought a baby so I pretended I was alright, but it took me quite a few days before I was. I didn't even tell my Mum as I knew she would worry.

We would all go into the woods on weekends and make little huts with the branches of the trees, and pretend they were our homes, taking our sandwiches and water for the day. We would visit a place called the Nap, a lovely stream with a little bridge over it surrounded by woods, and spend our time paddling and looking for dragon flies, beautiful blue and green ones shimmering in the sunshine. The cows and horses would also gather there when it was very warm to escape the annoying flies.

I was now doing cookery lessons at school, but when all the other girls were busy making pastry and cakes I always did my favourite dish, rice pudding, when asked to do our own meals. In fact it became quite a joke with the cookery teacher. She would say, "We don't need to ask Joyce Dowsell what she will be doing. We all know". I always had plenty of time on my hands on that day so I used to watch all the other girls who were all so busy making pastry or cakes.

I remember one girl - her name was Lillian Cullimore. She had a lovely new bicycle and on returning to the cookery lessons at the lunch hour she forgot about the clothes line that reached across the gateway, and, as she was riding rather fast, she had no time to stop. The line caught her across the throat, lifting her right off the saddle. She had a very bad cut for a long time. It was an awful shock for her.

Another time at school I felt very ashamed of myself. It was a gathering of all the pupils in one classroom and we were all singing. The headmaster's wife was playing the piano and I was busy chatting at the back of the room. The headmaster saw me and made me stand up for everyone to see. The upsetting part was that my niece was also present and I felt stupid.

There was one narrow lane between Hawkesbury Common and Inglestone Common with very high banks on each side, and if I was late returning home and it was dark, it was like the illuminations on a Christmas tree. The banks were covered with little moving lights. They were glow worms. I would stop and watch and marvel, but I never touched.

The evenings were long and light and the haymaking had begun. We would all hurry home from school, have our tea and then join the farmer and his farm workers. We would all get very hot and tired. The smell of the hay and the fresh air was wonderful. We would ride on the carts laughing and playing. The farmer would give us drinks and sandwiches, and then drive us home. The farmer's name was Mr Gale, and he had an orphan boy living with him. His name was Alan. We became very friendly. It was hard work for him. Early mornings and late nights we used to sit on the farm gate and chat, and I realized he was very lonely. One day he gave me a little parcel and said, "It is a little gift for you". On opening it I found a wristlet watch, my very first. I didn't know what to say. He wouldn't take it back. He said it was for my friendship. Not long after he disappeared and no one heard from him again so I treasured the watch for many years.

The barn was stacked ready for the arrival of the threshing machine. Oh, what a day that was! And what a worry for all the rats and mice that had made the stack their home with their own food store. As the stack was dismantled they would scurry hither and thither to safety with the farm dogs chasing them.

It was a very dirty job separating the corn from the chaff, but the threshing machine did a marvellous job. The men would have the occasional glass of cider to quench their thirst, and to tell each other stories, from which you could hear their happy laughter. The work would have to be finished in one day as the threshing machine visited all the neighbouring farms so there wasn't much time to rest.

One Bonfire night I stayed with my sister Milly so that I could enjoy the fun. All the people on the Common were there. It was a big occasion. Everyone brought fireworks and there was plenty of food. I was watching the big blaze. It was a dark night and the faces showed up very clearly in the firelight. There was a tramp standing on the outskirts and the children and I were a little afraid. He seemed to have popped up from nowhere. My sister Milly had not arrived so I went back to her house to fetch her. There was no one there. The house was in darkness. I became very worried and the joy of the fire vanished. I looked everywhere, scanning the people's faces. There was Freda, Esme but no Milly, so where was she? I was very upset. The fire had gone down and Milly had missed it all. Also, the tramp had joined us now which made me more anxious. Then he spoke to me. "Did you enjoy the bonfire Joyce?" Well, it was my sister Milly and she had dressed up for a joke. I vowed from that day that I would never play a joke like that on anyone as the pain and the suffering is not worth it. My whole evening was ruined, and I told her so. She gave me a kiss and said, "I am sorry you were so worried, it was just a joke", but it took me a long time to forget.

It was about this time that I noticed that Milly always seemed to be lying on the sofa when Freda and I came in from school. I asked her if she was ill. "Oh no", she said, "just feeling tired". But after a while I thought she didn't look well and I told my Mum about it. She called to see Milly who told her she was having trouble with her teeth, but she was afraid to have them out. Then Mum called the doctor who said she must go into hospital as the teeth had poisoned her body. She should have had them out a long time ago. She went into hospital for a checkup but peritonitis set in. She was only in hospital for three days and Milly died.

Mr Gale, the farmer, had given the hospital his 'phone number for emergencies. That same night Mum and I could not sleep. We felt something was wrong. All of a sudden one of the horses on the Common came galloping up to the cottage and started to kick the outside wall. Mum, who always had feelings about things, said, "That is a warning. I am very worried about Milly", and about half past two in the morning we saw the headlights of a car coming down the Common. Our bedroom window faced the road so our bedroom was lit up. We both knew it was about Milly and we were up and dressed before the knock on the door. Mr Gale said, "I have some bad news for you. Milly has passed away."

Mum and I were too stunned to cry then. We both quietly collected what we needed and then we walked in the dark at three o'clock in the morning all the way to Kilcot to tell my sisters Win and Dorothy. About four miles it was. I remember looking down across the Common as we walked along the hill, seeing little lights from the village windows, and I wondered if it was Stan's cottage we could see, and his mother's, and how did they feel.

Mum and I didn't speak a word all the way, each in our own thoughts. When we arrived at Kilcot and knocked up my sisters, well, it was as though a storm blew up, everyone crying, my sisters with their arms around Mum. What a night it was!

And then it was the funeral. I looked after Greta, Bessie's daughter at Orange End. The curtains were drawn, but I sat listening for the sound of the horse and special cart that took the coffins in those days. She was being buried at Hawkesbury Church cemetery. I could hear it approaching and I peeped through the curtains to have a last look, knowing that would be the last time my sister would pass by. The church bell rang a single DONG in keeping with a funeral procession. As it passed out of sight I broke my heart. Since then I have not liked the bells ringing joyfully or otherwise. I was about thirteen years old then.

Going past Milly's cottage on my way to school was terrible, and I couldn't call again at night as Stan's mother looked after Freda and Esme, and she could not have me for tea as well. The headmaster was very kind to me and didn't worry me about being late for school. I missed all the children, but somehow it wasn't quite the same. I didn't want to linger any more.

My sister Win moved next door to Mum, and I and Dorothy, Bill and Shirley moved to a cottage at Tresham situated on the hill as Bill worked on the farm. His father was a farm manager. So when Mum was working Win looked after me again. Win had her third stillborn baby. After the loss of Milly it was a great sadness. Mum said to me, "Don't go into the spare bedroom as the baby is in there waiting to be buried". But I was very curious and I just had to have a look. The baby was lying in a box. It looked so peaceful, like the dolls I had had. I wanted to lift it up and cuddle it and perhaps bring it back to life for my dear sister Win. I touched the little face. It was very cold and still. I left the room and went for a walk thinking about Milly and the baby and how death affects us all.

It was getting near to the end of my schooldays. At school I would stand by the gate with my friends, Jean Philpot and Vera Millard, too big for games any more, talking. The teachers stood in the playground chatting and watching the children at play. Suddenly I felt sad at what I would be leaving although I didn't really like school itself. The last day I rode my bicycle very slowly home. Even the woods were no comfort. So many thoughts rushing through my mind, and as I didn't have a job to go to, a little afraid.

CHAPTER 7

COALPIT HEATH

Mum heard about a job for herself at Coalpit Heath near Bristol, and she could take me with her - a living-in job helping to look after a little boy while the mother went out to business. So we left Hawkesbury Common leaving my sister Win behind. It was very strange for me after the wide open spaces and country lanes. I did not like it living with strangers. I had a big abscess come up on my right cheek. My eye closed up and it was very painful. Someone told Mum about a herbalist who lived not far away so we went to see him. He gave Mum some cream to put on it to draw out the pus and told Mum not on any account to let it be lanced as I would have a scar on my cheek for ever and to go back to see him in a few days. Well the abscess broke. I went back to see him. He was very pleased with the result, but Mum had to keep it clean until it had healed up. I had become a little run down and needed a tonic he said.

And then Mum heard that Dorothy and Bill had moved to Yate and he had left the farm and he was now a lorry driver for Mr William Febry, Old Sodbury. Dorothy asked Mum and I to go and live with them as there were plenty of jobs for Mum and me locally. So I was very happy about the move.

CHAPTER 8

YATE

It was lovely living with the family again. Shirley was about three years old and had lovely golden curls half way down her back. She loved riding her tricycle and we got on well together.

Mum had a job at Parnells cleaning the offices nights and mornings, and I worked in the Dope shop sewing the material onto the different parts of the aircraft and then painting it over. The smell was very strong. Also making seats for the pilots, filling them in until they were hard and firm.

Mum and I would pass each other mornings giving each other a smile as she went home to breakfast and I was just starting my day. No time to stop and talk as I only just had time to clock in and not be late.

Of course the war was on then, so everyone was busy. As I was new I was made the tea girl with another girl called Betty Fry. We would collect all the orders for cakes, rolls, sandwiches and tea, and with a tea trolley we would make our way to the canteen, but what a journey! We had to pass through the erection shop where all the young men worked. What a row! As soon as we entered, first one would bang his metal sheet then the next, and like Indian smoke signals the message would travel from one end of the shop to the other, everyone banging and shouting at two girls doing their job. I was very shy and that made them worse, shouting out and asking for dates, and that wasn't the end. After we had left the erection shop we passed a hangar where all the airmen trained. So once again we were followed by wolf whistles and calls. Into the canteen we went. I've never seen so many airmen at one time, and they would politely move away for my trolley. Twice a day Betty and I had the same thing happen, but I know that to the lads it was just good fun and we soon learnt to smile as we passed by.

I began to visit the Village Hall where dances were held, and I became friendly with a girl called Kay Prendergrast. We dressed alike and everyone thought we were sisters. Of course I always had plenty of partners as the airmen remembered the little tea girl and would ask me to dance. Every Friday, pay day, I would buy myself a new pair of stockings, wash my hair and then with a flower in my hair I was ready for the dance. I loved the music and, as the saying goes, I could have danced all night.

And then the soldiers were billeted in Yate. That was a problem as they would annoy the airmen and there were fights over who was dancing with who - too many men and not enough girls. There was a picture house near the railway station where we enjoyed many happy evenings.

My sister had two lodgers who came from Manchester to work, and every Saturday they would travel to Bristol just to have a bath as Dorothy did not have a bathroom. One of them wore a light pink coloured suit and was very jolly and his name was Charlie Gough. I once had a new hair style with short curls on the top of my head. He took one look at me and said, "What have you done to yourself! You look awful!" So I tried to comb my hair down again, but, of course, it was cut that way so I had to let it grow again and it took ages. He was always chasing Shirley for hiding his papers - all good fun.

I began to notice a young disabled boy who was always standing on the railway bridge watching the trains go by and then turning to watch the people as they left work in the dinner time rush. He had difficulty walking and he would fling his arms out for balance shaking his head from side to side. I never for one moment thought that he noticed me, and then one day as I passed he turned round and said, "Hello Joyce." What a surprise! I didn't know what to say, so I smiled and carried on. But

I took the trouble to find out who he was. His name was Jeffrey Powell and he lived at North Road, Yate. No one seemed to know what was wrong with him. Anyway the next time I passed him and he said, "Hello Joyce", I said, "Hello Jeffrey". Well, it was as though the sun came out. What a smile! And I know in my heart it was because I had called him by name. Each day the same thing happened and I knew he looked for me, and he would watch me out of sight. One night, taking a short cut across the airfield in the dark with a boy friend, someone came ambling towards us and as we all passed each other a voice called out, "Goodnight Joyce". Well, how he knew it was me I just don't know, and I felt very sorry to think of him always on his own. I have often wondered who told him my name.

We lived very near a chemical factory and when some bombs dropped very near to us Bill, my sister's husband, became very worried for his family, and one evening when things became rather hectic he loaded up his lorry and took them back to Tresham. Mum and I had to find somewhere to live as the lease of the cottage was in Bill's name, and we could not afford to leave our jobs. A friend of Mums gave us a bedroom, and we all lived in together, sharing the bills.

I met a young airman about this time. His name was Wilfred Lorton, and he lived in London. He wanted me to be his girl friend and to write to him while he was away, which I did.

I was very pleased when my sister Win arrived to visit us. She came with an urgent message from my brother-in-law, Stanley Bowen. He had lost his mother and there was no one to look after Freda and Esme. Would Mum and I return to Ingleston Common to help him. I said, "Oh please Mum do! It will be a home again with our own family". So we decided to go. Mum gave up her job and I would have to travel by train to Yate each day with a mile and a half walk as well. But the thought of living again in a country cottage was worth it.

CHAPTER 9

INGLESTONE COMMON

It was very sad to walk through the gate and into the cottage knowing my sister Milly would not be there. Facing me as I walked in was a picture of her standing by her open doorway. It was very hard for Mum also as it all seemed like yesterday when she was with us.

Stanley was pleased to see us as it had all been a great strain. Freda was nine years old and Esme about seven. It was like having sisters again. Also it was much better for Mum than working early mornings and late night shifts.

Wilf came on leave to visit me and enjoyed the countryside. We also became engaged, rather young but with a war on age did not matter.

It seemed very strange walking those familiar lanes again, and at night to hear the hoot of the owls as they searched for food, and the foxes barking as they called to each other. And then, when all was still, to hear the song of the maestro, the nightingale. What peace! What joy! I was really home again. The woods were only one hundred yards away. I could look out from my bedroom window to see them.

Win and Alf were now living in a cottage in a little place called the Barton. Just a few steps away from us there were five cottages in all, a little stream which ran through the gardens and at the bottom a big white gate to keep the cattle out. One cottage was a little shop as well where we bought most of our goods and sweets.

My sister Bess lived three cottages away. Her husband, Ernest, worked for himself cutting withy sticks from the woods for sale. He would come in many times with big bunches of wild orchids he had found. He knew the woods so well and all the secret places for the flowers to grow.

Mum would walk about four and a half miles to Yate to fetch our rations as there was more choice of goods there. She would carry her bag all that way and I am sure now that if she had done long distance walking for the Olympic Games she would have come first. What determination she had! I would hurry to catch the train every morning. I didn't need to cut out food to slim - I was always on my feet, running or walking.

My sister Bess and Mum would pick blackberries for the lorry which collected them for dyes. Happy days they were. My sister would hurry in, light the fire although it was a warm day as she had no other way to cook the meals. On would go the kettle. You would hear the clink of cups and saucers as she hurried to make a cup of tea and it tasted delicious.

Bessie's drinking water came from a pool in the garden and you could often see the baby frogs jumping around on the outside, so it was very important to boil all the water. We had a well in the garden. We would all collect the dead sticks in the wood for the fire and have lots of fun doing so.

The Italian prisoners of war were also working in the woods. The Irish came to cut down the trees as the wood was needed and the Forestry Commission girls arrived, measuring and also cutting down the trees. I would walk past and see the open spaces where the trees had been and feel very sad that the peace and quiet was no more.

The American coloured troops would march from Wickwar to the Common. You should have heard them! I wouldn't call it a route march - more like a nature walk with bits of greenery in their tin hats, chewing gum, and every now and then calling out, "Cuckoo! Cuckoo!" They must have heard it as they walked past the woods, and all waving at me as they passed by.

One day some English soldiers went past in tanks and lorries. I was sat in the garden. The tanks would practise riding up and down the rough parts of the Common. One tank came right up to the gate and out jumped a sergeant. Laughingly he said, "Can you tell me the time?", but I noticed he had a watch on his arm, but I went in to look and told him. He chatted for a while, asking me for a date. The other soldier called out to him to hurry up, but he took no notice. What a surprise he had when the tank took off without him, and he had to walk all the way back to Wickwar! Was he mad!

Stan, as we now call him for short, had been working at Wickwar Cider factory in charge of the engines, but he was now called up for war work at Trowbridge - the first time he had ever been away from home.

Stan's young nephew, Leslie Bowen, came down from Derby for a holiday with us. One evening when we were all sat round the fire telling stories, and Leslie was cleaning his gun at the same time, suddenly there was a loud bang, and we were all covered in soot and the fire began to blaze. Leslie had left the gun loaded and accidentally pulled the trigger and the bullet went up the chimney and dislodged a lot of soot. What a mess!

One weekend, when Stan came home on leave, Leslie brought a boy friend down with him bringing their tent for sleeping accommodation. They put it up just inside the wood. Stan, who was always up to jokes, waited for their light to go out then he dressed himself up in a white sheet and made howling noises round the tent. We all watched and listened. Not a sound, and then two frightened lads dashed out of the tent. Stan took off the sheet and we all had a good laugh. But even after that the lads would never admit that they were frightened.

I went to a dance at Wickwar village hall with my school friends, Jean Philpot and Vera Millard, and there I met my husband to be. I broke off my engagement to Wilf as I realized it was not really serious. His name was Arnold Kidman and he lived in Wickwar and he worked for an aircraft factory at Patchway, Bristol, as an engineer. We used to travel to Cherington Lake just outside Tetbury, Gloucestershire, in his Austin car, a lovely peaceful spot for people to swim and sunbathe. We also had a trip to Stratford-on-Avon. We hired a boat to row on the river. I had never rowed before and on a shout from Arnold I turned round and found I had been splashing the water up all over him instead of keeping the oars in the water. He was wet through and a little annoyed. We also visited Anne Hathaway's cottage, and places of interest concerning William Shakespeare, and finishing the day with a picnic by the river.

My sister Bess now had two boys, Colin and Tony. Tony was only about six weeks old. My sister Dorothy decided to live next door to us as when Stan's mother died it was left empty and as it belonged to the family Stan's brother said she could rent it. She arrived from Tresham and with an addition to the family - another little girl called Yvonne. She was very blond and someone else for me to spoil.

We all went down to the Nap one day for a picnic - Dorothy and her family, Bess and her family, Freda, Esme and myself. It was a gorgeous day, but some how fate always takes a hand. While we were all talking, paddling, and eating little Yvonne pushed the pram baby Tony was in and before we realized what was happening she had reached the bank and pushed the pram into the stream. Thank heavens the pram's hood was up as the baby was flung into it and that saved the baby's head. My sister Bess panicked. She stepped into the stream, lifting the baby out and searching all over for cuts or bruises. The baby seemed very stunned. That was the end of the picnic. We all hurried home very quiet and hoping everything would be alright which it was, but the shock stayed with my sister for a few days, and she wouldn't let Tony out of her sight for anything.

One day, after a lot of rain, one of the cows had slipped into a pond full of mud. It was awful. It could not get out. It was like a quagmire, and the cow was at the end of its strength. My brother-in-law, Bill, who had worked with animals, got a rope, tied it round the cow and tugged and tugged until they both reached the bank where they both fell back exhausted, the cows eyes large and white looking terrified. It managed to struggle to its feet and walked slowly away.

Jean and Vera asked me to go with them to a tea dance at the Berkeley Tea Rooms in Bristol. It was quite an experience. Every time the band started up this older gentleman would walk over to our table, very immaculate he was wearing white gloves and white spats and he would bow to me and say, "May I have the pleasure of this dance?" I had never had a chance to dance with anyone else there, but I must admit his dancing, like himself, was perfect.

We had a climbing rose bush outside our bedroom window and one morning, sitting up in bed, I saw a movement just outside. Mum, who slept in the same room, looked up just as our cat, Smudge, reached the sill. It must have given the cat a fright hearing Mum shout and seeing her in all her curlers. It looked so scared and it turned and half fell down the rose bush. I laughed - it looked so funny.

Mr Cullimore was our chimney-sweep. He would push the brush up and say, "Let me know when it comes out at the top", but after talking about this and that while he was working we would forget about the brush and only remember it when it was almost knocking on the front door. All that while Mr Cullimore was adding more rods to push it up. He was very jolly and knew everything that was going on. It took us the most part of the day to clean away the soot as it was all done by brushes in those days.

At Parnells we were all working away, chatting with `Music while you work' playing over the loud speaker when suddenly the sirens blew to warn us of enemy aircraft approaching. What a panic! People rushing in all directions to reach the air raid-shelters. One girl dropped her money. I picked it up to give back later still not really realizing the danger. I had just passed through the end of the Erection Shop when a bomb dropped on it blowing it to pieces. I certainly moved then, almost falling into the shelter with a lot more people. I cannot describe the awful fear of being underground and hearing the bombs dropping overhead. There were some people with us who came from Eastbourne and it was not the first time for them. Their tears and fears were awful. When the all-clear siren sounded, we were all so glad to hear it and to leave the shelter. There were ambulances dashing about, lots of blood everywhere and Parnells devastated. All I wanted was to return home. I caught the train from Yate to Wickwar and began my walk home. On the way my doctor passed me and stopped. He was Dr Dawes from Wotton-under-Edge. He said, "My goodness! You do look pale!", and I realised I was very dirty and still wearing my tin hat which I can't remember even putting on. He said he had heard about the bombing on the radio. Apparently the enemy aircraft had followed the railway line from Wickwar to Yate and there it dropped its bombs, after putting its wheels down as if to land, fooling the Defences, and blowing the watch tower to pieces. He told me to hurry home and to have a nice strong sweet cup of tea.

I was just crossing over to my gate when the door flew open. My Mum and my sister Win came rushing to greet me. Win looked so upset and as she had been washing herself at the time she only had on a vest and long knickers down to her knees. What with the bombs and how Win looked it was too much for me. We all cried and laughed together. "We thought you might have been killed", said Win, throwing her arms around me. I think until then I had been in a kind of daze, and to see my beloved family broke the tension.

It was quite a time before I had another job, and then I was directed for further war work at Wickwar where I was working on machines. And then Arnold and I were married. It was a lovely sunny March day, with a quiet ceremony, just family, at Chipping Sodbury Registry Office as it was wartime. Then we had a meal at Bristol. We also visited the zoo where Arnold was bitten on the finger by a rabbit, and I also remember there were some American soldiers on the Downs playing baseball. They were enjoying their game until one of the players hit the ball rather hard. It travelled through the air and landed in the back of an open army tank which was passing, so that was the end of their game. Were they mad!

Arnold now had a motorbike - a red Norton. I used to ride it myself up and down the Common and with Arnold the pillion passenger, but one day I caught my leg on the hot exhaust pipe. It was very painful, and I still bear the scar. And then we bought an MG sports car, a two-seater.

A Mrs Carter came to live in a caravan in the field beside us, and when we all went picking mushrooms - lovely fresh little white buttons, delicious for breakfast in a paper bag, Mrs Carter always took a sack and she would come back with mushrooms as big as dinner plates, but she would not tell anyone where she found them. We lived with Mum until we could find a house or a flat. Stan very kindly agreed to the arrangement as there was plenty of room while he was working at Trowbridge. Weekends in the warm days we would visit the local public house called the Fox and Hounds. A Mr and Mrs Stephens ran it and their daughter, Joan, who worked in the woods, measuring the trees for the Forestry Commission. Crowds of people would walk up from Wickwar and sit outside with their drinks, enjoying the company and the countryside. It was a treat for everyone.

One day we heard the sound of an approaching low flying aircraft. As it passed over the cottage we realized something was wrong. After watching for a few minutes there was an awful crash. Arnold and I dashed over the fields to see if we could help. The aircraft which was an American Flying Fortress had crashed into the side of

Cherry Tree Farm two fields away. When we reached the farm there was live ammunition all over the place. Arnold went into the aircraft and looked into the cockpit to see if there was anyone there, but it was empty. The American officials came from the direction of Wickwar in their jeeps and were very annoyed we were there first, asking if we had touched anything. Then my husband explained he was a Special Constable and had only been doing his duty which made them a little more friendly. Apparently the American airman had baled out over Bridgewater leaving the aircraft before it crashed. The young lad living in the farm had been asleep in bed, and, as he told me later, he didn't realize what had happened, but the poor lad had all his teeth knocked out. He was only about eighteen years old, and he and his mother went to live in a cottage next door to my sister Bess.

At this time I had given up work as I was expecting my first baby. One day, talking to my sister Dorothy, I had quite a shock. Until then I always thought babies were taken from the tummy. On asking my sister if the scar would be permanent and how the operation was done, she looked quite stunned at my question. "Don't you know where babies come from?" she said. I had to admit I did not and was I worried when she told me! I could not believe it, so I asked my Mum. "Yes", she said, "Dorothy is right". You see, we had never talked about those things in my family. Dorothy thought that I knew being as she had had children, but no one had ever told me exactly what happened.

I was very anxious about it all, as Dorothy explained, only certain people had their babies that way when the baby was not lying the right way round, but not to worry as it was nature's way, and everything would be alright.

I spent my last pregnant days walking round my favourite woods. I was just going to open the gate one day by the entrance when I spotted a movement in the grass. It was a warm sunny day and there in front of me was a family of adders basking in the sunshine. I had heard so much about their poison that I just stood very still. There were about five. They took no notice of me so I slowly and quietly backed away, but all the way home my eyes searched the grass in case I stepped on one.

My sister Dorothy had now moved to Hillesley so the cottage next door was empty again and a Mr and Mrs Crew moved in.

One Saturday morning my labour pains started. What an ache in my back! I just had to walk up and down the garden path. Then my water broke and Mum had me taken to hospital at Berkeley in Gloucestershire. What a night! I felt so lonely away from the family. I wanted reassuring and someone to hold my hand. I was all night in the labour ward and I realised that there was a problem to bring the baby into the world. And then I felt I couldn't stand the pain any longer and I think I must have passed out because when I came to I was alone, still in the labour ward, not having been washed or my hair combed, and no baby beside me as I had seen in pictures. And then the nurse came in and said, "Not to worry". I would see the baby later. So I was moved to another room and washed, and I was too tired to ask questions. After I had rested I asked about the baby. Again the sister said I would see it later. It was a little boy, seven and a half pounds. My doctor came to see me and said everything was alright, just to rest. But when the baby arrived and I looked down I had quite a shock. I could only see part of the little face because it was nearly covered in bandages and the head as well. It was the eyes that drew me - so intense and to me in pain. I will never forget that look, and then the nurse took the baby away as she said it was not well or strong enough for me to have yet.

The baby only lived two days. I was very sad and I thought of my sister Win. Was I going to be the same, not to have a baby? He was buried at Berkeley Cemetery with only my husband there - a very quiet affair. We called the baby Nigel.

And then my Mum arrived to see me. As she came towards me my sorrow rose to a head and I sobbed for she looked just like the flower seller of Drury Lane with a great big wicker basket full of primroses. All the children on Inglestone Common had gone out to pick me some when they heard I had lost the baby - each little posy tied with the lovely green leaves surrounding it. I have never seen so many flowers at one time.

Every window sill in the hospital had a vase of primroses and a big bowlful beside me. When my Mum left I lay and inhaled the perfume and thought about my baby, nine months waiting and then nothing to hold. Nigel was born on 22nd April, 1943.

And then having no baby to feed I had milk fever. The nurses used to bind me up across the breasts. I looked like a trussed up chicken. The bandages would stiffen like plaster of Paris and the smell was terrible. I felt very poorly. My mouth was covered in sores where I had bitten my lips having the baby, and every morning I was given salts to help stop the milk. I became very weak. I was in hospital for a fortnight, and even then they wanted me to stay longer to get stronger, but I knew my healing would quicken once I returned to my favourite Inglestone Common amongst the family.

Three weeks later my sister Dorothy had an addition to her family - a little boy called Royston which made me very sad when I picked him up.

My health slowly returned leaving me very thin with big black circles round my eyes. I looked like a Chinese panda. Then Arnold and I moved to a farm at Wickwar living in with the family but with our own bedroom.

CHAPTER 10

WICKWAR

Mr and Mrs Parker were the names of the farmer and his wife, and they had a daughter who was a nurse at Chipping Sodbury Cottage Hospital called Mary. Mr Parker was very jolly and he used to tease me, especially when Arnold cut my hair one day. He said it looked as if I had put a basin on my head and cut round it. I must admit it didn't look very professional. He also had a habit whenever we had lettuce for tea. He would shake the water from the leaves underneath the table and laugh, wetting all our legs.

One day Arnold missed his trilby and he could see Mr Parker's hat on the table so he guessed that Mr Parker was wearing his, so on looking for him he found him in the outside lavatory. It was rather funny as, not a bit abashed, he calmly opened the door, took off the trilby and passed it to Arnold. The exchange was made without a smile or a word. It was not until later we could all see the funny side of it.

Mrs Parker would gather fresh fruit from the garden and we would have it before breakfast with lovely fresh cream. She was a good cook and her veal gravies were always made with milk - very rich. She was a very feeling lady, and would get very upset about the ticks she found on the sheep, and she would spend hours removing them. It was a lovely old farm, and I would spend many hours wandering about it.

One day Mr Parker was standing by the front door with his shot gun when he spotted some crows across the way. He lifted his gun, took aim and fired. Well, what a deafening noise! I was standing right behind him and also by his side was his cat. Well, the cat just bolted through the gate and up the garden path and down the road. Mr Parker just looked calmly at me and said, "I always thought that bloody cat was deaf". Well, I had hysterics - it was too much for me. I was not working then as I still was regaining my strength. We only stayed a few months as we heard about a farm at Rangeworthy where we could have our own bedsitting room.

CHAPTER 11

RANGEWORTHY

As soon as we moved in we had a letter to say my sister Win had been taken to Southmead Hospital where she had her fourth baby born, eight weeks premature. The baby, a girl, was only three and a half pounds, so she was put into an oxygen tent. My sister was so thrilled and she called her Dawn Brenda. She was born on the 22nd April, 1944. It was a joy to see them together - such mother love after losing three babies!

I restarted work at the aircraft factory at Patchway, Bristol, and I would travel each day with my husband. We had bought another two-seater MG sports car which I drove as well. I found it very hard - the long hours, especially night work. I was a time clerk so I was kept very busy.

I remember we seemed to live on dried eggs as fresh eggs were in very short supply and our rations were very small. We bought a small primus stove to cook breakfast. Although we had the use of the kitchen in the farm it was awkward as we all seemed to need it at the same time as there were other lodgers besides us. The farm was called Bagstone and it was owned by a Mr and Mrs Smith who had two children, a boy and a girl.

One day Arnold said, "You can have a lie-in today, and I will make a cup of tea". I thought, "Oh good! I can sleep a little longer". But my rest was short-lived. Instead of methylated spirits to light the stove, Arnold had used petrol by mistake, spilling it all round the stove and on his feet. Well, when he lit it there was pandemonium! Everything was burning including his toes. He was doing a real high kick, shouting at the same time. I was out of bed, rushing around finding something to put it out. Well we managed to do so, but I was so worried that the stove might explode. That was the last time I stayed in bed and Arnold had some very sore toes for a while.

One night a lot of bombs were dropped around Rangeworthy and one of the ceilings collapsed in the farm. It was very frightening, and a few nights later Arnold and I visited the Lamb public house at Iron Acton for a drink where the elderly landlady whose name was Justina Brown still served behind the bar although she was very deaf. She was assisted by her nephew whose name was Bob Howes. For lighting in those days there was a big oil lamp hanging from the ceiling which every now and then needed pumping for a better light. Anyway, Justina asked Bob to take it down and pump it up. Everyone was standing around chatting and enjoying their drinks when suddenly there was a loud explosion and everything was plunged into darkness and all was quiet. Then out of the darkness Justina said, "That was bloody near!" But Bob shouted out, "That was no bomb! It was the bloody lamp that exploded!", so of course everyone laughed with relief and we finished the evening with flickering candles.

We had to give up our MG sports car as the petrol was rationed and it was very hard to obtain new tyres, so we both cycled to work - about six miles. But I found it very tiring, especially when I had to prepare a meal when I arrived home.

I cut my thumb on a meat tin I was opening and I had to go to the cottage hospital at Chipping Sodbury as I could not stop the bleeding. It was a very deep cut, but no stitches were needed. The next day, being a Sunday, Arnold and I walked all the way to Inglestone Common to have Sunday lunch with my mother, and back again - about five miles each way. I was away from work for a while as I could not hold the handle bars to ride my bicycle.

As Arnold had a week's holiday we decided to visit his relatives in Liverpool. We travelled by train, and then a taxi from Lime Street station to Great Crosby. We stayed with Moira, Arnold's sister, but I did not enjoy it very much. I felt so tired. When I reached Lime Street station on the return journey I fainted. Arnold had to find a taxi to return me to Moira's house. The doctor was called. He said I needed a long rest and I was anaemic. Arnold left without me and I travelled back to Bristol a week later, still very weary.

I also found I was going to have a baby again so, of course, I could not do the long bicycle ride to work every day so I gave up my job. But I found the hours very long with Arnold working all day and doing special constable duty at night. When he was on night work it was impossible with one room to live in not to make a noise, so we decided to find other accommodation.

CHAPTER 12

IRON ACTON

We moved to Chain Gate Lane, Iron Acton, to live with a Mr and Mrs Carter, friends of Arnold with whom he had lodged before. They had one son called Royston. Mrs Carter was a good cook and our meals, which we all had together were lovely. It was a big change for me, to sit by a nice fire and not to worry about the evening meals. My sister Dorothy had another addition to her family, a little girl called Christine.

Mrs Carter had a big red setter dog called Bob which I took for walks every day. We would walk all the way to Yate Rocks where there was a big pool called the Blue Pool where people would swim in the summer. It was very deep, but the lads would dive right off the high rocks - no fear at all. There was never anyone there when we had our walks, and the red setter would thoroughly enjoy a swim, and then, when I called him, swim to the side and have a good shake before we set off home again. We became a familiar sight each day as we set off, rain or shine.

In the evening Mrs Carter and I would listen to the Ink Spots on the wireless. We loved their song "Whispering Grass". Arnold was busy evenings on special constable duty. We only stayed a few months as my Mum suggested that we return to Inglestone Common to have my second baby as there was room as Stan was still working away at Trowbridge.

CHAPTER 13

INGLESTONE COMMON

How lovely to be back in my favourite place and with the family! My Mum would make creamy rice puddings cooked slowly in the oven on the side of the fire, made with fresh cow's milk where the cream was an inch thick on the top, and big pancakes that filled the frying pan - more like a main meal itself, which when eaten one was enough. She didn't bother to weigh anything - years of practice was enough. I soon became strong again. It was now the warmer days so I would walk in my favourite woods. It was a bit further for Arnold to go to work, but he managed to have a lift by car with another man who worked at the same place.

The war seemed to be drawing to a close and my time to have the baby. In fact I was taken in to the Chipping Sodbury Cottage Hospital while everyone was out celebrating the end of the war.

It was very hard to leave when everyone was enjoying themselves. Inglestone Farm, owned by Mr Chancellor, was giving a party on the lawn and everyone was there. But I was lucky because my nurse was Mrs Parker's daughter, Mary, and it was very nice having someone I knew. The doctor was very gentle. He was an African and he stayed with me during my delivery. I had a little girl, seven pounds, in the early hours, and it was so different from the first baby. The doctor put her in my arms, just as I had always imagined it to be. She had thick black hair and looked so peaceful. I just couldn't help comparing her to my first son and wishing that he too could have been with us. She was born on the 11th August, 1945. She was a lovely baby and loved me to dance with her in my arms, and she soon let me know if I stopped. I would take the baby for long walks, everybody, including the children, peeping in at her to say, "Hello". We called her Nichola Joyce.

About this time Arnold had a dog follow him home from work - a Labrador, golden in colour. He took it back the next day, thinking the dog would know its own home, but instead it followed Arnold all the way to Patchway where he worked and all the way back again. Arnold was riding a bicycle then. So we kept it home and Arnold called at the Police Station in Wickwar to see if anyone had lost a dog. The dog's paws were sore with such a long journey. Anyway, no one claimed him, so we called him Bruce and kept him. He used to get very excited when we went for walks and would sometimes jump over the pram. He couldn't understand that baby sounds inside and he wanted to have a better view.

It was time for Stan to return home so Arnold and I had to find other accommodation. We heard about a smallholding to let which was about two fields away (one mile), so we went to see the owner to see if we could rent it. How pleased we were when he said yes! It was very strange the first day, and we took Bruce with us. We unlocked the door and were just about to enter when Bruce went crazy. He chased into the house, dashing up the stairs and down the other flight of stairs. I thought he had a fit so I shut myself into one of the rooms until he was better. I think he entered every room of the farm barking furiously, and then Arnold, who was still outside wondering what it was all about, said he dashed outside, ran all round the garden and into the woods. He did not come back for quite a while. When he did he was out of breath but calmer. When I told my brother-in-law Stan about it he said, "Well, everyone around here thinks it is haunted". There used to be another cottage near by which had fallen into decay leaving just a few stones. Stan thought that Bruce had seen something that we couldn't see. But as we needed a home so badly, we decided to take a chance and rent it. Ghost or no ghost, I can honestly say we never saw anything to frighten us, so Bruce must have done his job well.

CHAPTER 14

WITHYMORE

The smallholding was called Bull Dog Farm. It was situated between Hillesley, Kingswood and Inglestone Common. Our post came from the Kingswood direction for a while and then from Hillesley. It was in the middle of the fields and on the edge of a wood - no proper path or road to reach it.

The day we moved in our furniture had not arrived. In fact it was a fortnight before it came owing to some confusion over the order, so we had to borrow a bed and use boxes for chairs. Were we glad when the furniture arrived on the back of the farmer's tractor on a trailer! I can remember one of the young lads saying to his mate, "Good gracious! She is only a young girl!" I think they thought I was going to be an old farmer's wife, living so far away from civilisation.

Bull Dog Farm was a large building and I suspect that it was two cottages at one time. There were two front doors, two back doors, two separate flights of stairs up to the bedrooms, and two flights of stairs up to the attic which was like two big bedrooms with windows on the side. There were very large outbuildings where the coal had been bought in ready for the year as the coalman could only reach the farm in the summer when the ground was hard. There was a very large garden with fruit trees and a field adjoining. We were very lucky that we had tap water instead of a well. Bruce enjoyed the run of the garden and chasing the birds in flight for fun.

It was nearing Christmas time and the weather not too good. I had to wear strong shoes to travel backwards and forwards to the shops two fields away in the Barton, and to the farm for the milk which I carried in a can. The landlord delivered and fitted a brand new range for the kitchen where we spent most of our time in the winter as it was small and warm. In fact, we used to get the top of the range red hot and just listen to the wind howling outside as we had no wireless then.

My sister Win baked us a Christmas cake for our first Christmas in our own home. Nichola was a good baby and always slept through the night, going to bed at about 6.30 pm so I kept busy as I was very often alone as Arnold left in the morning at about six o'clock and did not return sometimes until late evening, and on night shift work it was very rarely I saw him. So I used to make home-made butter by saving the cream from the milk in a big jar, and after a few days I would sit by the fire and shake the jar until I had separated the cream from the whey, and then I would salt it and make little butter shapes which were lovely on bread and helped with the rations. I also made cheese from hanging little muslin bags full of sour milk, and when all the whey had dripped out a little salt added would make lovely cheese.

I also made brawn which Arnold loved, and scones from sour milk which melted in the mouth, and sponges which were very light, the recipe given to me by my mother-in-law, and tarts of every description. Whenever Arnold had a bath I had to fill up the boiler for hot water and light a fire underneath. Our bath was like an old cattle trough. The people before us had made one out of rough stones and it was so rough that you had to sit on something soft or you would have a sore bottom. I didn't bother. I just had a good wash, but Arnold loved his baths and he would sit in it with a flickering candle for light. He did look funny! You could hardly see him for steam. The bath had been made in an old pantry room, so the water had to be scooped out of the boiler in a bowl and carried to the bath which made it a good half hour's work. Once a week was enough!

There were two front rooms - a very large one with an ordinary fireplace, and the one we used had an old fashioned red brick fireplace with a seat on each side. When we had a lovely fire going we would all sit round and talk and Bruce would sit on one of the stone seats enjoying the warmth. We would watch him slowly getting sleepy and his head drooping down, and just as we thought he would fall the jerk would wake him up, and it would begin all over again.

The front door sounded like an organ playing in the wind as it rushed round the corner, and the attic flight of stairs made an awful flapping noise as it had been sealed up with very stiff brown paper. But somehow the draughts would whip it up and down like a swan flapping its wings ready for flight, but we became used to it all.

The postman from Kingswood was an elderly man and if it was a wet day he wouldn't come right to the house. He would stand at the other end of the field and blow a whistle to let me know he was there. I would have to leave everything I was doing, put on wellingtons and go to fetch the post.

It seemed a very long winter and, of course, I couldn't take Nichola for walks in the pram as the fields and the Common were too wet for the wheels. So I was very pleased when the first signs of spring appeared. My sister Dorothy had another addition to her family, a little girl called Pauline. Arnold also had a little win on the football and he bought a little portable wireless which was heaven after so many long music-less evenings. At last we knew what was happening in the world outside. We seemed to be living on another planet - we made our own fun.

Arnold brought home a little box of baby chickens and baby ducks, all fluffy and chirpy. We made little runs for them. Bruce was very interested and would hold his head on one side watching them, and if you picked them up he would lick their little faces. Then Arnold brought home four geese who were very good at keeping the grass short, and they would roam about the garden. They became very good as watch dogs. We always knew if anyone was passing by as they always joined Bruce when he barked. The little chicks (bantum) were very friendly, in fact one would always eat the corn sitting on Arnold's hand. We also had laying hens, but we didn't seem to get any eggs, and I didn't realize for a long time why. Then one day I was standing outside, Bruce beside me, when I heard the hen making a loud cackling noise which I knew they made after laying an egg. Well, Bruce shot round the corner of the house, into the henhouse, and by the time I reached it he was having a good meal of the eggs. So now I knew why we never had any eggs! Bruce was the thief, but those were the last eggs for him.

The ducks soon grew up and they would all travel down the two fields until they reached the farmer's pool. It was a long walk and you would see them taking a rest every now and then, their little heads nodding in all directions as if they were having a pow-wow about the long journey.

The geese became as one with the family, and when I went shopping they would follow me down the Common and when I reached the stile to climb over into the field they would sit down and wait for me to return, and then, looking at me with their heads on one side, listen while I chatted to them all the way home. I had to carry Nichola most of the time as there was no one to leave her with. Later on in the year when the corn was ripening the geese would, in single file, leave the house, cross over to the corn field and there you would see the corn sheaves gently swaying as they walked amongst it, having a little snack, and then return to have a little nap. That was their daily ritual. I always knew where they were. Also just inside the wood there was a little pond where they would have a swim. They never went down to the farm pool like the ducks. Perhaps it was too long a journey for them. Also the stile was a deterrent as there were only little gaps for the ducks to squeeze through.

Bruce and the geese would play games together. He would dash about with a piece of rag in his mouth, and the geese would chase him, but I noticed the geese always won. They would surround him and after a while he would give in and lie down exhausted and with a few cackles the geese would walk away.

The foxes would pass by, but not too close as I am sure they were very aware of Bruce. They never killed any of the hens or ducks. We did have one mishap. We always put the bantam chicks into a chicken box at night which had slats of wood at the front to give them air, but on getting up one morning we found them all dead, and on inspection we found something had got into the box and bitten all their necks and killed them. It was very sad.

I had a little seat fixed on to the carrier of my bicycle for Nichola and I would visit my sister Dorothy at Hillesley, also my sister Bess and Win. Dawn and Nichola were great friends.

I started to dig the garden. The soil was very good. My cauliflowers were huge and Nichola soon found out how nice the strawberries were. You would find her in the middle of the garden helping herself. It was very lonely for her - no other children lived nearby so I spent a lot of time with her. We never hurried to the shops. We made it an outing as well.

One day, on reaching the stile, I saw a big white Shire horse feeding on the grass in the field. I didn't think much about it as I was used to the farm animals so I climbed over the stile and was walking down the field when I heard a thudding noise behind me. Imagine my fear when I saw this big Shire horse chasing after me! I took to my heels and just managed to fall over the other stile near the shop when the horse reached me. Was I glad Nichola wasn't with me! Arnold was looking after her.

I bought my goods and walked back up the little path, thinking the horse would be gone, but oh no! He was standing on the other side with his head resting on the stile. We looked at each other and I am sure when he showed me his teeth he was smiling! His eyes were huge and full of devilment. We stood for quite a while, testing each other. In the end I gave in and I had to return another way, right round the Common which was a longer route.

It was becoming a real test for me, each day trying to outdo the horse. One day he was under the big oak tree in the middle of the field, and I thought if I crept along by the hedge he wouldn't hear me, which I did, watching him at the same time. I thought, "Ha! I've done it!" when suddenly I saw him lift his head listening. He knew I was there and was only waiting his chance for me to get a little nearer. So there we were once again, our legs flat out chasing down the field. This time he nearly got me. I gave up after that, knowing that one day he would win.

He always knew when I was about. I would look across the fields as I went the long way round, and he would be there watching me. Just for fun one day I went back along the little path from the shop just to see if he did realize. There he was, head reaching over the stile, and when he saw me he gave a big neigh. I am sure he was laughing at me. The farmer's wife told me he only wanted to be friendly, but he was so big that I thought he might run me down so I always took the long way round after that.

In the front of the house there was a small garden, not very wide. In fact it was more like a border - just enough for a couple of rows of flowers - and then a long low wall with big round pillar stones at each end of the gate. The people who lived on Inglestone would all use the Common to feed their cattle, and the horses would roam about in groups. They would sound like thunder in the night, racing up and down, and then they would put their backs against the pillar stones until they fell off and what a noise they made falling off! I was always afraid they would push the window in.

My niece Esme came to stay with me once when Arnold was on night work, but one night we heard heavy breathing outside, and Esme drew back the curtains to look out. She gave a loud scream and let the curtains fall. I had a look to see what it was and there, leaning over the wall, face against the window, was a cow. I admit it was an awful shock for her to find herself looking into a pair of enormous eyes. She never came up again to stay with me.

Arnold bought a motor bike as it was easy to ride over the Common ground, and he would spend hours working on it.

I left Nichola with Arnold one Saturday to catch the bus from Hillesley to Wotton-under-Edge to do some extra shopping and to visit the chemist.

Arnold decided to paint the front room ceiling. What a mess I had to clear up when I returned! He hadn't covered up anything. Everything had splashes over it, and he looked like Picasso the painter, a beret on his head and an old shirt like a smock on. He was also covered in the white paint. And Nichola! Well! I could have cried! Apparently she had been looking in the bucket Arnold had been using and fallen in head first. I had an awful job getting it all off. I said, "In future please leave the painting to me!"

We had some lovely greengage trees loaded with fruit and damsons, and a grapevine growing on the side of the house. In the field we had Bramley apple trees. The apples were huge and we had a big old pear tree as tall as a fully grown poplar tree. The pears were small, but not good eating pears, so Arnold got in touch with the Wickwar cider company to see if they would like the fruit. A man came out with a load of sacks and looking at the tree he said, "I would think you have about a ton of fruit, but we are so busy ourselves that we will have to leave the sacks for you to fill and we will collect them later". Well! Who was going to get them down? Arnold would not climb the tree so I had a go. What a job! It took me quite a while to leave the ground as the trunk had no branches at the bottom to hold on to, so with a few pushes from Arnold I reached the first branch. It was very tiring shaking the pears off and when I reached the top of the tree and looked down it was very scary. I was glad when I finished, but then we had to pick up all the pears.

The man was right though - they did fill all the sacks - a ton in all. We informed the cider company. They were ready and they arrived with a tractor and trailer to collect them. By now though the juice was squeezing through the sacks and smelt very strong.

One morning, returning home from night work, Arnold arrived with an addition to the stock. The landlady of the Fox and Hounds pub had given him two baby goats. Apparently he had told them about the long grass we still had to cut. The landlady told Arnold that they would solve all our problems and also give us milk later on. He walked up the Common with them on long chains and looking from the window I thought they were big dogs. "Whatever has he brought now?" I thought. When I realised they were goats I was not very happy as I knew from experience what a problem they could be. Anyway, we decided to keep them for a while, as on the long chains I thought they would not do much harm. But I was wrong. They were always breaking off everything we tied them to. They would jump up on the sheds, reach for the fruit on the trees, and eat every one they could reach and then look down at us and spit out the damson and greengage stones. They were so agile. The vine they destroyed completely. The garden became a shambles - all my hard work down the drain.

One day, while having our tea in the kitchen, the windows wide open as it was a lovely warm day, we had quite a shock. All of a sudden, one of the goats jumped right through on to the table and out through the door. We shouted so loud with fright that it didn't quite know what was happening so it fled through the first open space it could find.

It came to a climax one night. I had gone to bed very tired. Arnold was still on night work when suddenly I heard the clanking of chains around the house. I thought about the place being haunted as we had been told and I was very afraid. In the morning, after a sleepless night, I opened the door to look around outside and there, looking up at me, were the two goats, their chains still on their collars. They were the ghosts! I decided there and then that I had had enough of them, so I gave them away to a Mr Crew who lived up by the Chapel, and was I pleased to see them go!

We rented the field out to a Mr Gardiner for hay for his cattle. It was so nice watching the grass being cut, and the lovely smell and when ready to collect in, the little hay cocks all around the field. A real country picture - a masterpiece.

It was very quiet and peaceful around the house. I didn't have any visitors as it was such an awkward spot to reach.

Win did bring Dawn up one day, but she was stung on the head by a wasp so it was not a happy evening with Dawn crying and her head all blue from the blue bag which we had put on to ease the pain.

We didn't have any outings or holidays, but we enjoyed all the simple things in life, and there was never any rush. Time seemed to stand still. We just drifted from day to day, Spring, Summer, Autumn, Winter. Every season had its different blessings and lessons. The last winter we spent there was very bad. The snow lasted until the following April. Even the baker couldn't reach Inglestone Common, so Arnold left the house early one morning to walk to Hawkesbury Upton with a clean sack to fetch the bread - about three miles. Of course, when the people knew he was fetching bread, everyone wanted a loaf. He didn't arrive home until late evening, tired out. He said the snow was so bad that he had to dig his way through with a spade someone had given him.

We couldn't leave the house for months to visit anyone. Unfortunately, Nichola was having ear trouble so I had to do my best to help her with the pain. She had a nasty abscess which eventually burst.

My Mum, who was now living with my sister Dorothy at Hillesley, came to stay with me just to sleep at night as she was so worried that I might need extra help with Arnold on night shifts. She would struggle up through the snow in the evening in the dark, and leave about six thirty in the morning as she had a job herself to do. You could hardly see her walking through the snow drifts with the edge of the wood for a guide.

I took a chance one day as Nichola wanted a walk, so I thought I would do some shopping and fetch the milk. Unfortunately we had a blizzard. My sister Win pleaded with me to stay with her instead of returning home, but I said I would be alright. I started back over the fields, but the wind was so strong and the snow blinding us that I soon became very tired. Nichola was crying so I had to bend down, get her on to my back, pick up the shopping bag in one hand and the milk can in the other, telling Nichola to hang onto my neck. What a journey! By the time we reached home we were both crying. I knew that if I slipped we would both have perished in the cold as no one would see us in the deep snow.

It was such a long winter. We ran out of coal and we had to burn what we could find. Thank heavens we lived by a wood! Unfortunately some of the branches we found were too thick to saw so we improvised. It was rather funny really. We balanced the branch on a box in the middle of the room, and as the wood burnt a little, pushed it onto the fire so that it would keep it going. Not very tidy, but when needs must, we do all funny kinds of things.

We were very glad when the snow began to thaw, but then we had floods. The little streams we had to cross had become like rivers. We would wade through them up to our knees and then it was very difficult to walk, as the Common had become very boggy. Mum walked down with me to visit my sister Bess, but she became stuck in the mud. Where the horses and cows had crossed the streams they had left deep holes in the ground where they had sunk. Unfortunately Mum had put both feet into two separate holes and she couldn't get them out. Well, she looked so funny swinging her arms around to keep her balance that it was like a comedy strip, and I might add she was holding up an umbrella against the wind and rain which blew inside out. Well, I just had hysterics. I put Nichola somewhere safe and tried to release Mum who by now didn't see the funny side of it. I tried to calm my laughter. I think that after so many hard winter days it was my way of releasing tension. Mum was covered in mud so we returned home to wash it off.

I had to do my cooking balanced on the logs on the front room fire where I had many mishaps, putting the fire out as sometimes the log would slip and over would go my saucepans. We did manage to carry up a few hundred weight of coal on the bicycle to give a base to the fire, praying that the ground would dry up soon for the coalman to deliver. I used to boil potato peelings for the ducks, hens and geese which even Bruce would try to eat, but the geese kept him away, lowering their heads menacingly. At last the warm weather had arrived. It was so nice to see the green grass after so much snow.

About this time Arnold was asked if he would like to be lent to the Royal Air Force as a special duty officer in charge of all the fighter aircraft engines in India. He was given the rank of Squadron

Leader as he already had experience as a leading tester in charge of various test beds at Patchway aircraft factory. He accepted the job.

So we gave away the farm stock, and Arnold gave Bruce to a friend as he didn't want to leave Nichola and me on our own in such a lonely spot. He wrote to his mother who lived in Liverpool and asked if we could live with her for one year, and she said it would be alright.

We put the furniture in store at the farm owned by Mr Chancellor. It was very sad saying goodbye, and also leaving my beloved Inglestone again. Arnold saw me off first at Wickwar station -- just Nichola and me and a big packing trunk. The journey seemed to go on for ever. I had never been so far away from home by myself, so everything was new and so strange. We arrived on Lime Street Station, Liverpool, in the late afternoon. I was in a dream - all the people rushing about, shouting, banging the train doors, whistles blowing, steam hissing from the trains. I just stood, a lonely figure with Nichola sitting on the trunk, thinking someone was going to meet me. In the end I managed to get a taxi to take us out to Great Crosby. But when we arrived there was no answer to the door bell. I was just beginning to wonder what to do when Arnold's sister Moira came hurrying round. She lived not far away. Apparently Arnold's mother had gone on a month's holiday, and I was to stay with her until she returned. It seemed to me like the last straw. Why hadn't I stayed where I was as I knew

I could have looked after myself in familiar surroundings!

CHAPTER 15

LIVERPOOL - GREAT CROSBY

Nichola was three years old now and I was twenty-three, but I felt I had already lived a lifetime. It was very strange - so many people after living in the wilds so to speak! Moira had a lovely home, everything you could wish for, and a maid called Alice who helped with all the chores, as Moira had four children, Ann, the eldest, then Tony, Pauline and Cheryl who was still a baby. Moira's husband, Doy Gepp, was Captain of a Blue Funnel ship called the "Machaon" which the house was named after, but he was away at sea at the time. His real name was Egerton Antony Hammond Gepp. He was born near Kew Gardens, London, and when he was taken for a walk in the pram the elderly residents passing by would stop and say, "Oh, what a pretty boy!", which he apparently was, and when he began to talk he would say "Doy", meaning `boy', and from then on the nickname stayed.

Great Crosby was a suburb of Liverpool, very pleasant with very posh houses. The people were all very friendly. Nichola found it very strange with other children to play with. It was like another world to her, and like me a little hard to grasp, but I watched, listened and I learnt. I was not a great talker, but I found being a good listener was just as good, and I soon joined in with everything.

Everyone seemed to be knitting which I hated, but I thought with help I would have a go. Of course, I was silly enough to choose a hard pattern, the wool a lovely gold colour and brown buttons. I thought it would suit Nichola's colouring. I can't remember how many times I undid it, but I was determined to finish it. But when I did it was too small for Nichola so we tried it on baby Cheryl. She looked lovely and she was very proud with my effort. Moira knitted all her children's cardigans and socks. She was always very busy and I grew very fond of her. We never had a cross word. She was like a sister to me. We would all trudge off to the shops and back with Cheryl in the pram and Nichola in a pushchair Moira had lent me. We also took the children down to Blundell Sands when the weather was good.

Doy, Moira's husband, arrived home on leave. I was a little apprehensive not really knowing him, also, would he mind my living in his house? He was very friendly to Nichola and me, not a man easily conned, but what a father! I have never seen such gentleness in a man. He would feed Cheryl, wash her, even change her nappies. I had never seen anything like it before. All the men I had known thought it was just woman's work. We grew to respect each other. Perhaps being at sea, lonely sometimes, was like living in the wilds like me. A kind of bond was formed but two people from two different stations in life. He would even make supper for Moira and me. He made me feel very welcome.

I was running short of ready cash so I thought I would visit the bank. What a journey! With careful instructions Nichola and I caught a bus from Great Crosby to Sea Forth Sands, and there we joined the overhead railway to Liverpool along the dock wall, passing Gladstone dock which was the dock for the Blue Funnel ships, and then passing the famous Liver buildings, getting off at the Pier Head. It was another experience, sitting with all the dockers on the train, but they were all very kind and helpful when we reached our destination, treating us with respect as we got off the train.

I then had to find my bank which was the National Provincial. It was the main bank, and very large. The day I entered there seemed to be a lot of high finance going on. All kinds of nationalities walking about with briefcases looking very important. I just stood for a while, watching and wondering which counter to approach, when a gentleman passing said, "Can I help you Miss?"

"Oh, yes please!" I said. I explained what I wanted. He took me over to one of the counters, introduced me to the man behind and left me saying, "I am sure you will now be looked after". The man in charge started to talk to Nichola, putting me at my ease, and giving her some sweets he had under the counter. He changed my cheque2 saying, "I hope we will see you again". Well, I walked out of the bank feeling like a million dollars, when I had in fact only changed a cheque for £8!

We boarded a bus and travelled to the great Lewis's store where we enjoyed looking round, but so many people milling around made me feel tired, so we had a little snack which we enjoyed. I have often heard people say you can be lonely in a crowd. That day I believed it, and I was glad to catch the bus back to Great Crosby.

My mother-in-law came back from her holiday, and Nichola and I had to move from Moira's which we were just getting used to. She also had a lovely home with very good antique furniture. Gillian, Arnold's younger sister, was still living at home. She had not decided yet what she wanted to do. She had a lovely soprano singing voice and my mother-in-law would play the piano and Gillian would sing her favourite piece of music, "Oh My Beloved Father", and Gillian would also sing "I'll Gather Lilacs In The Spring Again", a favourite of hers which brought back happy memories of a young German lad she had known.

She was a very sophisticated young lady, and many heads would turn as she passed by.

My mother-in-law was also very smart, and on her fingers were lovely diamond rings, sometimes two on one finger, and hats! Well, she had lots, all shapes and sizes and matching handbags. She was a great talker and for a while I used to get very tired listening, but I soon got used to it. She used to have a lot of Pekinese dogs and she gave one to Nichola to make up for losing Bruce. We called it Wong, and what a lovely good-natured dog he was. I would take Nichola for a walk in the afternoon in the pushchair. I had found a little path on the outskirts of Crosby which took me through some fields - just like being in the country - and then back through the traffic, doing a detour, with little Wong on a lead.

Moira had a Pekinese called Chung who had lost an eye fighting. Arnold's mother had two, Mitze and Cheeky. Well, after a while my mother-in-law realized that she could get rid of the dogs for an hour each day, so she would wait until I had disappeared round the corner and then she would let the dogs out to follow me. And then Chung, Moira's dog, joined in. He used to dash round, knock on the back door to be let in, and the same thing happened each day except I now had four dogs following me, but I must say they all enjoyed it. They were all very knowing dogs, but each had its different character. Chung and Cheeky were fighters, Mitze and Wong were very timid and loveable. My mother-in-law was a widow. I never knew my father-in-law as he died before I met Arnold. He also was a captain on the Blue Funnel Line, but in his later years he was the Chief Superintendent for the Blue Funnel Line in Glasgow. His full name was Hubert Charles Kidman. Nichola became very bored after leaving Moira's children and one day I missed her and after searching the house and the garden I became frantic with worry. Also, the back gate was open, so I thought she might get lost. I dashed down to the corner and I met Nichola coming back with a big ice cream cornet in her hand and a big smile on her face. She had travelled right through the busy traffic, crossing a main road, to reach the ice cream shop. I was too pleased to see her to be too angry, but warned her not to do it again. She had bought the ice cream out of her own pocket money.

Another day when I was busy cleaning the bedrooms my mother-in-law called me. "Joyce, just come and see what Nichola has done". I hurried downstairs, my heart in my mouth. "Oh dear! What now", I thought. Outside in the back garden stood Nichola, looking upset. My mother-in-law came out of the outside toilet. "Look! Come and see what she has done!" Someone had left a tin of green paint in their shed and some paint brushes. Nichola had shut the door, taken the lid off the paint tin and painted the walls and herself green. What a mess! I could only say, "I'm sorry", and I tried to clean up the mess, but we had to have someone in to do it properly later.

Moira suggested that I send Nichola to a playgroup mornings as it would be company for her while I was busy, so we found a place for her at a private school called Atherton House. I bought her the uniform which was a gray skirt, gray blazer and a gray hat with a purple band round it, and a purple tie. She looked very smart. Moira took her on the back of her bicycle as a treat, and collected her at midday. She enjoyed playing with the children. One day Moira was busy so I fetched her from school. I saw her little face watching from the window waiting for Moira. She looked right through me, not really seeing me, as her thoughts were for Moira. Then her eyes rested on my face realizing who I was and not very happy about it. "Where is Aunty Moira?" she said. As a mum I was very hurt for a moment as I was so thrilled to see her, but commonsense overruled and I explained that Aunty Moira would fetch her tomorrow.

It was Tony's birthday. He was five years old, and Moira hired a big hall for his party. All the little girls had party dresses so I decided to buy one for Nichola. We went down to Liverpool on the bus and we had a look round the big stores. I found what I liked in Lewis's store. It was white organza trimmed with blue satin and a big blue satin bow. Something like Little Bo-peep's dress in the nursery rhyme. She looked lovely and I bought her a big blue bow for her hair with new white shoes and socks. Ann thought it was lovely and that Nichola was the best dressed at the party. Tony unfortunately was taken ill and was laid out on two chairs with a pillow for his head and a blanket over him and a damp cloth on his forehead. He had a terrible migraine. Moira thought perhaps the excitement had been too much for him. Poor little dear! I knew how he must have felt, watching everyone enjoying themselves. Ann was always very good to Nichola and looked after her and I remember one time when I was a little sad her hand crept into mine just to show that she understood.

Every Saturday Nichola and I would travel into Liverpool, have a meal and a good look round the stores - all the different nationalities walking side by side, and all the different fashions, the sound of the trams clanging up and down, people getting on and off, bells ringing. It was one big family outing so to speak. I stood and wondered where they were all going, talking, laughing, arms full of shopping and all very friendly faces, always ready to give a helping hand if needed. It was a new experience for us, and one I will always remember.

I took Nichola on a trip to New Brighton. We crossed the river Mersey by ferry. It was a delightful crossing. Everybody was happy and a lot of young people were enjoying themselves. We had a lot of rides at the fun fair and laughs throwing at the coconuts to try to hit one off the stand. Afterwards we sat on the beach to eat our sandwiches, and then back again on the ferry to return home.

My sister-in-law, Pauline Grey, came to visit Moira from Glasgow, and she suggested taking me to visit the Reeces' dance hall in Liverpool. So the three of us set off one Saturday evening. The hall was packed with people, and to dance, well, you needed to be like the matchstick men and women in the Lowrie pictures. We did manage to find a seat, but we could not see a lot for the people dancing by. We danced with each other and then a young naval officer asked me for a dance. He was Polish and a perfect gentleman. In fact he was my partner for the evening. We both loved dancing and as he said, "Good company for the evening". We all enjoyed the night out.

Doy was now on leave and he said we had all been invited to a ball given by the Blue Funnel Shipping Line. It was full evening dress, and I did not have one so Moira lent me a mauve satin evening dress. It was a very grand affair with plenty of room to sit down and to move about. I danced with Doy for the first time and it was very amusing to me when after dancing for a while Doy, very seriously, looked down at me and said, "Well, I think I will guide you for a change!" You see, I had always taken the man's place when dancing with another lady, and it had become a habit. I found it very hard not to laugh, and for the rest of the dance I couldn't find anything to talk about. We also had the next dance and it was a spot prize waltz which Doy and I won, and we both had a small prize. It was a very enjoyable evening for us all.

My mother-in-law, Moira and I each week went to a whist drive and dance at St Luke's Hall. I had only played whist at home with the family so I was a little nervous. I found that the people took the game very seriously - a matter of life and death very often when wondering which card to play. I looked across at my partner to find two steely cold eyes watching, daring me to play the wrong card. Some of the people were like computers. They remembered every card that had been played before, and I am sure they knew what everyone was holding in their hands. To them it was winning that mattered, not a game, rather spoiling what was really a friendly get-together.

One evening, much to my amazement, I won a prize - three shillings and sixpence. I took no notice when I heard the name Mrs Kidman called out as I thought it must be my mother-in-law who was very good playing whist, then, "Mrs Joyce Kidman", was called out. I collected my winnings with everyone clapping and feeling very shy I said it must be beginner's luck.

It was the dance after I enjoyed. I would have liked to have been a ballroom dancer for as soon as I was on the floor I was lost to the beat of the music. A foxtrot was my speciality - not many people dance it well.

One Saturday my mother-in-law, Nichola and I visited a Chinese restaurant owned by a Mr Fong who had worked as a cook on my father-in-law's ship during the 1914-1918 war which was torpedoed, and they had spent quite a time in a ship's lifeboat before being picked up. Mr Fong was away at the time and the restaurant was being looked after by his son who told us to call again when his father would be there which we did. He was very pleased to see us, and he had made a beautiful iced fruit cake for us, and when we left he gave Nichola two one pound notes which she carried back all the way home in her hand. In those days that was quite a lot of money so, of course, she had many glances at her hand on the buses. I was rather worried, but she would not give them to me and I thought that if I took them they would be torn. She was so proud of owning her own pound notes.

After arriving home from a walk one day, I found my mother-in-law very angry. "Joyce", she said, "Whatever made you throw cake into the front room and lock the dogs in before you went out?" I was astonished. I had done no such thing, and I was as surprised as she was. "Well, if you didn't do it, then Nichola must have done it" she said, but Nichola said she hadn't. But I think that she was blamed as sometimes children do strange things, so I cleared the mess up and relocked the door taking out the key. I was very relieved when a policeman called to see my mother-in-law and told her a man whom they had interviewed had asked for a number of burglaries that he had committed to be taken into account. He also mentioned that he had broken into my mother-in-law's house, shutting the dogs in the front room with some cake as they were barking so much, so, of course, the mystery had been solved. Apparently my mother-in-law had disturbed him before he could steal anything, and as she entered the front door he got away through the toilet window on the side of the house. I was very thrilled that now Nichola was not the cause of the trouble, and everything had been cleared up.

Moira and Doy did a lot of entertaining, and one evening my mother-in-law was invited. She asked me to fetch her, and walk her back home as it might be rather late. Nichola was asleep in bed and Gillian was left in charge, so I set off through the well-lit streets. The air was lovely and fresh, and so peaceful as I walked along. Then I had an awful fright. A man stepped out of the shadow of a gateway, fully exposed and giving me some lewd suggestions. For a moment I hesitated then, swift as a thought, I turned and ran as fast as a deer with the hounds after it. I didn't stop until I reached Moira's house, then, with a good few rings on the bell, they let me in. Even then I could not speak. I was so out of breath. Then I did and told them what had happened. Moira rang the police station and in about five minutes the police were out. I had to repeat my story all over again, even to what kind of suggestions I had had which was very embarrassing in front of a lot of people. When I described the man the police said they had been looking for a man like that for a long time for many more offences, but they did not realize he was now in Great Crosby. The police took my mother-in-law and me back home, and as we got out of the car they said, "In future don't wander around at night on your own again. It is very dangerous". A few weeks later we heard that the police had caught the man not very far away from the house.

I thought that it was about time I returned to Inglestone Common as Arnold would soon be returning from India and I wanted to find somewhere to live before he came back. I wrote and asked my sister Win if there was anywhere I could stay for a while. She wrote back and said that Mrs Amy Winbow who lived in the Barton just across the way from her house would take me until I could find rooms or a house. I packed my belongings and ordered a taxi to take Nichola and me to the station. Wong we left behind until we could get settled. We reached Lime Street Station going a quick way, over cobbled streets known only to the taxi drivers, cutting out all the main traffic, and, once more, waiting with our trunk and suitcases on the platform waiting for our train. I felt so nostalgic for Liverpool as I waited. I would miss the sound of the ships as they travelled up and down the river Mersey sounding their horns when it was foggy. I used to be in bed and wonder what the noise was when I first arrived in Liverpool, sounding all through the night. Also the hustle and bustle of Liverpool and the friendly faces and the clanking sound of the trams.

Our train arrived and we were helped into the compartment by a young soldier who saw to our luggage as well. It was a long journey home, but the soldier gave us cups of tea and sandwiches.

We arrived at Temple Meads station very late and tired. The soldier got us a taxi and we were soon on our way back to Inglestone Common. When we arrived we were too tired to unpack so we had a nice hot drink and went to bed.

CHAPTER 16

INGLESTONE COMMON

Mrs Winbow was a very nice lady and made me feel very welcome. It was nice after breakfast the next morning and to cross over the way to see my sister Win and little Dawn. Win had not been very well and she had a very big swelling on the right side of her neck. The doctor said it was a goitre and she found it very hard to eat solid food. Nichola and Dawn played together and we went for long walks.

There was a new landlord at the Fox and Hounds pub, a Mr and Mrs Purvis, Dick and Doreen. I became friendly with Doreen being about the same age as myself, and she had a little boy a little older than Nichola. Doreen was very smart and when she wore her shorts in the warm days the locals were all agog as it was all new to them, but they were soon won over as she was so friendly to everyone. You could not help but like her.

Doreen and Dick had made the pub look very welcoming and lots of people travelled there for an evening out and their garden was full of lovely flowers.

Arnold had now returned from India after being away for twelve months. He was very brown, and glad to be home once more. Doreen's friend was a warden at Tortworth Open Prison near Wotton-under-Edge, and we were invited to a dance there given by the Governor of the prison. I wore a long black dress with white accessories. It was lent to me by Moira, my sister-in-law. It was a good evening - good band and company.

One evening Mrs Winbow, who had lit the coal fire, decided to brighten it up by putting on an old wireless battery without my knowing, and we were all sitting talking when suddenly there was a loud bang and the coal was shooting out of the fire in all directions. For a moment we did not know what was happening except to jump out of the way. It was like a machine gun - bang, bang, bang! We were all rushing about trying to pick up the hot pieces so as not to catch the room on fire. But we did laugh after it! It must have looked very funny with us all jumping about. Poor Mrs Winbow had quite a shock, but like the woman she was, she soon made light of it. As she had had the battery for such a long time she didn't think it would do any harm.

My sister Dorothy had an addition to her family - a little girl called Sandra, and she had moved to a bigger home in Hillesley as the cottage was too small for them all. Sandra was born in September, 1949.

Arnold returned to work at Patchway, finding it a big change from India. The winter months passed very slowly and we were all very glad to see the spring. Win was still very poorly and Mum very worried about her. I was also having a lot of pain in my back. The doctor sent me to see a specialist who said I needed an operation. It was a woman's complaint. I was sent to a hospital on the Bristol Downs called the Chesterfield. My Mum, who was now living with my sister Dorothy as Freda, Esme and Stan could now look after themselves, offered to look after Nichola as she was now staying with Win to help her and Dawn until Win felt better. Dawn had already started school at Wickwar, going by bus each day, not having to walk like we did all those years ago.

While I was in hospital my friend Doreen came to see me and told me my sister Win had been taken into the General Hospital in Bristol, for an operation on her neck. They found she had cancer, and owing to the weak state she was in she would not live very long. I was so upset and feeling very weary after my own operation. I broke my heart. The sister gave me a sedative to calm me down. Mum fetched me by taxi from the hospital to go home on the weekend and, although I felt very weak, the next day I went in to see Win. I didn't have time to buy anything to take in so I picked a bunch of her own wallflowers from the garden which she had planted in the autumn.

When I looked into the ward Win had her eyes closed and she seemed to have tubes everywhere. I stood looking down at her and softly said, "Win, can you hear me?" She slowly opened her eyes as if with a great struggle. "Look," I said, "I've brought you some wallflowers out of your own garden". She looked at me. The tears rolled down her cheeks unchecked. Her arms reached out to me, and then fell back again. She was so weak. The sister said, "Don't stay too long. She has just had her pills which are making her sleepy".

I returned home, broken hearted, feeling so useless. Then we had a 'phone call from the hospital to say she had passed away. A week later she was buried at Hawkesbury Church Cemetery, not far away from my sister Milly's grave. I had lost a sister, a second mother, and a friend, and she was only in her forties.

This is a poem I wrote later in memory of my sister and that last day in hospital.

The Wallflowers

Whenever I see a wallflower display
My mind returns to a bygone day
When with hands of love the seeds were sown

Underneath the window of my sister's home.
"Just wait until the spring", she said,
"And then you will envy my flowerbed.
With lots of colour and perfume bold
It will be a picture to behold."

The winter passed, then came the spring
With wallflowers abloom and birds to sing,
But no sister dear to enjoy the pleasure
Of what had been a pastime leisure
For in the hospital she lay,
Not knowing of the hour or day.
And so I took the wallflowers for her to see
But what should have been joy was calamity

As with one look her tears did fall,
Her heart just broke at what she saw,
No garden that she had planted free
But a bunch of wallflowers to smell and see.
She could not speak, her emotion so great,
Her arms reached out for mine to take.
And I know now that in Heaven above
The wallflowers are tended by the sister I love.

Alf's brother Jimmy and his wife Nora said they would look after Dawn, jut a cottage away, and Mum returned to my sister Dorothy at Hillesley.

After a while, Arnold, Nichola and I moved to a small cottage at Hillesley situated in the main street, taking our furniture that had been stored at the farm.

CHAPTER 17

HILLESLEY

It was a very small cottage with two bedrooms, living room, kitchen and a small garden back and front. It was nice to be living in Hillesley - so many childhood memories. It had not changed at all except all the people were a little older. It was nice having our own home again and doing our own thing.

We decided to visit Liverpool for Arnold's holiday and to bring back Nichola's little peke, Wong. We hired a car for the journey as we did not have our own transport. We all enjoyed the long journey, stopping for sandwiches along the way.

It was very nice seeing Liverpool again. One day on our way out shopping and while waiting for my mother-in-law we were scraped along the side of the car by a Liverpool bus. In fact we were blocked in by all the traffic as it was so very busy.

After the police had taken all the particulars of each driver of the incident, out of the shop comes my mother-in-law, unaware of all the trouble, saying, "Where are we going now?" Of course we felt like returning home, but decided to have a little trip to Ainsdale beach which is on the way to Southport.

We had a nice day, Nichola enjoying the sea and the sand, also a nice picnic. We gathered together our deck chairs to leave and to find the car. It was just not our day, for the tide had come in and our car was sinking in the sand. It took a long time to release it, but with a little help from other people we managed it. I think my mother-in-law secretly enjoyed all the excitement. We also had a day trip to Southport. We only stayed a week in Liverpool and then we returned home with Wong.

It was nice living near my sister Dorothy and family. Also, Nichola had Pauline to play with. There was only one year's difference in their ages. Nichola would treat Wong like a doll, wheeling him about in her pram and he loved it. We also took him for long walks up the hill towards the Hawkesbury Monument which was erected in memory of General Lord Robert Edward Henry Somerset GCB KTS, a member of the Beaufort family. Wong was always a long way in front. I think that after being in a little back garden to him it was sheer heaven smelling all the long grasses and hedgerows. On the way back I would stand and look down on Inglestone Common with so many memories going through my mind. I would just see the little cottages and also Bulldog Farm. It was such a peaceful walk - no cars dashing up and down, just the odd tractor or lorry, and the sound of the cows as they called to each other.

Arnold bought another motor-bike so that he had transport for work, and also to do our shopping at Gloucester. Also we would have a little trip to the cinema at Dursley when Mum could look after Nichola.

It was quite something to go to the doctor's surgery on a Saturday morning. The County bus would be almost full when it reached Hillesley so most of us had to stand all the way to Wotton-under-Edge, and many times we thought that it would never reach the top of Alderley Hill - it was so steep, especially in the ice and snow. But everyone would be chatting away, mostly about their ailments and medicines. We had about two hours to do all our shopping, and to see the doctor. The surgery was always full up, but the doctors took their time, listening to our tales of woe, and then back on the bus, standing all the way again, our baskets loaded with the things we could not buy in Hillesley. It was such a friendly atmosphere.

We bought our bacon and cheese at the shop belonging to Mr Hopkins. He would bring out a big piece of bacon and then he would sharpen his long knife, talking all the while, and then proceed slowly to cut long thin slices of bacon. It really was a work of art. And then a big round cheese was placed on the board which he cut with a long piece of thin special wire. He did not need to measure very often as he had done it so many times he always knew just how much to put on the scales. When I left I was always fully informed of the day's events. In the evenings he would fill his van full of fresh bread, and with a Mr Smart, who helped him, they would travel to Inglestone Common to deliver bread to all the cottages and farms. It was nothing to see Mr Smart, who had bad feet, struggling down the Common in the semi-darkness with a big bread basket as the car could not be driven over the uneven ground of the Common. The people always enjoyed the fresh bread for their supper. Although the two bakers worked very late, they were always up early the next morning, baking their bread again.

My other groceries I bought from Mr and Mrs Coates as they always had such a good variety such as their own doughnuts and buns. They were very nice people and always had a friendly word for everyone. Their shop was just around the corner near the Church.

My milk was delivered by Mr Arthur Davis who carried a large milk pail and a measure. The required amount was poured into my jug. He had a friendly word and a smile for everyone on his round.

The Post Office was run by a Miss Jewell, an elderly lady who was a very happy person, and she always hummed as she served. When she retired it was taken over by a Mr Clutterbuck whose wife delivered the letters around the village after Miss Werrett retired. There was also a petrol station owned by a Mr Walker. There were two public houses, The Fleece, run by a Miss Jotcham, and The Port Cullis, run by a Mr and Mrs Carter, and an old established firm of builders by the name of Werrett. Arnold used to have his haircut by a Mr Stone who had a sweet and paper shop three doors away. He would cut the people's hair in his living room. There was always a queue of men and boys waiting for a short back and sides.

Lillian Cullimore, who I used to go to school with at Wickwar, lived two doors away, and she was now married with three boys.

I remember Nichola who had always wanted her hair long like her cousins in Liverpool, had now graduated to two little plaits. When the Vicar of Hillesley called to welcome us into the community, all the time he was talking Nichola would keep saying to him, "Look! Look at my plaits!" which of course made him smile. She was very proud of them.

Nichola was now attending the village school which was a Church school. She came home for dinner as it made a little break for her, and it was not far for her to walk.

Mum had come to live with us but she still went out to work to earn a little extra for herself. She looked after the cleaning of the Church. She always said that she felt a great peace while doing so. She also cleaned the bus shelter. It was not any old bus shelter. In fact it was built of Cotswold stone. It had a lovely polished seat which was my Mum's pride and joy and she did not like the children standing on it. The land it was built on belonged to a Mr Mervyn Coates who gave it to the village. The village bought a lovely clock which was installed and enhanced the bus shelter. Unfortunately the clock disappeared one night not long after. Someone must have fancied it, thinking that it would look better on their wall than in the bus shelter.

One day the scrap man called to see if I had anything to sell. I decided to let him have my old bicycle as there was no room for it in the cottage, and it was not used any more. I told my Mum, "You can have the cash for it as you bought it all those years ago". I wheeled it to the front door to the waiting lorry. The man said, "I haven't any change at the moment. I will pay you on the way back." "Alright", I said, and Mum and I waited at the window to make sure we did not miss him. Suddenly the lorry came into view and instead of stopping, belted past. On the top was my bicycle, upside down, with the wheels spinning with the vibration. My Mum said, "Well, I'm buggered! That's the last time I give anything to a scrap man!" As for me, I suddenly felt very sad at losing my old friend who had served me so well for so many years.

One evening, while sitting by the fire reading to Nichola, a knock came at the door. On opening it I found my brother-in-law, Alf, with Dawn. He asked me if I would bring Dawn up with Nichola as it was difficult as he was living alone. I agreed wholeheartedly to look after her. She was seven years old at the time. And so Dawn was like a sister to Nichola going with her to the village school, but, I might add, not with the same headmistress that I had had years ago. My Mum left to look after a cottage my niece Shirley and her boy friend, Ray Crew, had bought for when they got married as our cottage would not now be big enough for us all. So things worked out very well.

There was one very loveable character who lived in the village. His name was Lionel Chappell. He was not able to do a full-time job, but he helped everybody in the village doing odd jobs. His sister, Dorothy, looked after him after their father died, and when she and her husband moved to a cottage not far away his brother Cecil and his wife Ruby looked after him. He was very loveable in the home and he would help out doing the potatoes, emptying the bins and doing the shopping. On a Sunday he would ring the Church bells, calling the worshippers to the Church, and then dash down to the Chapel to hand out the hymn books, standing by the door so proudly. He also liked a drink with the lads who generously treated him. He knew everybody and passing me in the street he would call out, "Hello Joyce!", and stop for a little chat. He loved being with a lot of people, enjoying a laugh, even if it was at his expense. It was all done in good fun.

It was now the year of Queen Elizabeth's II coronation - 1952. There was great excitement in the village. There was a carnival with everyone taking part. Dorothy's girl, Christine, was dressed as a Union Jack, and Pauline and Sandra were a bride and groom for which they won first prize. Nichola was Little Bo-peep and Dawn was dressed as a gypsy. There was a tall letter box in the Carnival and we all wondered who it was, and then, right at the end, the little flap opened and a voice said, "Hello, Joyce!" What a surprise it was! It was my neighbour, Cyril Stinchcombe! And what a good costume it was! There was tea and dancing in the streets and all the children had coronation mugs. It was a very happy day.

I joined the Women's Institute and won a prize for a fancy knitted tea cosy, much to my surprise. It was all very interesting and you met a lot of people.

Arnold came home from work one day with an awful pain in his tummy. We called the doctor who said it was appendicitis so an ambulance was called from Wotton-under-Edge to take him to Gloucester. I quickly packed a case and off we went, Mum looking after Nichola and Dawn.

The sister looked at my case when we arrived and said, "You can't leave that here", which I had no intention of doing. It was the first thing I picked up in my hurry - a holiday suitcase. It was like talking down to a little girl instead of making you feel at ease. I just looked at her. Words failed me. I left Arnold sitting up in bed waiting for his operation, very worried. The ambulance gave me a lift back to Wotton-under-Edge, and then I had to walk about two miles, nearly midnight, back to Hillesley. I was very glad to reach home.

Arnold had his operation which went well, and the girls and I visited him in hospital, going by bus. I always remember one day leaving the hospital and I could hear someone yelling my name. The girls and I looked everywhere in the street and then, on looking up, we saw Arnold shouting from the hospital window. So we all waved back. He told me after that the sister had told him off for making such a noise. He was very glad to return home as he was such a long way away from us to visit every day.

We sold the motor-bike and bought a baker's van so that we could take the girls shopping and for picnics. It had big bars on each side and the girls used to swing on them as we drove along, getting bored if it was a long journey. We had a lot of fun in it, not having to worry if we scratched any of the paintwork. We also collected dry sticks from the woods at Kilcot for lighting the fires.

One lovely day we had a trip to Weston-Super-Mare, stopping at Cheddar. We enjoyed it in the caves and eating lots of ice-cream and strawberries

- too many I'm afraid as Nichola was very sick by the time we reached Weston, and it spoilt her day.

We all went by coach to a pantomime at Bath including Dorothy and her family and Mum. We had seats in the front row. There were two comedians on the stage trying to make all the children laugh, but it was my Mum who had not been to a pantomime before who started all the laughing. When the Baddie crept up behind the Goodie my Mum could not stand the suspense and she yelled out, "He is in the cupboard Simon!" Of course everyone laughed and from then on the comedians played up to Mum sensing that children loved it. It was a pleasure to see my Mum's face, a picture I shall never forget.

Dorothy's girls and mine joined the Brownies and looked very smart in their uniforms. On listening to a programme on the wireless from Luxembourg advertising Ovaltine Nichola and Dawn sent away for special badges to wear and they would sing, "We are the Ovaltinies, little girls and boys", the signature tune. In the end all the children in the village joined, flashing their badges on their blazers.

My sister Bess had an addition to her family, a little girl called Susan, in the year 1954.

When Arnold was on night-work, in the daytime we would visit the Blue Pool near Yate Rocks as Arnold loved swimming.

One evening after we had had a lot of rain, we were sitting by the fire when suddenly Arnold said, "Whatever is all that water coming in?" It was flooding into our sitting room. After a quick inspection we found that the huge water tank outside the back door had overflowed. What a mess! It took a few days to clean it up properly. And talking about water I might add we had to fetch our drinking water a little way up the street in a bucket, and we had no proper sanitation. But in those days many people were the same.

As the girls were now getting older and their bedroom very small we thought we had better move to a bigger house nearer Arnold's work. We were offered a house at Stoke Gifford and we decided to take it. My Mum was very sad to see us leave and I must admit, sitting in the furniture van looking back at her standing by the door, we also were in tears. The girls did not want to leave their friends and familiar places and for one moment I too wondered if we were doing the right thing.

CHAPTER 18

STOKE GIFFORD

We arrived at our new abode. The house seemed very big after our little cottage and we would need a lot more furniture. The village was very pretty with a large village green situated on the outskirts of Bristol near Patchway. It consisted of three shops, a public house, a garage, a post office, a Church, a Chapel and a village hall.

Nichola started at the village school, and Dawn started at Patchway Secondary Modern School. She went by bus each morning. Arnold had a lift each day to work as we had got rid of the van. It was very strange not knowing anybody after being with my family for so long. In fact Dawn did most of my shopping. At first I was so busy doing the garden.

The girls found friends and they were out most of the time. Dawn made friends with a girl called

Pamela Rowland whose grandmother made home-made wine. On meeting her I thought I would have a go. There was a lady in the village who had a stock of quart bottles and when Arnold told her I was going to make some home-made wine she gave him as many as I needed. I prepared all the fruit in a large container. I bought some wine-making equipment and special jars for the wine to ferment in.

I made damson, dandelion, orange, beetroot, rice, and carrot wines. I must say I had very good results. The beetroot was just like sherry and the orange better than any champagne. In fact all the wines were very moreish. I used to test the wine while changing it into clean bottles, and many times going downstairs I missed the last step owing to the strength of the wine and so many sips when mixing it. You see I used to make the wine in the little box room upstairs and if I was called to the door I didn't have time to linger.

I never drank a lot of wine myself, but it was a pleasure to offer my friends a drink when they called, and I must say they always left very happy. With any fruit I had left over I made jam, sometimes thirty pounds at a time. The damson jam was lovely, especially on buttered scones.

Going back to the wine making, one day, while I was putting the wine to ferment in the jar, Arnold came home from work and, seeing a glass of red home-made wine on the table, decided to drink it. He did not realize the yeast was still working in it.

Well! He thought he was going to die! He lay on the bed in agony and all we could do was to wait until the uncomfortableness had passed. He never did that again, but, of course, the girls thought it was a huge joke seeing Arnold in such a state.

Everybody thinks that home-made wine doesn't hurt you, but it is very strong. A friend of ours wanted some of our small dust coal for his greenhouse stove. He arrived with a small sack on a bicycle. We offered him a drink which I am afraid led to another and another. He was alright until the fresh air hit him. What a job getting the sack on his back! He kept throwing it over his shoulder. In the end he managed it and rode unsteadily home. He said afterwards, "I really don't know how I managed to reach home, and when I did I went straight to bed."

We bought Nichola a budgie, bright blue in colour. It was just a baby from a friend of Arnolds at work. We bought a nice cage with a mirror and lots of toys for it to play with. When I was on my own I would talk to it. As it grew older we let it out to fly round the room, and when Arnold was writing a letter he would stand on the paper and peck little pieces off. We called it Georgie. If anyone came to the door he would whistle out, and if I changed my dress downstairs he would give me a wolf whistle. He would stand on my head and peck my hair lovingly and walk up my arm and kiss me on the cheek and say, "I love you Mummy". He sometimes said, "Hello Mrs Kidman".

Nichola went to dancing lessons, tap and ballet, and Georgie would call out all the movements in French. We never taught him that - he just picked it up after hearing us when Nichola was practising the movements. He became a real member of the family and it was a sad loss when we lost him after catching pneumonia. He was very poorly for a week and the vet said there was not much chance for him. My Mum was staying with me on holiday. She never had a lot of time for pets as she was always so busy, but she didn't like to see Georgie ill. He was lying on the bottom of the cage panting away, so I lifted him gently out on to the palm of my hand, and we both gently smoothed his feathers. He struggled up my arm until he reached my face, and then he gently kissed my cheek, looking right up into my face saying, "I love you Mummy". I put him gently just inside the cage to put the kettle on and when I looked back in Georgie was in a little crumpled heap on the bottom of the cage. Mum said, "Well, I have never seen anything like it Joyce! He kissed you goodbye. He loved you." I couldn't believe he was gone. I called him by name, but I knew it was in vain so I made a little box for him and I buried him in the garden. But I did so miss my little friend. He was so loveable.

Nichola was now going to the Secondary Modern School at Patchway with Dawn, but she still went to dancing classes and also visited different halls to give dancing displays, dressed in fancy costumes.

Wong would roam around the garden, but I am sure he missed the long walks he had had at Hillesley. He also was a loveable dog -never any trouble.

The garden was very hard work with clay soil, but I managed to grow some lovely roses in the front and some vegetables at the back. One day, arriving home and looking out of the back window, I thought my garden was on the move. Mrs Palmer, who lived next door, had let her pigeons out to fly, and they had spotted my young cabbage plants. They alighted and all I could see was movement on the ground, but when my eyes really registered I realized it was the pigeons moving, and they had eaten all my cabbages right down to the stalks. And then the next day the farmer's cows broke in through the back hedge and went through all the gardens. Mr Palmer tried to chase them out, but they became so afraid of all the noise that one of them fell in my hedge, breaking it right down. But still, like all things, I persevered and grew lots of vegetables and some tomatoes. Missing the country and the woods, I spent a lot of time in the garden and when that was tidy I would be painting in the house.

Arnold had the chance to buy another car from an Israeli pilot. He went to collect it and I waited for him to return as we had decided to take the girls for a run. Well, suddenly this big white car came round the Avenue and I said to the girls, "Oh my goodness! He has bought a bus!" It was so large!

We all got in and very excitedly drove out of the Avenue and we visited some of the little country places we had known. But when we returned we were all as black as tinkers - our hands, clothes and faces all black. The seats had been covered with material and that was what had caused it. Perhaps the car had not been cleaned for a while or, as I said for a joke, perhaps the previous owner had been collecting coal in it. Anyway, I found some new material and recovered the seats. They were like new. Arnold painted the car black and, as it was so big, we called it the Brab after the big Brabazon aircraft. It was like sitting in a bus it was so high, but it was a lovely smooth ride. It was an American car called a Hudson.

We took the girls to visit a friend of Arnolds, someone who had been in India with him, but who now owned a chicken farm near Chippenham. His name was Percy Hillier. It was a great coincidence that on the way, on passing a field where there were a lot of sheds, Arnold said, "That looks like my friend in there". So we backed to have a look, and was he surprised to see us after such a long time! He had his brother-in-law with him who helped him out at the weekends. He said, "Follow me, and then we can have some tea and a chat". He used to have his food prepared by his sister, and it was to her house we went.

It was near Christmas time, and the table was already laid. "What a lot of food!" I thought. There was food of every description. I'm afraid the girls must have been thinking the same and Nichola said, "Well, whose blooming birthday is it then?" I felt very embarrassed, but everybody laughed and I am sure the sister was very proud of the remark about her laden table.

Percy then took us to see his chicken farm, but I did not like to see the chickens in the batteries. What a noise they made, all cooped up together, and just their heads moving up and down to eat the corn - not as I remembered them, strutting about in the sunshine and lazily picking at this and that. Percy also had pigs, but they were roaming free. Nichola always had a love for little pigs. They looked so pink, and very clean I might add. We enjoyed our day and said we would call again.

One evening, being very cold, I built a nice fire to last the evening. Nichola, Dawn and Arnold were enjoying the warmth and I was busy in the kitchen. I popped in to see if everything was alright and if anyone wanted anything. I heard this roaring sound and I said, "Whatever is that?" Arnold said, "I think it is a motor-bike outside". I listened and said, "It is not coming from that direction." Nichola was seated on the floor in front of the fire. I said, "Just a minute, love, move back. I think it is coming from the chimney". I bent down and looked up as far as I could and what a shock I had! The chimney was just a ball of flame ready to drop at any moment. Well, it was action stations with everybody rushing around to move the furniture. We did not have a 'phone then so I said to the girls, "Run up to Mr Knight's and ring the fire brigade". Well, the girls were so shocked that they could not remember at first where Mr Knight lived although he had lived two doors away for a long time. I was just as bad. I didn't know what to do first. We all seemed to be rushing around in each other's way. Mr Knight was having a Council meeting at the time, and after ringing the brigade he brought all the councillors down to help. There were people I had never seen before walking in and out of the house carrying the furniture out on to the lawn - all very helpful. I rushed next door to Mrs Phillips and borrowed a piece of metal to hold in front of the fire to stop the red hot soot from falling out, holding it in place with the poker. It was so hot that the metal burnt away looking like a piece of burnt paper.

There were some people walking up and down the stairs as though it was open house, but mostly everyone helped. The fire brigade arrived and soon had the fire under control. In fact the firemen did a marvellous job of cleaning up after, with plenty of hot cups of tea.

There was one strange incident - we never found out who directed the fire brigade to our house. The firemen said it was someone wearing a cap waiting on the main road. We asked everyone, but no one knew who it was so we thought of it as one of those strange things that happen in life. You see, even our next door neighbour did not hear the fire siren and did not know about it until the next morning, or that her piece of metal I had borrowed from the garden was no more. She even took all my lace curtains and washed them for me and said, "Just forget about the metal".

That was the last time I had a coal fire. I never really got over my fear that it could happen again, like all those years ago when I lived at Kilcot.

All the girls and boys were dashing about on roller skates. Diana Phillips gave us all a laugh one day. She was wearing her roller skates and she also had the dog on a lead. The dog was alright while she was standing still but, when she moved, off went the dog, a little too fast, and they both disappeared up the Avenue like the wind. Arnold, on hearing the story, said, "Oh, I am marvellous on roller skates". The girls said, "Alright! Show us then". He put on a pair of their skates, but when he got up off the chair it took all of us to hold him up. In fact he was more horizontal than vertical. We were too frightened to let him go in case he fell down so after that, every time he boasted about what he could do, we all shouted out, "Roller skates!"

About this time, the girls took up the fashion of wearing very stiff petticoats and hoops which they wore in their skirts. I was washing them every day and starching them. In fact, before the girls came in to tea they would march down to the line and feel the clothes, making sure I had done a good job. But they did look very nice when they went out with their friends, but I must say all that washing and starching was a bit of a bind and I was glad to see the fashion go. Arnold brought home a lot of baby hedgehogs he had found on the airfield. They were alive with fleas. We put them in the back garden giving them some milk to drink, but they all disappeared although even now we see an occasional hedgehog on our path. Perhaps it is a descendant of the same family. I hope so.

Dawn would bring home privet slips from a friend's garden - a bag a day. The man was cutting his hedge and I put them all round the garden, keeping them well watered. I must say I was very lucky -they grew into a very strong hedge as the years passed by.

CHAPTER 19

The girls had now left school, Dawn was working as a typist for Mr Simmonds, a builder at Hambrook, and Nichola as an apprentice hairdresser at Filton. Of course they both had boy friends now and we did not have them with us so much.

My Mum was now living in a cottage at the top of the street in Hillesley called Rose Cottage, not far away from where I used to live. She found it very hard though living on her own and very lonely so we would take her on picnics which she loved, and she would stay with each of us sisters in turn for a break.

The Brab was now beginning to be a lot of trouble. Wherever we went the cooling system was faulty and the water would boil so that we had to carry our own water with us and keep filling up the radiator. Also we seemed to be pushing it all the time to get it started which was no pleasure as it was such a heavy car. It came to a climax one day when Arnold, who had a shed to keep it in belonging to a Mrs Dent, was doing a repair job and unfortunately did not put the handbrake on. The car started slowly to move and, before you could say, "Jack Robinson", it had gone right through the side of the shed which eventually collapsed on top of it. Mrs Dent said, "Don't worry about it. I don't use the shed for anything." But to us it was the last straw. The Brab just had to go.

We sold the Brab to some young lads who were interested and we bought a second-hand cream-coloured Anglia. Unfortunately I had only a provisional driving licence from years ago and I had not renewed it so I had to take a driving test for the Anglia. It was like starting all over again, and also there was more traffic on the road to deal with. It took me eight driving tests before I passed. I sat with the examiner through the sunshine, the rain, the ice, the fog, the snow, spring, summer, autumn and winter. I took tranquillizers that made me feel so sleepy that the examiner had to put on my windscreen wipers in the rain. In fact I did everything wrong as soon as the examiner sat beside me.

On my third driving test I had a smash. A van ran into me and smashed the mudguards. The examiner said, "Would you like me to drive you back to the Test Centre?". I said, "No, I can manage". At that moment I was quite calm. I think it was the examiner who was shaken.

On my tests I used to drive along Whiteladies Road, and I swear everybody knew I was out as every crossing was full of people and obstacles, but I persevered. I am sure that if I had had the same examiner each time I would not have been so nervous. It was pure shyness on my part that was holding me back.

So I decided to have some lessons from a driving school. The first day the man took me out he said, "We will go out into the country and I will see what you are doing wrong." We only got as far as Winterbourne and he said, "There is nothing wrong with your driving - perhaps a few bad habits picked up from your husband who has been driving a long time." So we went down to Bristol through the traffic. He was still impressed with my driving and said, "All you need is a few lessons to learn to drive by the book - little things that the examiner will look for."

Well, I had five lessons and then it was time for my eighth test. The examiner called my name. This one I liked - so friendly. Everything was perfect - no mistakes. I just could not go wrong, and I passed with flying colours. I was so pleased. I said to him, "Would you like a cigarette? No - have the packet! You've made my day!".

Arnold was on night-work at the time and when my instructor took me back home Arnold was in bed asleep, but I just had to tell someone so I drove to Nichola's hairdressing salon full of excitement. On going round a corner my passenger side door opened. What a fright I had! I realized that just because I had passed my driving test I was not perfect and had to go carefully. That is when you really learn to drive - when you are on your own.

Going back to when I was first learning to drive the Anglia - I gave the family a few frights. One day at Filton I was turning into the little row of shops, past the Bank, but much too fast, and we all nearly ended up on the butcher's slab. On another day, as I was going down Gloucester Road, just as I drew alongside a parked bus it pulled out and only by putting up my speed did I manage to pull past it. I might add that my passengers never spoke a word.

Wong used to sleep in the shed in a wicker basket filled with soft blankets until one year when it was particularly cold. I would find him sleeping in the coal compartment, all huddled up and looking very afraid. I looked around to find the reason and then I thought perhaps he wanted his blankets renewed or shaken up, but, on doing so, I had quite a shock. Between the blankets was a nest of little baby mice. So that was the reason! Even the mice found it too cold outside and they had turfed Wong out of his bed. After that I let him sleep in the house. In those days animals did sleep outside in kennels or in the shed, but as

Wong was such a clean little dog there were no problems with him sleeping in the house.

Nichola and a friend of hers decided to enter a beauty competition for Miss England. We travelled through the Brecon Beacons. It was a glorious day and the scenery was lovely. Nichola's boyfriend, Michael Maggs, came with us. They were always known as Mick and Nick for short. The competition was held at Aberavon and the girls wore bathing suits. Nichola's friend won third prize and Nichola came sixth. At the last moment Nichola became very shy being looked at by so many people, and, of course, lost points on poise and confidence. You need to be very sure of yourself on these occasions, but it was all good fun.

On the way home Mick became very thirsty but there were no shops to buy anything so we stopped at a cottage and asked for a drink of water. A Welsh lady opened the door and said, "Would you like a cup of tea instead?" "Oh yes please!" we said. "Well come on in my dears", she said. "Sit down while I lay the table", which she did, talking all the while about our trip.

We sat down to fresh bread and butter and home-made cakes. I don't remember ever enjoying a tea so much. We were all so very thirsty and hungry. "Eat it all," she said. Just as we were finishing some friends of hers called to take her to the pictures. She said, "Don't hurry, my dears. Just shut the door when you leave." We asked her how much we owed her for the meal. She said, "Forget it. It was a pleasure, and very nice to meet you." We just could not believe it. She was so trusting and kind. So we left some money on the table for her, and every time we hear a Welsh choir singing "We'll keep a welcome in the hillside" we remember the little Welsh lady and her generosity.

One year we had a trip to Scotland to visit Arnold's sister Pauline who lived in Glasgow. We picked up Arnold's mother in Liverpool on the way. It was a long journey by car and we stopped to have a main meal at an hotel. I met Foster, Pauline's husband, for the first time. He was a very nice thoughtful person. He had contracted polio in his left leg and he had to wear a leg support, but he still played a lot of golf and he did his own gardening. He was the manager of a shipping office. We also met Sheila and Colin, their children, but their other son Ronald was away at college. We stayed a few days and then made our way slowly back home, stopping at all the places of interest. From Glasgow we visited Loch Lomond where Arnold's father used to take the family for trips, and then to Loch Ness where we had bed and breakfast. We did not see Nessie, but the loch looked very deep and dark. There were lots of people with cameras sitting about just hoping to catch a glimpse of Nessie. Then we stayed at Inverness at a beautiful bungalow for one night, and on to Poolewe which was a headland jutting out of the sea with only one cottage in sight.

We passed Granton-on-Spey and then on to Balmoral. The Royal family were away at the time so we had a good look round the estate and we stopped a little way away on the edge of a pine forest to have our sandwiches, but we were very careful as there were signs all over the place of BEWARE OF ADDERS. Then we went to Braemar, and as we passed by there were some highland games in progress, and then on to Edinburgh where we stayed a night. We looked round the castle with about one hundred other people, but it was very interesting to see all the Scottish relics and regalia. Actually we made it a round trip. We travelled for days, not seeing another car - the peace was sublime. We then made our way back to Bristol. We had collected a dozen steak knives on the way given to us by some of the garages with every five gallons of petrol we bought in Scotland.

We lost Wong after he contracted dropsy. The vet put him to sleep to save him more pain. It was a great loss, and to see him carried out in a bag and taken away was very upsetting.

Then a letter arrived to say that Dawn's father, Alf, had passed away, and he was buried at Hawkesbury Church Cemetery, leaving his house and contents to Dawn and some more sad memories.

Arnold and I booked a caravan at Weymouth for a week's holiday. At the last minute Dawn and her friend Joan Kelly decided to have a caravan on the same site, and would we give them a lift. Well, the Anglia was not very big for four people's luggage so I ended up by having a suitcase under my feet, and when I reached Weymouth I could hardly stand up after having my legs in such an awkward position.

We had a lovely sunny holiday and the girls I know had a jolly good time, and it was very hard to leave at the end of the week.

A month later Arnold and I went back to Weymouth for our next holiday. This time we travelled around more to see the various places of interest such as Portland Bill, Chisel Beach, and to see all the yachts in the harbour which were very picturesque, and we still had lovely weather. We also looked up some cousins of Arnold's mother, Victor and Doris Digby, who lived at Preston, just outside Weymouth. He was the sole fruit importer and exporter in Weymouth.

Nichola and Mick had gone to Guernsey with Mick's parents for a week and on the way back they decided to stay overnight with us at Weymouth. Victor and Doris invited us all out to dinner at the Royal Hotel in which Victor had a financial interest. It was a lovely ending to our holiday.

My sister Dorothy and her husband Bill had separated, and she was now living in Bath with her new partner, Jack Archer, who she had gone to school with, and they had a young son called Timothy born in 1963. I would travel to Bath on a Monday morning, pick Dorothy and Timothy up in the car and take them to see Mum in Hillesley, and sometimes I would take Timothy for a walk along the lane. He was a pretty little boy and very good to look after.

Both the girls were now engaged, Nichola to Mick and Dawn to Michael Foss who was a cousin of Joan Kelly. So we didn't see much of them. Nichola was now working at a Gloucester Road hairdressing salon near Bristol, owned by a Mr Champ.

Arnold and I used to visit our friends at Tuffley, Gloucestershire, Dave and Trixie Thomas. Dave was a police sergeant. In fact we followed them wherever they were moved to, and we had many pleasant evenings together in the Cotswolds. We also had a lovely holiday together in Cornwall. We visited Jamaica Inn, of which there was a film on the television - a very lovely place. Our weather was not very good so we spent a lot of time just driving around looking at different beauty spots and eating sandwiches.

We arrived at King Harry's Ferry which crosses the River Fal, and anchored out in midstream was a Blue Funnel Line ship. Alongside the ferry there arrived a ship's life-boat, manned by a small crew and an officer. Arnold made himself known to them and said that he had sailed in the Blue Funnel Line as an engineer officer and that his brother-in-law was the Chief Superintendent in Liverpool for the Blue Funnel Line. The officer was very interested and he invited the four of us on board for a meal.

We all got into the little life-boat, but I was very afraid. The water was very deep and dark. The boat rocked so badly that I thought it would keel over at one point. I grabbed Dave's arm and later he had a great bruise on it.

The lifeboat reached the ship and that was not the end of my fears. Confronting us was a big ladder rising steeply up to the deck for us to climb up. On reaching the top and looking down we saw the Chinese crew looking up talking and laughing. Of course Trixie and I only had short skirts on and Arnold said, "I know what they are saying! Hi, yi, yi yi, knickers!" which made us all laugh.

We had a lovely meal served by the Chinese stewards, but I disgraced myself again by putting my knife and fork down in the wrong position, and the meal was whipped away from underneath my nose. I had to sit through the first course as though I had done it on purpose while everyone said how lovely it was. It was like being Royalty, the stewards surrounding the table watching our every move, but I am sure I saw a suppressed smile every now and then. For the sweet I kept my spoon in my hand. It was a great experience and we were shown over the ship afterwards, Arnold being very interested.

Then we made our way back the same way. I was very glad to reach firm ground, but it was a great experience for us all and one I will never forget. As we made our way home the sun began to shine making us all wish we were staying on.

CHAPTER 20

Dawn and Michael decided they would like to get married. Michael was a Roman Catholic and, of course, he wanted to be married in a Roman Catholic Church. Dawn did not want to change her religion, but on talking to the priest she let him know she had never been christened, so he said that she must be before he could marry them.

Talking it over with Dawn, I said, "Well, if that is the case, we will all be christened together", Dawn, Nichola and myself. You see, I had travelled about so much that Nichola had never been christened. Like my Mum before, we always meant to do it, but never got round to doing it. I had been to different churches and chapels each time we moved, so, of course, we put off the christening until we were really settled and, as I said before, it was never done. So perhaps now was the time, I being forty, Dawn twenty and Nichola nineteen. I might add that at about this time in my life I had become conscious of something that I should be doing. It was something to do with religion. I would find myself listening to the religious vans that came round and the sermon on the television, but somehow I knew that that was not what I was looking for. And always, as a young child, I felt that I must always do the right thing and always speak the truth. So perhaps the christening was what I needed to be a part of.

Dawn knew a friend who went to a church in Bristol and she introduced her to the Vicar, a very nice man. He invited us out to tea to get to know us all, and he said it would give him a great pleasure to christen a mother and her two grown-up daughters, as, of course, I had always been a mother to Dawn.

We were christened at Christ Church, Bristol, not far away from the Grand Hotel. We stood in a row, with me in the centre, while the Vicar blessed us. The Church was full as I think the story got out about our christening. It was such an unusual happening. Nichola's boyfriend's parents were witnesses. It was all written in the Church magazine. We stayed friends with the Vicar for a long time.

Dawn was married in the spring of 1964 at the Pro Cathedral, Clifton, Bristol, with close family and friends. She looked very lovely in her long white dress and veil with tiara. Nichola was her only bridesmaid. She was dressed in peach satin with ribbon threaded through her hair. They both had matching bouquets of roses and carnations. She was given away by Arnold, and Mick was the best man. Timothy, Dorothy's little boy, who was dressed in a blue velvet suit, gave them a silver horseshoe. Afterwards there was a big reception at the Beaufort, Stoke Gifford, and then we all followed Dawn and Michael back to their new flat at Clifton.

My sister Bess had had a divorce and was now married to Steven Watts, and they lived in a new bungalow at Hawkesbury Upton. She only had a daughter at home now, Susan, as her other children were now married.

Dorothy, Jack and Timothy had now moved to a house at Streamleaze, Thornbury, which was a lot nearer for me to pick them up to take them to see Mum at Hillesley.

Nichola and Mick decided to build their own house at Hambrook near Mick's parents who had given them the land to build on, so of course they were very busy evenings and weekends so we did not see them a lot. I always remember the laugh we all had. I had invited Mick round for a meal and I had made some sausage rolls. For a change I decided to make puff pastry instead of short. I had made rather a lot and the pastry I had left I rolled into one sausage roll. When I opened the oven door it nearly came out to meet me. Well! You've heard of the biggest Aspidistra in the world! Well, mine was the biggest sausage roll in the world, and |I had a job to get it out of the oven. I had forgotten how much the pastry would swell. I am afraid it was the joke in the family for ever after.

Nichola decided to learn to drive as Mick had bought a mini van. She had an instructor and she passed on her first test.

The days rolled slowly by and Nichola and Mick decided to get married. They were married at St Michael's Church, Stoke Gifford, on June 11th, 1965. It was a lovely hot summer's day, and it was attended by close family and friends. Nichola looked lovely in a long white wedding dress with tiara and veil. She was carrying a bouquet of roses, carnations and Freesias. She had two bridesmaids dressed in pale green satin with flowers in their hair and matching bouquets like the bride. Timothy was the page boy dressed in blue velvet.

The reception was held at the Cricket Pavilion, Hambrook. Nichola and Mick went to Cornwall for their honeymoon. I felt very sad as I saw them leave, knowing I had lost another daughter, but I was lucky as they would be living near me when they returned.

My sister-in-law, Pauline and her husband, Foster, came down from Scotland, and Moira and Doy from Liverpool, so it was a family gathering with my Mum and my sisters.

While the house was being built, Nichola and Mick lived in a caravan near Mick's parents. Nichola now had a little black and white kitten called Smudge that was very knowing and loveable.

Dawn had her first child, a little girl called Debra born September 27th, 1965, the same date as my Mum's birthday, and Sandra's, Dorothy's daughter.

CHAPTER 21

Mum decided to stay with Arnold and me for Christmas 1965 so I prepared all the food ready and I bought a few bottles of wine to celebrate. I decorated the house with holly, mistletoe and trimmings, but I knew that it would not be quite the same without the girls.

I picked up Mum on the Wednesday as Christmas day was on the Friday so that she would not have to rush about at the last minute. When I arrived at Hillesley she was ready with her bag full of goodies and presents.

We stopped on the way to see my sister Dorothy and to have a cup of tea, then we set off for home. It was a wet evening and the traffic was very bad, especially near the aircraft factory at Patchway. I had promised to pick up Nichola from her hairdressing salon so I had to travel towards Filton. I was stopped and waiting in a queue of traffic leaving a space for the workers to leave the factory at one of the main gates when, out of the blue, there was a terrific bang. My car was pushed past the gateway into the line of waiting traffic on the other side. There was the sound of smashing glass and my car engine was roaring. Mum was thrown on to the floor and I was caught behind the steering wheel. The ambulance arrived and Mum was taken to Southmead hospital for a check-up. I was very worried about the smash. In fact I didn't know what was happening. Luckily the police arrived. I knew one of the policemen, a Mr Jim Watts who was very kind and understanding.

The car was pushed on to the side of the road and I was taken to Southmead hospital to see Mum. I was wet through and carrying all the parcels. Mum was very upset but as there were no bones broken she was allowed to leave with me.

The policeman took us home and I had to give evidence of how it happened. All I knew was that someone had run into me and I was told it was a bus with workers in it that had skidded when the driver had braked suddenly, pushing me about seventeen feet into a line of waiting traffic.

I remember ringing Nichola to say what had happened. She hurried home, very upset, and I sat down and she dried my hair and set it with pins. I was in a daze. Arnold arrived home and, seeing me so upset, he didn't really know what to do. We didn't want to eat our evening meal.

We retired to bed very worried about the car and what was going to happen. At about two o'clock in the morning I awoke with an awful pain in my neck and back. I got up and sat by the fire not wanting to wake up the family. The pain was so bad I didn't know what to do. In the morning I went to Southmead Hospital for a check-up. I was given a collar to wear and I had to go back for treatment twice a week. The car was a write-off and yet not one window was smashed, yet the other driver I had been pushed into had all his windows broken, and he said he thought I was overtaking him. Our car was three inches shorter and the chassis was cracked after the impact, so now we had all the worry of the insurance claims and getting another car.

Our Christmas was spoilt. There was plenty of food, the coffee table laden with drinks and goodies and yet no one wanted to eat or drink. In fact our nerves were so bad that when Arnold accidentally dropped the radiogram lid we all shouted at each other. In fact, even now I can't stand a loud noise behind me, or a sudden bang.

Mum also saw a specialist later for the insurance company as her back was painful. I went with her and it really was a third degree. You would have thought Mum was making it up. Like all things, with illness it comes back to your age. You can expect pain after your forty years of age, in other words not much sympathy. But Mum never felt the same after that. Her back was very painful at times.

I went for my treatment - neck exercises and heat treatment. I remember one day leaving the hospital covered in red spots all over my face. I am sure the heat did not agree with me, and while waiting for Arnold outside the factory gate I felt so poorly that I just lay my head on the steering wheel to rest when I heard a deep voice say, "You can't park here Miss. You are on a double yellow line". I looked up and there was a policeman leaning against the car. For a moment I could not focus and then I started to stutter from embarrassment all about not feeling well and just leaving the hospital. Seeing my predicament he smiled and said, "I can see you are not feeling very well so this time I will let you off, but don't do it again", and he rode off on his bicycle smiling.

I was having very bad headaches and taking pain killers. My energy was sapped. I could not keep going for very long - everything was a trial. After the hospital treatment there was not much improvement, but I was informed it would take time.

We bought another car, a 1965 Ford Cortina, so in a way the smash had been very expensive, and we were the losers as our Anglia could have lasted for a long time and my mother's health would not have been impaired. I would sit about the house, not caring about anything. Then a friend suggested I visit an osteopath who had helped a lot of people like myself. So once a week I went for treatment, and after a while he suggested I take off my collar as it was restricting my movements. What a relief to take it off! But I was rather scared in case I was doing wrong. But as the days rolled by I found that I was moving a little better although the neck was still very stiff and painful with any sudden turn, my headaches were still with me and I could not bend too long with the pain my back, but as the days passed by I learnt to some extent to live with it.

Dawn now had a second child, a little boy called Andrew born on the first of October, 1966, so she had plenty to do.

CHAPTER 22

Nichola was now working in Stoke Gifford. The lady who had owned the Post Office retired and she rented one of her rooms to a Mrs Stenning who was already doing hairdressing from her caravan near her home. It was much better for Nichola as it was not so far for her to go. The Post Office had been transferred to a Mr and Mrs St Quentin who had a grocery shop next door.

Nichola would walk up to have her lunch with me so we saw much more of her. She was now living in her house, but there was still a lot to do.

I still went to see Mum once a week, and we would go for a ride and sometimes weekends Arnold and I would take her for a picnic and a drink on the way home afterwards which she enjoyed. She loved company and she found it very lonely living on her own. In fact, one day I went to see her and she wasn't home. I looked everywhere. Then a neighbour said, "I think you will find her along the lane. She went off with the potato pickers early this morning". So I drove along the lane and I waited outside the gate where the potatoes were growing. Then along came a crowd of young people with their baskets full of potatoes, but no Mum. Then I heard one of the women say, "That's Joyce Dowsell by the gate. I expect she's come to pick up her mother". They all passed me by, smiling and laughing with one another, so I waited, and waited. Then round the corner of the field came my Mum. She could hardly walk with her basket of potatoes. When she reached me she said, "Don't bloody say it. I know I should not have been in the fields and I can hardly walk and am I glad to see you and to have a lift home!" I said nothing. I could see that although she was tired she had enjoyed being with the other women having a laugh and a gossip.

I took Mum home and made a cup of tea and when I left her she gave me a bag of potatoes that was my Mum - she always shared everything. She was a real character. Another time I picked Dorothy and Timothy up and took them for a visit. Mum had one of those big black fireplaces which she would clean until it had a lovely shine on it. Well! Clever me, anxious to help, accidentally knocked the boiling kettle off the hob, and oh what a mess! The fire was nearly put out and the fireplace and I were covered in white ash. All that polish for nothing! Poor Mum. She gave me a good dressing down, but in the end we all had a jolly good laugh. It was all such a mess. Even my hair was white.

Dawn and Michael had now moved to a house in Downend, just outside Bristol, which was a lot better for them and nearer to me. The two children were now good company for each other.

We had some very sad news from Scotland. Foster, Pauline's husband, had had a heart attack and he had died. He was only forty five years old. It happened as he was walking down the street. It was a very upsetting time for the family. Also my mother-in-law, who had been very poorly for quite a while, passed away in 1967. Arnold and I journeyed to Liverpool for the funeral. So many memories crowded my mind as I saw all the familiar places. It was such a sad time to return, and for two deaths so close to each other in one family.

Nichola decided she would like to learn to swim, and would I go with her. Everybody said it would be a good idea for all my aches and pains as swimming was a very good exercise for all parts of the body. So I decided to learn. So Mick and Nichola picked up Arnold and me once a week in the evening and we joined a swimming class at Bristol North Baths, Nichola in her bikini and pretty flowered hat and I in a black one-piece with a white fluffy hat. Arnold and Mick were good swimmers and they enjoyed the evenings. Nichola and I didn't like putting our faces under the water.

It took quite a time for Nichola and me to learn to swim and the instructor said that I looked like a lazy frog. My arms would pull but my legs were very lazy. Nichola on the other hand was good. Her legs were very strong. We spent a lot of time on the edge of the pool just holding on to the bar. Nichola said that I looked like a seal in the water when I looked up underneath my fluffy hat.

We had a lot of encouragement from the other swimmers, and it was all good fun. On the way home we would buy fish and chips for our supper as the swimming gave us such an appetite. I used to feel exhausted for a few days after, but I persevered.

One evening we used the University pool as our pool was being cleaned. The students used it for their canoes and some parts were very deep. In fact I thought I was going to drown. Not being familiar with the new pool, I was walking slowly along thinking it would just be up to my waist when suddenly I went under. I lost my cool and each time I came up I shouted to the other swimmers who thought I was joking and they just waved back and went on swimming. On the third time Arnold noticed my difficulty and swam quickly over. He lifted me on to the side of the pool and started to bang my back as I was coughing so badly - choking in fact with the water I had swallowed. It took me quite a time to control myself, and what a nasty feeling it was! I felt that my poor old tummy would never be the same again. But, like all things, we do recover given time. If Arnold had not seen me ..... well, it doesn't bear thinking about.

Our own pool was ready again, but I was very nervous and I swam near the bar, but I did manage to get a certificate for swimming 100 yards. Nichola did not really enjoy the swimming. She still had a fear of the water. At about this time Mrs Stenning lost her husband and moved away. Nichola decided to buy the shop as she knew all the customers, but she was very sad to lose her boss who had become such a great friend.

CHAPTER 23

Nichola found that owning the shop took up much more of her time. Every Monday I would drive her into Bristol and collect all the items required for the shop, and then we would look through the stores and do most of our shopping and then back to Nichola's house for lunch.

I remember one day, while waiting for Nichola to return to the car, I shut the door with a bang on my finger. For a moment I just stood stunned with the pain, but I knew I had to open the door again to release my finger which I did, but the pain was agony and it took a long time to heal. Even now it aches at different times. Another time, returning home, I said to Nichola, "Oh dear, I have left my umbrella in the stores". I remembered I had put it down to pay the bill, but halfway up the Gloucester Road Nichola started to laugh. I said, "Now, what is it?". She pointed to the bonnet of the car, and there, resting against the bottom of the windscreen, was my umbrella. So I must have picked it up in the shop and then laid it on the bonnet of the car while I put all the shopping in the boot. How it stayed on so long beats me as there was a lot of traffic about so it was stop and start all the time yet it remained secure. I said, "When we stop the next time I will let down my window, reach out and lift it in". I did not realize I was being watched by the other drivers who, when I had retrieved the umbrella, gave a cheer and blew their horns, everyone smiling.

Another time, after parking the car, we went into the Ladies to freshen ourselves. We thought we heard someone in the toilet trying to open the door. We asked, "Are you alright?", and a little voice said, "I can't open the door". Well, we tried to help, but the door would not be moved. The lock had jammed. We were just going to get help when a big man entered the Ladies and asked, "Have you seen my wife? I have been waiting for ages outside". The lady shouted out, "I am stuck in the toilet. Can you open the door?". After trying for a while he said, "Well, stand back, I will try and break it down". He stood back and then rushed at the door. On the second rush the door collapsed with the man falling on top of the lady on the toilet. Well, it had to be seen to be believed! For a moment no one spoke, and then we all had hysterics. It was like the comedy, Some mothers do have 'em, with Michael Crawford.

To help Nichola I used to wash all the hairdressing towels and once a week I would clean her house, doing the little jobs she didn't have time for. That was when I became a Country Western Singers' fan. Mick would put a lot of records on the record player for me to listen to as I worked as he also enjoyed Country Western music. Smudge would also keep me company.

One weekend, when it was raining hard, Nichola suggested we take the towels to wash to the launderette. It was the first time we had been. It was quite an experience. We sat down watching the machines and seeing the washing whizzing round. One lady had put a teddy bear in to wash with her clothes, telling us that she had found it in her attic and she was going to wash it and send it to her granddaughter in Australia. Well, after a little while watching the teddy going round and round as it had now become the focus of our attention, Nichola and I, at the same time, said, "Look! I believe the teddy is breaking up!". As we watched, first the head went round, followed by the body, and then the arms and legs - all separate. The lady, seeing it, said, "Oh dear! Now I will have to sew it all together again before I can send it away". She wasn't a bit worried.

Another lady, who had been searching through her shopping bag for ages, said, "Please keep an eye on my machine for a minute. I think I must have left my cigarettes on the shop counter". When she came back smoking we thought she had found them. Her machine stopped and, as she started to take out her washing, she cried out, "Here they are in the machine!", and what a mess! All her washing was covered in pieces of tobacco. She had put the cigarettes in with her clothes. Nichola and I had a good laugh, and we said to the lady on leaving, "We must come again. It is better than the pictures!".

Nichola bought me a bicycle for my birthday as she thought it would help me to travel quicker when Arnold had the car. I was very pleased with it, but I nearly had an accident the first day I rode it. I had forgotten that it was a long time ago since I last rode a bicycle. On the way out of the Avenue I nearly ran into a little boy coming round on his bicycle. He was going very fast and at the last minute he changed direction and passed over in front of me. I lost my balance and had to jump off very quickly so as not to fall. After that I was very careful until my balance returned.

Dorothy was now married to Jack and living at Falfield, and Timothy was at school so I did not see him so much. One day Dorothy said to me, "I saw your Anglia the other day go past. It was your number". I said, "You must have made a mistake as the car was a write-off". We then had a letter from the police in London to ask if we still had the car, and, if so, why had we not licensed it. We wrote back and explained why and we heard no more about it, so what it was all about we did not know.

Arnold and I decided to have a little trip around north Wales, taking our chance on bed and breakfast accommodation. We stayed a few days at Harlech, looking around the castle and various places of interest. We stayed with a blacksmith and his wife. They were very friendly people. The blacksmith showed us all over his blacksmith shop explaining everything, and, just as I passed the furnace, there was a terrific bang. I nearly jumped out of my skin, but he roared with laughter. Apparently he always did that every time someone new visited the forge to give them a fright, but, as you know, bangs are not my speciality, and I nearly fainted. I tried to smile, but it was an effort. He did not say how he made the bang. It was his secret and his sense of humour.

We passed by Conway and Caernarvon, and a few other Welsh towns. Our weather was not very good so most of the time we were in the car, but it made a change for us both.

Mum was now living in a new bungalow at Hawkesbury Upton, not far away from my sister Bess, who went round to see her every day. Bess made her special little cooking treats, did the main washing and her shopping. Mum still liked to do as much as possible herself. Dorothy and I would visit and also help all we could. Mum would always say to me if she wanted something new, "Joyce, see if you can get me this on your travels". It is a little saying we always remember when we think of Mum.

One day leaving Mum, Nichola and I travelled along Sandpits Lane from Hawkesbury to Horton. At the end of the lane were twin roads, both going down to Horton, with a patch of grass in the centre. As we started down a bus full of workers came up the same road but in a flash Nichola, who had been driving, swung the car quickly into the second road just missing the bus which had stopped on seeing us. It was so sudden that some of the people in the bus had their mouths wide open, but as we waved to them that it was alright they waved back. We didn't expect to see a bus at that time of day.

Nichola then had the bright idea of going horse riding and asked me if I would go with her. So one evening we went along to the Riding Stables, North Woods, Winterbourne, which was owned by a Mr and Mrs Irish, and joined a riding class. We bought our riding hats and whips, but we decided we would not buy full riding kit in case we did not like horse riding, so we just wore trousers and sweaters as near enough in colour to the real riding kit.

The first evening we were very nervous. My horse was very tall and I had to stand on a step to get on his back. His name was Jack and he had a wall eye. Christine, the young lady who took the class, was a very likeable and helpful girl. We trotted down the lane feeling very nervous of the horses, but when two young gentlemen passed us on their own horses raising their hats we felt like one of the crowd and we quite enjoyed it. But the next day we could hardly walk. The tops of our legs and hips were very stiff. In fact it took quite a few days after that first ride to get over the stiffness.

Nichola had had a smaller horse and she joined in with the other riders quite easily. The second time I rode Nichola's horse, quite the opposite to Jack. In fact my feet were very near the road, which was covered in ice patches that day. The horse was slipping a lot of the time and I was scared he might fall down. Looking back at me, Nichola thought I looked very funny on such a small horse. In fact afterwards she said, "Were you riding the horse Mum or walking with it?".

CHAPTER 24

Arnold and I decided to prepare Mum's garden so that we could put down the grass seed. But what a job! The ground was very stony, and very hard to level, and the back garden was worse. There was a big pile of stones that had been left by the builders which we had to move before we could start. It took fifty barrelfuls to move it, and by the time we finished, as it was a rather warm day, Arnold and I were worn out.

My back and my neck started to trouble me until I could hardly walk. I became so frustrated that I threw my rake across the garden swearing. At the same time I said, "Oh please God help me", and he did answer my prayer.

The following Sunday Arnold, on reading the News of the World, called out to me, "Joyce, come and read this. Perhaps this man can help you". On the front page was a photograph of a man in Anglesey healing a patient. His name was Harry Harrison and he worked for Lord Boston. As he said, "I work for two Lords and I have had a lot of success with my healing with the laying on of my hands". There was quite a story about him by the reporter. Arnold decided to write for me to see him. We had a reply by return of post, but the thought of the long journey with my back was not very inviting.

In the end I said I would go. I had tried everything else so I couldn't go wrong. It was a nice day to travel. We took sandwiches and hot coffee with us. We did not hurry, enjoying the scenery as we drove along through Chepstow, Monmouth, Hereford, Leominster, Ludlow, Welshpool, Llanpyllin and Llangynog. We stopped by a lovely lake at Bala to have our food and to stretch our legs, then on to Ffestiniog, Betws-y-Coed, Bangor, and then Moelfre where Mr Harrison lived.

We travelled through the village and Arnold said, "I will ask where `Caer Borth' is". That was the name of Lord Boston's house. But I said, "No, it is a little further down the road", and so it was, with a little road winding down to the sea. How I knew was a mystery, but later on I knew I was guided there.

We found a place for bed and breakfast and the next morning Arnold and I looked around the village, and then we found a beach on the opposite side of Lord Boston's house where we spent a few hours waiting for my appointment. I was worried about what might happen, and if he asked me a lot of questions about the Bible I would not have all the answers. In fact I felt like returning home. Arnold said, "Don't be silly. He is only human like us, and he might be able to help you". With that we left the beach and travelled down the little winding road to the big house.

What a shock we had when we arrived! The drive was full of cars and people walking about. "Oh dear!", I thought, "another long wait". We saw a gentleman in the field walking a dog, a big black Great Dane, whom we realized after was Lord Boston.

On looking up at the door it was written that the house was built in 1965, the same year as I had had my accident - another co-incidence. A lot of people came out looking a lot happier than when they went in, and one man was not using his walking stick any more which gave me courage.

Then the door opened and my name was called. Arnold came in with me for support, but I need not have worried. A very pleasant man stood up and shook hands with us both. Then he said, "Take a seat and tell me all about yourself", which I did, leaving nothing out. Then he said, "There is nothing to worry about. I am just going to lay my hands on your back and neck, and I am going to send out some prayers for you to get better".

I sat very still, waiting, and then I felt as if someone had punched me on the back and my mouth became very stiff and I could hardly move my jaw. Mr Harrison said, "Don't worry. People do feel different things when I am healing them, but I am sure that it will be for the good. I started to cry then, and he said, "Don't worry, but just before you reach home you will feel a great depression as sometimes you have to get worse to get better, but remember what I said, and don't let it worry you too much as it will only be for a little while.

On the trip back home my mind was full of all the things Mr Harrison had told me, and I was a little apprehensive of the depression I would have. Just before we reached the Severn Bridge we stopped to have a cup of tea from a flask. While drinking it, it happened - such a feeling of depression that I did not know what to do with myself and all I wanted to do was to reach home quickly.

For three weeks I cried every day. I could not talk about my meeting with Mr Harrison without crying. Arnold said, "He has made you worse, not better", but I remembered the feeling I had when he touched me and what he had said I would have, so I persevered, waiting for the depression to pass.

Then one morning I felt as if a great big black cloud had lifted and taken my depression with it. I was not free from all the aches and pains, but there was a difference. I found I was singing again as I always did while working. And then one day, sitting alone, I knew that I wanted to thank Mr Harrison for helping me, but what could I do or say? And then, out of the blue, this poem came to me.

To a Friend

To you I came in grief and pain
My body most tormented.
A smile, a word, a touch, you gave,
I went away contented.
The days rolled by, my hopes were high,
My tears fell fast and free.
Just like the clouds up in the sky
I wandered aimlessly.
And then the sun began to shine
My heart was most uplifted.
No more to sit, and mope and pine,
My strength to me was gifted.
And now my friend, my thanks to you.
With God's help I am well,
And all the things you taught me true
Will forever cast a spell.

I also wrote a poem to Lord Boston. In fact I wrote four poems in one morning. I had never written poetry before or been very good at any kind of writing, so it was a great surprise to me and the family.

To Lord Boston

A Lord is he with a heart of gold
Who gives his house with wealth untold.
His open door will ever be
A Way to God eternally.

He was very pleased with the poem and he sent a word of thanks through Mr Harrison, and according to Mr Harrison he kept the poem on his bedside table. I must add that when I wrote these poems I felt great humility as I did with every poem I wrote afterwards. I am sure I was being guided.

Mick's mother lent Arnold and me her caravan for a week at St Agnes, Cornwall. The site was owned by a lady whose ancestors had been smugglers. Her arms were covered in silver bracelets. She was a very nice lady. She even had her own pottery wheel and she made her own pots of different shapes and sizes.

It was a glorious week of sunshine. We were very close to the beach and the perfume of the wild flowers was wonderful. I had not seen so many wild flowers for a long time. The hedgerows were alive with colour, and the cliffs dropping down to the sea had a lush carpet of heather and clover. There were little paths for the people to walk on and to enjoy the scenery, the sound of the seagulls as if they were welcoming us and the hum of the bees as they flew from flower to flower.

You could hear the sound of the children as they played on the beach and swam in the sea, and as I sat on the cliff relaxing in the sunshine and listening to all the sounds around me, the words of this poem came to me.

A Summer's Day

Summer sun and gorgeous smells
God's own rockery excels.
Bumble bees and birds of prey,
Children laughing - what a day!
The rocks steep sharply down to sea
With little paths invitingly
Winding round and round the bay.
I feel I want to kneel and pray,
To thank you God for all I see
As peace I feel steal over me.

St Agnes, Cornwall

We were very sad when it was time to leave. We felt we could have stayed there forever, but, like all good things, they do not go on forever. But every time I read my poem I return.

CHAPTER 25

Nichola and Mick decided to have a divorce. It was a very sad period for us all. Perhaps they were too young when they got married, and with far too much responsibility, working day and night so to speak with no time for relaxation. We all had a very unhappy Christmas, each trying to comfort each other. It took quite a time to bring the smile back to Nichola's face and for life to return to normal.

As the days rolled by we slowly came back to life again. I took Nichola up to Anglesey to see Mr Harrison who gave her a healing and words of comfort. It was a very cold journey. Ice and snow covered the roads but we felt it was necessary.

Nichola returned to live with us and, as she still had the hairdressing shop, there was plenty for her to do. She brought her cat Smudge with her who became one of the family. She also bought herself a second-hand car, a white Austin A40 of which she was very proud. One day she dropped her keys down the drain near the car and, just as we were wondering what to do, a council man came round in his lorry and got them out for her, having the right kind of tools at the time to clean out the drains. Nichola was always lucky with things like that - always something or someone turned up to help her when she was in distress.

We still went up to help Mum and to spend a day with her and she came to spend different weeks with us and at Christmas time. But she had become very tired and found it very difficult to walk and she slept a lot. I planted some roses for her in the garden, and I did my best to keep it tidy and to cut the grass once a week.

Nichola did not like leaving Smudge out at night in case he got lost and went back to his old home so we kept him in the house with a dirt box, just in case he wanted to use it. He had the run of the house. But we had a lot of sleepless nights with him. He would jump on to the wardrobes and the dressing-tables as he always came to life at night. One night it came to a climax. I had left my window open and there, in the middle of the night, was Smudge. Hanging upside-down outside the window! It took me a long time to get him back in as he was so frightened. When I did I said, "This is the end! Out you go at night!". So the next day I made him a nice bed in the shed. I put a cat flap on the door so that he would go in and out, and that was the end of our troubles.

One day I could not find him, and I thought, "Oh dear, what will Nichola say? She will be very upset", and then I went upstairs to make my bed and there, right underneath my quilt, was Smudge, fast asleep. Every day after that he would wait until I had made my bed and then he would tunnel underneath the quilt with just his face looking out. He looked so contented that I didn't have the heart to move him. Also, we were all having peaceful nights at last.

Nichola and I still enjoyed our horse riding. I didn't realise that horses were so strong-minded though. When we arrived at the stables all the horses would gather round us for a lump of sugar, and they would push and shove each other, just like little children when they want something. There was one big chestnut horse who tormented Nichola as she passed in front of it. He would lift his front foot up as though to kick her, and when she passed behind him he would do the same with his back feet. I was sure he was smiling.

One day when we went riding it was very wet and windy. Christine took us down a little winding path. She rode in front followed by Nichola and then me. There were some horses in the field alongside the path and they all decided to join in the fun. I am not sure what really happened but suddenly Nichola's horse took fright, dashed in front of Christine and galloped down the path.

Well, it was panic stations! My horse followed with Christine trying to get back in front of Nichola. The horses in the field galloped alongside the hedge enjoying the fun. We were hit in the face by all the low growing branches from the trees, and every minute we thought we were going to fall down. Christine managed to slow Nichola's horse and bring her back to see where I was. Well, I had slid off my horse and I was standing in a pool of water. My foot had slipped out of the stirrup. It was very funny really. Nichola's face was all black from her mascara and we were all wet through. As if that wasn't enough, on the way back down the path someone was shooting rabbits and a bullet just whizzed behind my head. If it had happened a second before I would have been shot.

I had made friends with all the little children. They would ride with me and tell me what to do, and when we did jumping they would turn to watch me and give me words of advice. There is no doubt in my mind that the time to learn anything is when we are very young as there are not so many fears of what could happen. Sometimes when we rode in the field to learn how to train our horses in obedience there had been a silent watcher, a fox, half concealed in the long grass. I made a point of looking for it and I was never disappointed. I would always see the lovely long brush resting on the grass, and the quick movement of its head as it was always very wary of us as well. Added below is a poem I wrote.

The Friendly Fox

The first time we saw you, oh what a thrill!
A golden glow in the grass so still,
A suitable audience for our riding spree
A front seat fan, your admission free.

You seemed to enjoy our shouts and fun,
No fear you showed although you were one
As if you were lonely and wanted to share
Our fun and games without a care.

Your golden brush behind you span,
A tempting gift for greedy man
Who doesn't see your beauty wild
And wants to conquer like a child.

To see you thus without a fear,
Your presence oh so very near,
Fills one with a love and awe
Of one so cheeky, and yet so small.

But please beware of the circus fray
When the redcoats come with the hounds at bay,
And when you hear the horn please hide
As they are not your friends that ride.

And next time we ride our eyes will look
For the friendly fox from shady nook,
And our hearts will be gay to see our friend
Alive, and well, with brush on end.

Another time, while jumping obstacles in the field, Nichola was riding a white horse called Eclipse. She was just preparing to jump when the horse stood up on its back legs and threw her off. She went down like a sack of potatoes. I was very worried in case she had really hurt herself. She was very sore for a long while, but no bones were broken.

One lady rider, who had been riding for a long time and who wore all the proper gear, thought she was the cat's whiskers. She never spoke to us or to anyone else. But as I said before, horses are very intelligent and have minds of their own. Well, on day we were all riding in the field when she passed us, head in the air as usual. She rode straight for the stile to jump it but the horse had other ideas. Just as she reached the jump the horse lowered his head and threw her in the hedge instead. Nichola and I just looked at each other. I bet you can guess our thoughts, but we felt very sorry for her. We asked her if she had hurt herself, but without a word she got up and remounted the horse and rode away out of sight. I think it was really her pride that had been hurt.

I was beginning to experience a foreknowledge of what was about to happen. For example, a friend of Nichola suggested that she should go riding with him. He knew of a riding stable that would hire out horses for the day. She agreed to go, but the night before I had a picture shown to me like on a television set, and right in the centre was a big chestnut horse. He looked very fiery, tossing his head about. So I said to Nichola, "If you are given a chestnut horse, don't ride it."

At about tea time they returned home and the gentleman was covered in blood. I was too scared to look at Nichola in case she too was the same. I said, "Whatever happened?" She said, "Well, I was offered the chestnut horse but, after what you said, I declined to ride it and my friend said he would ride it being an experienced rider." But, while riding through the woods, the horse took fright at something in the grass and he threw Nichola's friend on to the ground, scratching his face on some thorns. He looked a real sorry sight but, after bathing his face and having tea with us, he said he was alright to return home.

CHAPTER 26

Nichola had a new boyfriend. His name was Colin Dickinson and he came from Leeds, Yorkshire. He worked at Rolls Royce. After a whirlwind courtship, they were married at Chipping Sodbury Registry Office attended by close family and friends. Nichola wore a mauve suit on which she wore a spray of freesias. The wedding breakfast was held at an hotel in Chipping Sodbury. They had a flat in Redland, Bristol, so once again Arnold and I were on our own. Nichola had sold her hairdressing salon as she wanted to make a fresh start.

One day when I was busy sewing I picked up my glasses to see better, but unfortunately I had the sewing needle in my hand and as I put the glasses on the needle went straight into my left eye. Oh, what a sharp pain! I dashed to the mirror to see the damage and to find my eye bleeding. I rang

Mr Harrison in Anglesey and asked him for a healing which he did while I was on the 'phone, but he said, "Go to the Eye Hospital for a check-up just to satisfy yourself." The eye had stopped bleeding, but I decided to go to the Eye Hospital as Mr Harrison advised me. I went just as I was - no coat and with my apron still on. I sat in a queue for a long time before my name was called. I was given a thorough check and found that there was no permanent damage done to the eye. But I knew that the healing had started before I went to the hospital and I rang Mr Harrison to thank him.

Arnold felt that he would like to visit Great Yarmouth where he was born, and to show me his old school. We set out on our journey, Arnold full of the stories of childhood days.

We passed through Cambridge where there was a big sign saying "The American War Cemetery". We had passed by when suddenly I felt I had to stop and look inside. We turned and parked the car just outside.

I had never visited a war cemetery before and I find it very hard to explain the feelings I felt as I saw all those little white crosses. I just stood and the tears fell down my cheeks.

Arnold and I walked round and round looking at the statues which looked so life-like - just young boys who had died fighting for their country. There were pools full of lilies and goldfish that swam. You were afraid to cough in case you disturbed the peace. In fact we did not feel like talking. Our hearts were very sad.

We went into a room where all the names of the servicemen were listed. All those names! It must have been very hard for the parents and families to visit England and to search for their loved one's name, and then to walk amongst all those crosses to find their last resting place.

We sent up a prayer for them all, and we left feeling very sad as we continued our journey.

But suddenly words started to form in my mind, and I wrote this poem below on all the different scraps of paper I could find in my handbag.

The American Cemetery, Cambridge

A Mother's Thoughts

Little white crosses marking each grave,
All that is left of a love that you gave.
A blanket of green to cover your bed,
A sky of blue above your head.
The peace that you fought for is surely yours,
And God himself will heal your sores.

But as I stand and look at all the names,
And think of all your childish games,
My eyes fill with tears for such a waste.
I am filled with horror and distaste
As I know now that your love was in vain,
No lesson was learnt for the life that you gave.

The statues, all magnificent and serene
Of a soldier, sailor, airman and marine,
For a parent to look and visit a while,
Their hearts full of tears for a face that can't smile,
For a voice that can't whisper endearment and love
For a body to hold that was sent from above.

A pool full of lilies and goldfish to swim,
Lingering walks where thoughts will creep in,
A hush that is felt by each single one
As we each have our memories of a loved one.
I wonder if we all are thinking the same,
That war itself is a hell of a game.

A garden of remembrance is all very well
But how much better if no horror to tell.
Our children alive and with us each day,
Not rotting beneath a garden of clay.
As we all know now, their fight was in vain,
No lesson was learnt from the life that they gave.

I now know it was meant for me to stop and visit the cemetery so that I could relay through my poem the devastation of war. We reached Great Yarmouth where we visited Arnold's Aunty Margery who used to be a headmistress. She was very pleased to see us and, after giving us some tea and all the news, she suggested we stay at the hotel of a friend of hers nearby as it was too much for her to have guests at her age.

She came out with us to spend a pleasant evening, talking over old times, and to enjoy an evening at the hotel and to meet many of her friends there.

The next day we visited the graves of Arnold's grandparents, Grandfather and Grandmother Milburn with whom Arnold had lived as a child. They had owned fishing trawlers and drifters, and they had been well-known in Great Yarmouth. Arnold remembered that there had always been plenty of fresh fish to eat. And then on to the graves of Grandfather and Grandmother Kidman who had been herbalists, but with whom he had not spent so much time.

Arnold had relations in Australia. In fact there was a Sir Sidney Kidman who was an Australian millionaire who owned many sheep and cattle stations. A book was written about him by Ion L Idriess and he was called the Cattle King. He owned and had interests in vast tracks of land in Australia, and he was a great friend of Lord Vesty who lived at Stowell Park, Gloucester. Sir Sidney's son, Walter, sent Nichola a koala bear when she was two years old, and we corresponded for a long while.

We then visited Arnold's old pastor college at North Walsham where Lord Nelson went to school. We went inside and a teacher showed us round. Arnold was very interested although there had been no changes since he left. I was glad to leave as I had picked up a great sadness as I stood in the quadrangle. Did I pick up the sadness of a new recruit, sad at the thought of leaving his loved ones for the first time?

We also looked at Grandfather Milburn's house from the outside which was now a hotel.

Arnold was surprised at the absence of the many fishing boats which used to line the banks of the River Yare when he was a boy, and he took me to many places he had known in his youth.

I found Norfolk very flat after my own Cotswold rolling hills, but it was a change of scenery and many memories for Arnold.

The months rolled by slowly with just every day more or less the same, and when we heard that Nichola was having a baby, something she had wanted for a long time, we were all pleased for her. As she had so many steps to climb at the flat I suggested she return home to have the baby which she did. It was also nearer for Colin to go to work.

The day arrived for Nichola to go to the hospital, Southmead, as her labour pains had started. It was an anxious time for us all. She had a rather hard time especially as she had blood pressure problems. The baby was born in the early morning of the 28th of February, 1973 - a little boy.

It was most unfortunate that at the time of his birth there was a hospital strike and, while I was washing up the breakfast dishes the next morning, there was a knock at the door. I nearly collapsed with fright to see an ambulance outside and the driver standing by the door.

He said, "Don't worry. I have just brought your daughter and baby home as there is a strike on at the hospital and there is no one to look after them." The baby was put into my arms. Nichola was still in her nightdress and dressing gown as her outdoor clothes had been brought back home. So much for a nice rest in hospital, poor dear! But anyway, mother and baby were back with their loved ones. Nichola called her son Neil. He was a lovely boy, but it was a big challenge to have a baby in the house again.

Nichola took a long time to feel better so I did most of the running about and looking after them. When the baby was restless I would hold him in my arms, singing all the old songs which always had a soothing effect. Nichola gradually regained her strength and began looking for a home of their own.

CHAPTER 27

Nichola and Colin bought a cottage at Over Lane, Almondsbury. It had a large garden so there was plenty of work to do. I went down every day after lunch to give her a hand, and we took Neil for long walks, rain or shine. He was always happy to be out although Nichola and I used to get very tired pushing the pram up all the hills that are in Almondsbury. Whichever way we went we had to climb one. It was very picturesque with lovely views of the River Severn as the cottage was built on a hill. At the top of the hill was a grocery and paper shop, a public house and a post office. At the bottom of the hill was a war memorial and a garden centre.

There were little paths that meandered through the woodland slopes down to Lower Almondsbury, passing the Vicarage and down through the cemetery where there was a lovely old Church and a village green. Just around the corner was a very old inn called The Bowl which looked so attractive with its white-washed walls and pots of lovely flowers decorating the front. It was built by the monks in 1132.

There was also a dentist and a grocery shop at the bottom of the village. It was a very peaceful village - very much like the village of Hillesley.

There was a forge near the school which always seemed very busy, and we would stand and watch the sparks flying through the open doorway. There was also a village hall which was used as a play group school for tiny tots.

Behind Nichola's cottage was a rambling old house that is now a residence for the elderly with a lovely olde worlde garden with lots of flowering shrubs and trees. In the spring it had a carpet of daffodils and bluebells. There were little seats to sit a while, a goldfish pond and a lovely old summer house. You could imagine what it must have all looked like years ago. Even so, just to walk around it you could feel the peace and tranquillity.

Nichola had a lot of wild flowers growing on the garden walls which attracted the butterflies, and in the summer evenings the outside wall of the cottage would be covered in Red Admiral butterflies. In fact there were so many that you could hardly put a hand between them, and Nichola had to keep the windows shut as there were so many flying around outside that every time she opened the windows or door they would fly in.

One weekend we took Dawn, Andrew and Debra up to Anglesey to meet Mr Harrison. We stayed at an hotel just outside Anglesey, making it a nice change for us all. Dawn suffered very badly with asthma and Andrew also had symptoms of it. With the long journey Debra was sick in the car coming back. We had to stop and wash out the car. There were no immediate healings as things don't always work out that way. Sometimes it takes time as it isn't meant to be.

Another weekend Mr Harrison invited Arnold and me to stay with him and his wife. On arriving he said, "We will drop formalities and call each other by our Christian names. I am Harry and this is my wife Jenny." Jenny was the cook for Lord Boston and she made us feel very welcome.

In the evening we all went out for a drink at the Kinmel Arms public house, Moelfre. I was sat down at one of the tables when suddenly I turned to watch Harry ordering the drinks. His hair was down to his shoulders, wearing a loose jacket, brown trousers, bow tie, colourful shirt and brown sandals. He was leaning against the bar and, as if he felt my gaze, he turned and looked at me and suddenly I knew we had met before. In fact the words `The Christ' came to me.

After that I found myself watching him and listening to every word he said, trying to sort out this new experience that I felt. I felt that it was what I had been waiting for and that Harry was the key to unlock the door for what I had to do. I did not mention this at the time, not even to Arnold, as it was something I wanted to sort out in my own mind. So on the homeward journey my mind was full of questions.

A little later we went again to Anglesey as Harry had a big healing session. There I met another healer, Mr Alfred Bridger, and his wife Doris who came from Ringwood in the New Forest. He told me a lot of things about myself which were true. Mr Bridger had met Harry when he was healing at Sway in the New Forest. In fact he had seen him on the television. From all the people he was healing he looked exhausted so Mr Bridger immediately went to help Harry as there were so many people still waiting outside in the pouring rain who had come from all over the country after seeing Harry on television.

The long hours had exhausted Harry, and when Alf arrived to help him he was resting and relaxing before healing again. Mr Bridger showed him his NFSH membership card and said he had come to help him. Harry was very pleased to see him and said, "I have been praying to God for help and now that help has arrived." Harry's brother Jack was also helping him, making sure he had plenty to eat and drink and greeting the people as they arrived.

One afternoon, while waiting for Arnold to return from work, I was suddenly aware of the dining room door being pushed open and Smudge came into the room, or so I thought since the cat was black. I bent down to stroke him and nearly fell off the chair as my hand went straight down to the floor and the cat had gone. I looked all round the house for him but there was no sign of him. On looking out of the window I saw Smudge outside on the lawn and at the same time it struck me that he had a white flash on his face whereas the cat I had seen was all black.

Then one night I saw pictures of a young boy with a mask-like face and, as I watched, he smiled at me. I also saw pictures of old Egyptian furniture. These things I saw for about a week and I was puzzled as to what it was all about, but not for long. Suddenly on the television was the story of the discovery of King Tutankhamun's tomb with all the treasures that were buried with him. They were exactly like what I had seen with one exception - the young king was very much alive and smiling at me. I also saw pictures of a Roman soldier seated on a gold throne. It was just like watching a television screen. I mentioned to my friend Alf, the healer from Ringwood, about seeing these things and he said, "You are going to experience a psychic happening in the near future. Sometimes seeing the black cat is the forerunner of another psychic happening."

About a fortnight later I was busy washing the kitchen floor when suddenly I heard a hissing sound. Remembering what Alf had said I was very scared. I thought, "Oh dear! If it is Martians descending what can I say to them as I don't know the language". But my fears vanished when, on looking out of the window, I saw a hot air balloon travelling very low over the house. In fact it came down just a few yards away, but it really took my breath away at the time wondering what I would do.

On the weekend Arnold and I fetched Mum to stay with us for a week's holiday. She always brought a bag full of goodies and some cigarettes for Arnold as she always liked to think she was paying her way. She never forgot anyone's birthday and at Christmas time you would find her wrapping up all the little presents for the family even though she could have done with the money herself. It gave her great joy.

Nearing the time Mum was getting ready to leave for home again, one afternoon she was sleeping in the armchair and seeing her so comfortable I thought that I too would have a rest. So I went upstairs and just lay on the bed relaxing my body when suddenly I felt a great vibration and my body started to lift. It was as though I was in a lift, then there was a kind of humming sound. I was rather afraid when I remembered Harry saying to me, "If you are ever afraid ask me to hold your hand", which I did, and the fear went. And suddenly I was being projected up to the sky. It was as though a hand rested on my back holding me.

Oh, but what a wonderful feeling! No pain, no aches, no tiredness - just pure freedom and ecstasy. The clouds made a pathway for me and I could feel the lovely breeze on my cheeks. Then some great impulse came to me to look down. Well, I have never liked heights and I was not sure, but the impulse was so strong that I did, and to my surprise I was looking down on a beautiful sun. It was so big and I thought, "But how can that be? I am above it". And as I was trying to work it out I suddenly was back on my bed again, but knowing that I had experienced something wonderful and remembering what Alf had prophesied - that something psychic would happen to me. It was such a glorious feeling that I wrote this poem knowing I had had my first astral travel.

My First Astral Travel

As I lay down my head to rest
I felt my body rise
Like an Apollo mission test
I was projected to the skies.

I called my friend to hold my hand
And all my fears were stilled,
And as the sun set over the land
My heart with joy was filled.

For a little while I gently floated
Like down on a summer's day.
The peace and calm is what I noted

As through the clouds my pathway lay.

Like a figurehead on ancient ships
My way was steered with care,
The breeze a caress against my lips
That nothing can compare.

But all too soon my journey ended
As if at first my fears to shed,
And back to earth my body wended
With such wondrous knowledge in my head.

Next time I go I hope to see
Much more of all the glory
That I can write of wonders seen
Into a poetry story.

About two weeks later the same thing happened to me. I felt a great impulse to relax my body after being busy in the garden. I just lay on the bed, letting my body and mind relax, and I felt my body vibrating again and the same feeling as before. I heard the humming sound and felt the pressure on my back as I was gently lifted up.

Once more I went up to the sky and through the clouds. I was always aware of what was happening. This time I was taken to a rocky place and I saw a cowboy picture being shown. I thought, "Whatever am I being shown that for?", and then, after a few seconds, I felt a presence on my left, and turning to look I saw someone who had been seated there and who now stood up to face me.

Tall and stately in white apparel, he was a glorious sight. Just like the pictures in the Bible but surrounded by a mist. As I stood and looked I was filled with a great love and humility. A gentle smile spread over His face as He lifted his hand to bless me, and I knew that somehow little me had been in the presence of our Great Saviour, Jesus Christ.

Thinking back on the astral travel, I was still puzzled about the cowboy picture, and then, as if to set my mind at rest, I saw the film on television the same week. Suddenly I knew why it had been shown to me - to prove that what I had seen was no fantasy but fact. I had seen the past and the future to prove to me that it was not imagination. So once again I wrote my experience in poem form.

My Second Astral Travel

Once more I was gently lifted high
Up through the clouds into the sky.
This time no sunset do I see
But a rock place to welcome me.

And as I looked about with awe
A movement on my left I saw
As someone who had been seated there
Arose and faced my inquisitive stare.

Tall and stately in apparel white
To me he was a glorious sight.
As of pictures in the Bible old
He was a picture to behold.

Surrounded by the mists of time
No distinct features to define
And with one hand so gently raised
As if to bless my honoured days.

Seeing the gentle smile on His face
I felt my troubles all erase,
And as I awoke I knew that I would be
A child of God eternally.

CHAPTER 28

Neil was christened at Almondsbury Church by the late Vicar Byron Thomas. The christening was attended by Colin's parents, his brother and sister. Also Alf and Doris came from Ringwood in the New Forest. It was a very pleasant day for us all.

Alf and Doris stayed with Arnold and me for the weekend, and Alf related many healing and psychic stories and also gave Nichola and myself a healing for various aches and pains. One night I was awakened by the sound of my late sister Win's voice calling my name. I had heard her calling me in the past and I knew from experience that she was troubled about something. I sat up in bed and suddenly I saw a shape by the open window which came into the room, but as quick as it came it disappeared back through the window. I felt that it was my Mum and that she was trying to reach me because she was in trouble. So the next day I had the car and drove up to Hawkesbury Upton and there I found dear old Mum sitting by the fire with her arm all bandaged and a cut on her nose.

Mum had fallen down in the night. My sister Bess had gone round the next day and found her all upset. After a cup of tea and a little chat she said to me, "Do you know, I was in a strange bedroom last night." I said, "I do know. It was mine. That is how I know you were in trouble". She looked at me very straight and I found her watching me every time I looked up.

Mum was very distressed when I left and she felt that nobody cared. As I drove home I knew that somehow I must show her that I did, so I wrote this poem to her.

To My Mum

Although my love I seldom show
I write these words to let you know
How much I do appreciate
The loving care you always take,
The way you share each little thing
Instead of hiding from your kin.

When as a child you sang to me
As I did sit upon your knee
Each song a story it would tell
The words I knew so very well
For as a treat you always said,
"Just one more verse and then to bed."

And as I grew older I knew just how much
You must have missed a loving touch,
For all your worries you bore alone
And your tears you shed inside your home,
But a smiling face you always gave
To show the world that you were brave.

But now with age you cannot hear.
You sometimes shout to hide your fear
For it is hard for one to contemplate
Unless they too doth share your fate,
But underneath is a heart of gold
And I know too well what warmth it holds.

And now as you sit in your chair
With only memories to share
Forget the worries and the pain
And that you did not rise to fame,
And remember instead, Oh Mother dear,
Your daughter loves you, and will always be near.

On the way up to take it to her the next day I was driving through Chipping Sodbury Common when I felt the passenger door of the car open and someone got in beside me. I was not afraid, in fact I felt a great peace and I thought, "Now, what is going to happen?" Well, just as I reached Horton Hill where there was a rather blind corner, I was told by thought to blow my car horn which I did, keeping my hand on it. Suddenly a car came sweeping down the hill around the corner, in fact to pass me it had to drive into a farmyard opposite thus missing me. What a look of fright on the man's face! But he drove back onto the road and straight on without stopping. So you see, once again my Guardian Angel had looked after me, and, as I drove on, I sent out a prayer of thanks, and my Guardian Angel left me the same quiet way he had arrived.

Mum was looking out of the window when I arrived, and by the time I reached the door she had the kettle on. We sat and chatted and I did a little bit of shopping for her. I also bought us both an ice-cream which we both sat and enjoyed by the fire. When it was time to leave I said, "Mum, I have written you a poem which I would like you to read while I am here". "A poem for me!", she said. "Don't be silly! Whatever would you write in a poem for me?" I said, "Well read it and see", but she would not read it, so I said, "Well, I am going to leave it on the table. Read it when I am gone". Mum smiled and said, "Perhaps when you have gone I will have a look". She waved goodbye to me from the window, and as I drove along I wondered how she would feel when she read it.

A week later I went up to see Mum again. The poem was not on the table where I had left it so I assumed she had read it. After being with her for about an hour she said, "I read your poem as soon as you were gone and after reading it I broke my heart. I could hardly read it for crying, for I realised how true your words were, and for the rest of the evening, sitting alone, I read and re-

read it many times remembering days gone by when we were all living together as a family and I had my health and strength. I will keep it always to read when I feel a little low", she said and, "Thank you very much".

Sometimes it is very hard to show your feelings and love for someone, but it does make such a difference just to say, "I love you", and it doesn't cost anything. As I drove back home again I felt that I had given her extra strength knowing that she was really loved and that someone did care.

Neil was now getting a big boy and very heavy to carry about, but we always had long walks when it was fine and he liked being in the garden watching Nichola cutting the grass or weeding the flower beds. I was sitting on Nichola's garden steps looking at the cottage and I said, "You are going to have a lot of trouble with your water pipes" "Oh no!", she said, "Don't say that! I don't want to spend any more money on the cottage just yet". But a week later she had water pouring through her dining room ceiling from the bathroom from leaking pipes. And then she had trouble with her water pipes underneath the sink. So I was right. She always became anxious when I predicted these things as she knew they always came true. In fact, when the plumber passed me I knew exactly what he was thinking. I told Nichola, and for a joke she told him what I had said. "Oh dear", he said, "That was exactly what I was thinking. I wouldn't like to do jobs here often with all those steps, having to carry all the tools from my car", and he added, "I will have to watch my thoughts in future when I pass your Mum".

Nichola bought a pushchair for Neil. It was a lot lighter than the pram, and we could take it in the car and also show Neil all the cows in the fields and the horses which we would stop and talk to. We found a track which was called The Marshes where it was so peaceful and we only passed a farm tractor. If we went into the fields all the cows would follow us which Neil loved.

Harry invited Arnold and me up to Anglesey to stay with him and Jenny at the cottage where they had been living on the estate after Lord Boston had passed away and they had been retained to look after Lord Boston's house until the new Lord Boston arrived from Australia. Also Harry had lost his brother Jack.

Harry was a natural artist and he had had lots of buyers for his pictures. In fact that weekend he had a display of pictures at a local hotel. I was going to ask him if he would paint me a picture of the view from his cottage so that we could look at it and remember our visit to Moelfre. While we were having breakfast the next morning Harry said, "What were you going to ask me Joyce?", and I was most surprised that he had picked up my thoughts so far away, and more surprised still when I saw the exact picture I wanted displayed with his other pictures. He looked at me and smiled, and taking down the picture he said, "It is yours". He also showed me a big bundle of letters he had received from people he had healed from different parts of the world. Jenny was always very busy and she helped out at the Ship's Bell Hotel, Moelfre. When Harry took Arnold and me out we always took his Great Dane Sukie. She would sit on the back seat of the car and I am sure she enjoyed every minute of it. She was a very big dog and filled the back seat completely.

Harry had two children, a boy and a girl who were now grown-up and married, Peter and Kathleen.

Harry had hurt his hand and it was all swollen, and while we were all sitting around chatting in the Kinmel I said to Harry, "Let me see if I can help you". Taking hold of his hand I sent out a prayer for it to get better. Harry said, "Did you feel anything?" I said, "I felt as though I was in a bit of a trance. Did you feel anything Harry?" "Yes", he said, "I felt as though I was being lifted up". Anyway we finished our drinks and returned to the cottage where Harry related the story to Jenny. The next morning Harry's swelling had gone down.

Harry said, "Do you know, Joyce, you are a healer, and I would like you to come out with me the next time I go healing." I thought to myself, "Oh dear! I am not very good with the chit chat like Harry", always having been rather shy in the company of other people. Harry said, "You will soon lose that shyness when you see the pain and the suffering of so many ill people." But watching him and the easy way he put people at their ease I soon realized that it was also how you felt inside that mattered, and sometimes just a smile and being able to listen was very important. I had always been a good listener so Harry was to talk and I was to listen, making it a great team.

As Arnold and I left for home we felt that a great bond had been forged between us all, leaving us all very sad on parting.

CHAPTER 29

One day on visiting Mum I found her very weary, but she felt like having a little walk as it was such a nice day. So she put on her coat with my help, left on her slippers as her ankles were swollen, and we walked slowly across the field together. But we did not get very far before Mum had to sit down on the bank for a little rest, and then back to the house for a cup of tea. But she did enjoy it although while I was with her she was dozing - all the fresh air had relaxed her.

She was now becoming very weak on her feet and Bess, Dorothy and I would help in turns to be with her although Bess, being nearer, went round many times in the day to visit her and do her shopping and washing. Dorothy had a job so it was not so easy for her to visit every day.

Mum was very poorly one day and Bess called the doctor. Mum had to stay in bed which she hated.

We took it in turns to stay with her, sleeping on a camp bed.

One day, when I was looking after her and Bess was with me at the time, we heard her singing a hymn in the bedroom. We looked in and there she was, singing her little heart out, struggling with the words. When she had finished she said, "Did you see that choir outside on the lawn? They were singing lovely." And looking straight at me she said, "He has called me now".

A week later Mum was taken by ambulance to Glenside Hospital, Bristol, for the elderly as she needed professional care. She passed away there a few weeks later aged 86, the year being 1975. She was buried at Hawkesbury Upton Church Cemetery, not far away from Win and Milly. It was a very peaceful cemetery away from the madding crowds. It was a very sad day for all the family. Mum was a great loss as she had always been there to give a helping hand.

All the wreaths were the same colour - blue irises and yellow daffodils, a vivid splash of colour - and, as we all left the cemetery, hardly a word was spoken, each in our own thoughts.

Harry had been staying with us and, as he said, "Don't fret Joyce. She has gone out of her pain and misery and you will see her again one day."

A couple of days later Harry, Arnold and I sat talking in the dining room when the mirror on the wall behind Harry began to swing backwards and forwards very powerfully as though someone was pushing it with all their strength. It stopped as suddenly as it had started and Harry said, "Does the mirror have a story, Joyce?" I said, "Yes. When I bought it Mum was staying with me. She was asleep in the chair and I thought I could put the mirror up without making a lot of noise. So intent was I doing it that I banged a bit harder and I woke Mum up. Half asleep she said, `What in the world are you doing now! Couldn't you wait until I was awake before putting up that silly mirror instead of disturbing me'. But after making her a cup of tea she agreed that I had done a good job, but after that we often made a joke about the mirror disturbing Mum and waking her up."

Harry said, "Perhaps shaking the mirror is her way of letting you know that she is still around you."

Added is a poem I wrote remembering Mum's last few days with us before she passed away.

It is not Goodbye

Dear Mother as you lay so worn and frail,
Your body tired of worldly pain,
Your mind wandering down memory lane
Of what you would not do again.
Our eyes not seeing what you see
As you gaze so openly
As into space you see anew
A world of happiness for you,
As we are only here our characters to make

So really worldly goods we can forsake

For they are only trivialities
For one to goad and one to tease
So what you did not have in goods
I know you did make up in love,
And, as you said that day to me,

"I can go home now for `He' has called me."
And so, dear Mother, I will not fret
As this is not goodbye.
One day I know we will meet again
So it is not for me to cry.

So to all who lose a loved one
Let me a message bring
Do not waste your time in fretting
As this is not the thing.
For life goes on forever,
And the One who is Father of all
Will help His children to find their soul
Because He loves us all.

CHAPTER 30

Smudge had been having problems with his throat and all the time he would be trying to swallow so I thought I would try my healing power on him. I picked him up and gently caressed his throat, sending out a prayer at the same time. He sat very quiet. As a rule he did not like being picked up. He seemed to know I was trying to help him. I did this for a few days and then one morning, on looking at him, I noticed he was not having problems with his throat and eating his food with relish. I was very thrilled to think that I had helped him. Also, after that Smudge became very attached to me, trying to sit on my lap when I was watching the television.

One very windy night, when I opened the door to let him in, he dashed to the fire, sat down shaking his head and body like a small child, turned round and, looking directly at me with his large green eyes he said telepathically, "It was lovely out there in the wind tonight", and suddenly I knew we were one. There was no need of actual words - it was pure thought from one mind to another, and all the love I had given Smudge was returned tenfold just by those few telepathic words.

Arnold and I went in to Bristol shopping and the traffic was very bad, so we parked the car and walked to the shops, crossing the busy road from Lewis's store. We were directed by a policeman on a horse to stop and wait, which we did until it was safe to cross. And then another strange thing happened to me. I felt myself walking over towards the policeman on the horse. He thought I was going to ask him the way, but I looked directly at the horse and said, "Hello, Beautiful". Well, I don't know who was the most surprised, me, the policeman or the horse, as I am sure the horse picked up my telepathic thought as well and wanted to follow me. The policeman had a job to control him, and every time I glanced back the horse's head was turned, watching me walk away. So perhaps someone, once again, had given me two examples of telepathic thought with two separate animals.

Another time I was out walking with Neil. I had just reached the bridge that passed over a busy motorway near Winterbourne when along came a man and a woman leading a horse. The horse would not cross over after hearing all the busy traffic passing below. His eyes were large and frightened. I heard the man say, "Well, I don't know what we are going to do to make him cross." I said to Neil, "Now please be quiet while I talk telepathically to the horse to try and still his fear." I stood very quietly and told the horse not to be afraid, and to cross over as there was nothing to hurt him.

The horse went very quiet and stopped tossing his head about and became very calm. "Come on," I said, "It's alright", and the horse looked at me and gently trotted over. The man said, "Well I'm buggered! After all that struggle we had he has decided to behave." But Neil and I knew differently.

Alf and Doris invited Arnold and me for a weekend in the New Forest, which we all enjoyed, seeing new countryside, but unfortunately Alf had hurt the back of his neck while working on his car. The bonnet had fallen down giving him a nasty bang on the back of his neck which was very painful. He asked me to give him a healing, which I did. Then I remembered something Alf had said a little while ago - "The people you went to see for a healing will come to see you for a healing." Of course I had been to Harry, and then gave him a healing, and now Alf, who also had given me a healing. So Alf's prophesy had come true.

Arnold, Nichola, Neil and I had been out shopping one morning, and, as we arrived back to our house, we were all very surprised to see the curtains parted and a lady look out. Our first thought was that we had not locked the door and someone had broken in. The curtains closed and

Arnold dashed to the door, thinking we had burglars. Nichola and I were a little afraid of going in. After a while Arnold called out, "There is no one here." So we went in and we looked everywhere - underneath the beds and in the wardrobes, but not a sign of the lady. I can only assume that it was a psychic happening and someone had been waiting for us to return home. Whatever it was, we felt no fear in the house.

We were still having our long walks together. Sometimes we would travel down the little paths through the woodland with Neil trying to climb the very high banks and picking wild flowers. We had also seen many foxes, but they hurried away if we got too close. Sometimes we would walk down to Cattybrook brickworks and watch the trains going by.

One day we walked up the hill and along the A38, and after about one and a half miles we followed a road down to Tockington. It was a very hot day and we became very tired. Unfortunately we didn't have any money with us or we could have given Arnold a ring to come and fetch us. After sitting for a little while, we saw the country bus coming towards us. I said, "Quick! Let us hurry to the bus stop and perhaps the driver will let us get on and we can pay him another time or when we reach home", as the bus travelled past Nichola's entrance.

The bus stopped and I explained our predicament. The driver said, "Don't worry my dears", and he put his hand in his pocket and paid the fare for us and said, "Have that on me." Neil hadn't been in a bus before and he thought it was wonderful driving along the lanes. I think the people on the bus enjoyed it as well as not every day do you meet such a kind stranger. He dropped us at the top of the hill, all hands waving as he left.

Another little walk of ours was travelling down the little path to the cemetery where we would pick up all the fallen apples and take them back to feed Lucy, the goat that was tethered in a field by the forge. Neil loved to see and hear her munching the apples. One day Neil got inside with Lucy, and before we could get him out Lucy had butted him and he was flat out on the grass. But he only laughed and called out, "You big bully!". I think he thought it was a game - Lucy also.

Another time Nichola, Neil and I were walking in the big garden behind Nichola's house and we decided to look in the summer house. We sat inside for a few minutes, enjoying the peace and talking about what it must have looked like all those years ago, and then we heard the sound of horses on the stony path outside. I said, "Quick! They are coming in here." We dashed to the open doorway and although we could still hear the horses' feet on the path we couldn't see anything. In fact, it was so loud that it seemed to echo all round the garden. I said to Nichola, "We must have picked up something that perhaps happened when the summer house was used. Perhaps the owners rode their horses round the garden as I believe their stables were attached to the big house." As if to verify my story, on one of the photographs of Nichola, Neil and me taken in the garden, if you look carefully you can see the outline of the horses with riders that are children. So, once again, we had experienced a psychic happening.

Also, around three in the afternoon every day we would all hear the outside gate click open and shut. In fact, we could set our watches by it. Years ago, workers living in the cottages used to take a short cut to the big house, passing by the window. We had also seen a cloud of fine white mist drifting past the window and up the steps into the garden and over the garden wall into the garden belonging to the big house.

One day when Nichola and I were having a cup of tea, we were amazed to see a shadow come through the doorway. We both watched as it entered the room and sat down on the settee. We asked if there was anything we could do, and we both sent up a prayer for help for whatever was needed. After doing so, the shadow stood up, in fact you could see the cushion fall back into shape after the weight had gone, and we knew that whatever or whoever it was had left us. Nichola had become very psychic, also Arnold, and we would all heal one another for various aches and pains.

Neil surprised us one day. After giving him a healing for a very bad headache, I said to him,

"Did you feel anything?" He said, "Yes. I felt very cold and I saw Grandpa and Uncle Keith talking outside on the patio." We said, "Are you sure you are not making it up?" "No," he said, I saw them." Well, the next day Uncle Keith arrived unexpectedly as he was on his way to France. After looking around the cottage, he was outside on the patio talking to Arnold when Neil said, "I told you I saw them talking outside on the patio", and he was very thrilled to think that he had prophesied it.

Nichola found an early sixteenth century black mudstone in the garden, and it had a mermaid drawn on it. As Neil was a Pisces, Nichola decided to have it built into the centre of her stone fireplace. It seemed very strange that Nichola found it just lying on the top of her garden wall. Many people over the years must have passed by and not seen it. In fact, Nichola herself had planted flowers and not seen it, but that morning it just stood out. She took it to the museum in Bristol who said it was very unusual and early sixteenth century and they wanted to keep it.

One evening I had a very vivid dream. I saw Mr Harry Edwards, the spiritual healer, healing someone on the television, but he was dressed like the ass in Shakespeare's Midsummer Night's Dream. I thought, "What a strange thing to show me", as I knew Mr Harry Edwards had helped a lot of sick people, so why was he portrayed to me as someone stupid. Anyway, a few nights later there was a television programme on about a healing Mr Harry Edwards was doing, and it was being put on television for everyone to see. But, as I watched, I realised it was my dream, and I felt that Mr Harry Edwards was out of his class trying to impress people who did not really believe anyway. I felt that in such circumstances he would not concentrate, and, as he glanced back towards the camera looking rather at a loss, I realised what the dream was trying to tell me, and I vowed, there and then, that I too would not be made such a silly ass of if ever my chance came to heal in front of a lot of people. You see, Mr Edwards was a genuine healer, not a bogus one, and a laughing stock for all to see.

Smudge had not been very well and his paws were turning inwards with arthritis. The vet gave me some pills for him to ease the pain, but I had rather a job making him take them. In the end I rolled them in with his liver, thinking he would not see them but, whenever I washed his dish, there was the pill left on the bottom. He would sit on the back step, grumbling at the birds as he could not chase them any more, and I said to Arnold, "I do wish he had a little friend for company. I sent out prayers that if it was not meant for him to be healed could he at least have another cat for company.

One night calling Smudge in, sat outside on the doorstep was another cat with him, a rather wild looking tabby, long haired and with very long legs and very knowing big amber coloured eyes. He walked more like a dog than a cat. As I opened the door he followed Smudge in. I said a he, but it could have been a she. I did not know.

Smudge walked to the fire and sat down, and the tabby cat sat just behind him, just like you would do if you were invited into someone else's home, letting the owner have the best seat. The tabby had a way of looking right through you as though it knew all the answers, giving me a kind of oneness. We fed both the cats, very happy to see them together, with the tabby cat looking after Smudge. Arnold said, "Let's call him Nimrod", why, I don't know, but Nimrod it was.

About one month later Nichola and Neil arrived to take me to visit Dawn, but Smudge was not very well, and I didn't really like to leave him. He just sat about with his head just drooping towards the carpet as if there was no more energy left. But in the end I thought, "I won't be away long", so I picked him up and put him outside so that if needs be he could go into the shed for shelter. We had only been at Dawns for about half an hour when I said to Nichola, "Smudge is dying. I can feel it. Such a despair and pain is flowing over me." I was glad to return home, but when I could not find Smudge I called all night, but there was no sign of him. Even Nimrod had gone. The days passed by, and I felt very unhappy, not knowing what had happened. I can only surmise that Smudge must have wandered away and was too weak to return and had died under a hedge or somewhere. I blamed myself for leaving him. At least I could have buried him properly.

But, as if to put my mind to rest, he returned to me one night. Arnold and I had just settled into bed when we felt something jump on to the bed and cuddle down between us. I said, "It is Smudge come back." Then Arnold said, "But how could he? The window and the doors are all shut. He couldn't get in." I said, "Not the Smudge as we knew him, to feed and look after, but an astral Smudge", proving to me once again that spirit-wise we go on living.

Smudge came to us most nights, and I could feel the warmth of his little body against my back. Then one night I awoke as Smudge jumped on to the bed, and being only half awake, I said, "Oh Smudge, get off the bed and let me sleep." After that incident he never returned and once again I felt guilty for being angry. But after thinking about it, I knew that he could not stay forever as we must all travel on to evolve, and knowing also that real love is a very strong bond, be it human or animal.

A little while after my neighbour's elm tree contracted Dutch Elm disease, and she had to have it cut down. I felt very sad as over the years I had grown so used to seeing it. Many times sitting on the lawn or gardening I had listened to the wind blowing through the branches and all the birds singing their different songs, and seen the glorious colours of autumn and in the winter looking like a Christmas tree, all covered in snow. But I was totally unprepared for the depth of despair I felt when the man began to saw through the main trunk. I could not leave the window, and the sound of the saw was like a saw in my own heart. I cried all the way through, and as I heard it fall, I felt as though I went with it. Once again, I was being shown we are all part and parcel of the whole. Below I have added a poem which says everything.

Death of an Elm Tree

Oh stately elm! your time has come,
For I'm afraid the beetle has won.
The man with saw has just arrived
And rope around your neck is tied.

To hear the grating of machine,
As through your heart it cuts quite clean,
And with a crash your body falls
Into the field, you overawed.

Your grandeur gone. No more to hear
The little birds that would appear
Way up in branches, close to the sky
Where blackbirds sang their lullaby.

No more to see your Autumn tinge,
Or hear the wind when on a binge
Giving you a playful shake
To test your strength, and stand you make.

And in the winter, frozen white,

No more to give a glorious sight
Like Christmas tree with silver paint
Where starlings, like toys, would congregate.

So through my tears I see you go,
And know that I shall miss you so,
For as you fall upon your face
You leave a gap for our future race.

CHAPTER 31

Arnold and I decided to visit Moelfre to stay with Jenny and Harry. We had packed a suitcase and sandwiches for the journey, but just as I was getting ready to go I felt very faint. I didn't say anything, thinking it would pass over, but in the end I had to say that I could not travel until I felt better. Arnold was very disappointed but agreed that it would be silly to go. So to bed I went and Arnold rang Harry to cancel our visit. Harry was also very disappointed as he had been looking forward to seeing us again.

So I lay in bed thinking of all the lovely scenery I would be missing, as the trip up to Moelfre was a holiday in itself, taking our time and picnicking by the wayside, suddenly I found my body vibrating and I knew I was going on an astral journey. But what a surprise I had when I realised I was on my way to Moelfre, and there I saw my friend Harry standing deep in thought looking out to sea. For a moment I watched, and then I returned to my bed and by the evening I felt a lot better. I realised I had been given a healing.

We decided to leave the visit as Harry had told Arnold he would be coming down to Bristol the following week, and once again I have added a poem below describing my third astral journey.

My Third Astral Travel

My case was packed, the weather fine
To visit my friend whom I had not seen for some time.
But my breakfast did not seem the same,
My excitement and joy began to wane
As a feeling of faintness swept over me
Leaving me weak, and my eyes not to see.

I knew I could not my journey make
The thoughts of reunion I had to forsake.
Instead to bed I wearily went
With eyes all blurred, my body spent,
Not driving through the mountains free,
But wrapped up in blankets with misery.

My husband rang my friend to say
We could not make it that same day,
Who being a healer for all humanity
Said he would say a prayer for me.
And not to worry, but just to rest,
And he himself would do the rest.

And as I lay with mingled thoughts
My body rose to find the healing it sought.
My friend was standing looking out to sea
Just the merest glimpse to satisfy me,
And then to return to my own dear abode,
Knowing my friend had done wonders untold.

So you see, once again, to you I have proved
That all your fears and anxiety can be soothed
If only your faith will always abstain
What a load of wealth you can obtain.
For we are all God's children, with the same
chance to win
If we all love each other and forget the word sin.

Then all illness will cease and life will be joy,
The blind to see, the deaf to hear and the lame
their legs to employ.
No need to pray for futile wars to end
If already each person was really your friend.
No need for hurt to ever be done
If we always think good and to help everyone.

A few nights later I saw a picture of a very big hand. I was beginning to wonder why when the hand turned over, showing me the other side, and written all across each knuckle were the words, "Look to the heaven for the signs", which, of course, I did each day, wondering what I would see.

Harry arrived on the weekend and he said he would like to stay for a week as there were so many people he would like to visit, which of course delighted us. Of course, he brought Sukie who by now had become our pet as well. We would all visit the people's homes where it would become a social evening, and Harry the life and soul of the party. Everybody loved Harry. He had that special kind of charm that drew all ages and made each one feel in a class of their own - in other words, someone important - which means such a lot to someone who feels ill, unwanted and afraid. He would soon have them laughing and feeling at ease.

One afternoon we were sitting in the dining room, which really is my favourite room. Arnold and Harry were chatting and I was facing the window just listening, when suddenly I saw a great big cross appear in the sky. I watched for a moment, then I said, "Look! Can you see what I can see in the sky?" They both jumped up and looked, and Harry said, "Well, if you can see a cross in the sky so can I", and Arnold agreed. In fact, we all stood and watched. It was a very clear day with a clear blue sky. There were no clouds whatever about, and suspended from the blue sky was a white cross, and as suddenly as it appeared it disappeared.

But I continued to watch the sky, and then I saw a colour just like one of my pictures in the front room, a dark gold, drifting across the sky, and then a face looking directly at me, such a kind gentle look, and eyes that smiled. Dark-haired with a small artist-shaped beard is how I would describe it. I was just going to call Harry and Arnold when that too disappeared. So I suppose that was only for me to see. Also what the hand had told me had come true, "To look to the heaven for the signs."

That same evening we all went out for a drink at the Wheatsheaf public house, Winterbourne. There was quite a crowd sitting at our table and somehow the conversation turned to healing. One gentleman said that he had had a nasty pain in his face and neck for about a week and pills did not help the pain. Well, whether or not it was what I had witnessed and seen in the sky giving me courage I don't know, but I suddenly got up, went round to him and said, "Would you like me to try and help you?" "Yes please", he said, and I placed my hands on the painful spot and sent out my prayers for the pain to go. After I took my hands away I said, "Did you feel anything?" He said, "Yes, my face is like it is on fire." I said, "I hope you are soon better and we will all send out our prayers for you each night at 10 pm."

The next weekend we again went to the Wheatsheaf and there was the same gentleman I had healed. He came across to me and said, "It was rather odd. After you had healed me my face became all swollen, and on going to the dentist the next day I had a lot of poison coming out of my gums for which I had to have treatment and the tooth taken out, but now it is all better and the pain released." So once again, sometimes a pain has to be worse before it can get better to get rid of all the impurities before healing can begin.

CHAPTER 32

Neil is now growing up fast and enjoys swinging on his tyre hanging from the apple tree. Also Nichola bought a proper swing which was more comfortable. One day she was very worried as Neil had gone for a walk with his friend Warren Smith. She looked everywhere, and then she thought of the marshes, a place he loved. She drove down in the car and there they were, just ambling back home, and their shoes and wellingtons were thick with mud, but their faces were wreathed in smiles. Neil loved to wander about on his own and time meant nothing to him.

One lovely day we all went on a trip to South Cerney near Cirencester where people did a lot of water ski-ing on the man-made lakes which had originated after all the gravel had been dug out. Neil enjoyed paddling on the edge of the lake where it was not very deep. We then set up our picnic table and put the kettle on the little gas stove. Arnold bent over to take it off and then there was a terrible explosion. The stove blew up in his face, cutting him on the forehead, burning his eyebrows and also a big hole in his vest. As it was such a warm day he had taken off his shirt. It gave him a great shock and he said, "Never again will I use one of those gas stoves."

Nichola, Colin and Neil went for a week's holiday to Leeds to visit Colin's family, and Arnold and I decided to visit different members of my family. Driving along the A38 to see my sister Dorothy, I was overwhelmed by a feeling of despair and I said to Arnold, "Please turn the car round. I want to go back home." "Whatever is wrong?" he said. I replied, "Nichola is in trouble. I have seen her face and it is full of doom, so I will sit quietly and send out my healing thoughts to her." The feeling stayed with me for a long time, and I prayed she would ring me and tell me all about it, which she did in the evening. Apparently they had all gone to visit Temple Newsam Park and Nichola had left Neil with his grandmother while she went to buy some ice-creams. When she returned Neil had disappeared. They all looked everywhere, even the police who had been looking round the Park. Nichola was so afraid that he might have fallen in one of the lakes which were very deep. In the end they found him talking to some horses near the Park, unaware of all the trouble he had caused. I told her how all her fears had transmitted themselves to me and how glad I was that everything was now alright.

We all decided to visit the Bristol Zoo after Nichola's holiday in Leeds. We had not been for a long time and we thought Neil might enjoy it. It was very full of people as the weather was so good. We drifted along with the crowd, looking at all the animals and the different kinds of birds with their lovely plumage, the children running about calling to their parents to come and see. We had just reached a cage where there was a big crowd surrounding it, and we realised it was a pair of white tigers that was causing all the interest.

I stood and watched, and then one of the tigers sat down and looked around at the crowd, just like your every day cat and dog, but as its eyes reached mine, and for a while interlocked, I suddenly felt on a par with it, sensing all the misery and pain of an animal that was not free any more. Instead of running wild with its kind, it was a prisoner just for people to stand and look at for about fifteen minutes before they passed by and back home to their own freedom with no bars. It was so beautiful, another of God's lovely creatures, that was put on this earth to be free - not to be put in a cage.

After seeing such a sad picture, I said to Nichola, "I don't want to see any more. Let us go home". She agreed after also feeling the same sadness as me. I think it was the quickest visit we had ever made anywhere.

The winter is now upon us, and looking out of the window one morning Neil was thrilled to see the snow falling. By the afternoon he was tobogganing down the hills with Nichola and Colin. The field was very steep and I used to worry in case he fell off. He would walk back up the hill, his face all red with the cold wind, matching his red woolly hat, scarf and gloves.

Then he would help Nichola to make a snowman in the garden. It was all good fun, with plenty of snowballs flying around. He was around four years old at the time and full of mischief.

From Nichola's house down to the main road was a very steep path, and it was covered in snow and ice and very dangerous. Colin thought he would carry Neil in case he fell and hurt himself, but unfortunately it was Colin who fell and Neil, who was on his back, fell off and hurt his right elbow. It was very swollen and Neil was in a lot of pain, so Nichola and I took him to Southmead Hospital. He was taken for an X-ray. In fact, we were waiting there all day, and every time we saw a nurse or doctor we asked them how long it would be. It was a very upsetting day, not knowing what was going on.

Late in the evening the specialist came to see us and Neil was with him, looking very pale. He was very thrilled to see his Mum and me, some friendly faces. His arm was in a sling and the specialist said that they were not quite sure if he had a very bad fracture or a chipped bone. There was nothing they could do at the moment, but perhaps in later life, around twenty-one years of age, he could have it attended to, and to give him Disprin for the pain. The poor little lad had some very bad days and sleepless nights for a long time, and he had very bad pain in his arm. In fact he could not do all the things that little boys do at his age. It was always a weakness for him. He went to the hospital for physiotherapy once a week for about six weeks, and then he was told what to do so that the strength could return to his arm. But even after all that he suffered a lot of pain, and he could never use his arm properly again.

Nichola bought Neil a rabbit which he called Bright Eyes after hearing the song on television. It was a lovely white rabbit with pink eyes, and he would spend hours with it in the garden. It was a very knowing rabbit and it would always show off if you went near it.

I was still visiting people who needed healing, and sometimes I did not always help the person I went to see. In fact, many times I would heal someone else who was in the room with them who would afterwards ring me and say that I had taken away a bad back, headache and lots of other things. Also animals. One day I went to see a lady with a bad back, and while we were talking I noticed a movement underneath one of the chairs and, bending down, I looked right into the eyes of a very frightened little dog. I thought to myself, "That little dog is mental and needs help." We looked at each other for what seemed like eternity, and then it dashed out of the room as though the fox hounds were after it. I thought no more about it until the lady rang me. She said she felt a lot better, but the funny thing was that, since I had called, her little dog, who had always been rather on the silly side and very nervous, was now a completely different dog, and she thanked me for making it better.

I am always so thrilled to hear good news, especially about animals who can't ring and ask me for help. It is always done by chance because I happen to be there, but I also know I am guided to such places, and that a feeling of true love passes between me and the animal - a gift which most of us have lost.

Also a man came to see me about his very cold feet. He had no feeling in them. As he was talking to me I felt that the trouble was in his back. So when he had finished telling me about the doctor he had seen and the specialists, I asked him to sit on an upright chair, telling him at the same time to relax. I then placed my hands on his back and sent out my healing prayers. Afterwards I asked him if he had felt anything. He just looked at me for a moment and then he said, "Well, it is the first time I have had pins and needles in my legs for a long time, and my feet are like toast. He sat down, overwhelmed with it all, his face flushed with excitement, and then he got up again and jumped about on his feet. "What do you think was the trouble?" he said, and I said, "I felt that somewhere in your back was a trapped nerve which the healing has released." Whatever it was, it made him a very happy man.

Sometimes I would also have a picture of the person who came to see me for a healing in advance, while in bed or working about the house the day before, like one man who had booked an appointment with me. The night before I had seen an aircraft with parachutes dropping all around, and then the face of just one man, and when the gentleman came to see me it was his face. On telling him what I had seen he said, "During the war I had to parachute out of an aircraft that was on fire and I hurt my back on landing. I find that having little stories that are true gives the person confidence in you and also helps the healing, for which he was very grateful as since that time he had had a lot of pain in his back, and at last he was cured.

Also a fireman came to see me who had hurt his back fourteen years ago, and had been pensioned off. Once again I put my hands on his back and sent out my healing thoughts and his back was cured.

I also find that I say things and they come true just in natural talking without meditating. There are so many incidents like this that I have ceased to be surprised any more.

CHAPTER 33

Harry rang to say he would be down on the weekend for a week's stay with us, which we all looked forward to. When he arrived he gave us a big jar of fresh mussels which he had collected himself the day before. I surprised him by saying, "Yes, I know. I was with you when you collected them. I was walking behind you on the rocks, and you were showing me which ones to pick up and which ones to leave. And I would put the little baby ones back in the water on the rocks." For a joke he said, "You are too clever Joyce. What don't you know."

A little later, while talking to Harry, I had quite a surprise, for suddenly a man materialised between us and, for a second, we just looked at each other, and then, as suddenly as he had materialised, he disappeared. Harry said, "Why are you looking like that? Did I say something wrong?" I said, "No. For a moment you were not there, but somebody else was, and I tried to describe what I had seen - a man in a gray suit with dark hair and blue eyes and, as he first materialised, he looked kind of transparent, and then he became clear, like something you see on the `Out of Space' series when the transparent figure becomes clear.

We talked about it for a while, but it did leave me puzzled as to what it was all about.

Harry used to visit the Bowl Inn at Almondsbury at lunch time as Arnold and I always went down to see Nichola and Neil every afternoon. He used to enjoy the company of many friends he had made while visiting us. One day he told us he had met a Mr Gordon Hodsell, his wife Doreen and his daughter Norma, and he had arranged for us all to meet at the Bowl Inn, the landlord being Colin Lambourne, in the evening. When we arrived Gordon and his family were already there. I am afraid I left most of the talking to Harry as usual, but I did feel that Gordon was very psychic and very interested in all of Harry's stories. We met each evening while Harry was with us and talked about many things.

Gordon hurt his hand and I felt that I had to give him a healing, not Harry. After I had touched and held his hand and sent out my prayers, Gordon was in a lot of pain, worse than before, which does happen sometimes. In fact he left the room and went outside for a while, and then Harry went out to bring him back in again, and the pain was not quite so bad.

But the healing had brought Gordon and myself closer together, more than perhaps we had realised at the time. I only knew that a bond had been made between us, and I always knew when Gordon was sending out his thoughts to me while meditating, and he always knew when I was troubled. One morning, while having a morning cup of tea, I saw a man with a long white robe standing by Harry, an oldish man with white hair and blue eyes, and around Harry's hair was a greenish colour and his face was mauve. Then in front of Harry appeared three more men - just head and shoulders, but too quick for me to really describe as my eyes were mostly on the man in the white robe. He looked at me very intently, as though he was appraising me, and then they all disappeared leaving me with the wonder of it all. Harry had no answer for it saying it was something for me, and perhaps I would know at a later date what it was all about. So with that I had to be content. When it was time for Harry to leave again we found the house very quiet, and we all looked forward to his next visit.

One morning, when I was in the kitchen, I heard a shot outside, and it was so close that I opened the door and looked out. Looking all around I could see nothing amiss, and then, as I looked down on the path, I saw a little sparrow. I picked it up and I felt the little body all soft and warm with blood on the tiny feathers. There was nothing I could do to help it, so I picked it up and held it between my two hands and I said, "God bless you, little one", and I wrapped the little body in soft paper and laid it in its last resting place, feeling very sad at such a wanton killing.

A few nights later I went on another Astral and I found myself on a grassy slope with hundreds of birds around me. The sparrows were looking so big and full of life, and as I lay and watched them, once again, I felt that oneness which I have always felt for all creation. Below I have added my astral poem describing my experience which I am sure was my reward for my love and kindness for a little dead sparrow.

My Seventh Astral Travel

I find myself on a grassy slope, the colour a luscious green,
And around me hundreds of feathered friends.
The common sparrow could be seen.
I lay and watched their antics gay, no fear of me they showed
As I was one with them that day in their heavenly abode.

For they all knew that they were safe. My love they knew was pure,
And no harm could ever come to them, of that they were so sure.
They looked so big and full of life as they strutted to and from,
With me right in the centre, like in a first class show.

I know that I was honoured to be included with such trust,
But love I gave them from the start, not cruelty and lust,
And through my healing and my faith I will help mankind to find
The love and peace I felt that day amongst the feathered kind

As no greater power there is on earth than love for one and all,
Starting from man, king-size to all creatures, big and small.
For animals and humans, we are all the same to Him,
And so I say, "Be kind to all, as cruelty is sin".

Neil has now started school at Easter Compton about one mile away as Almondsbury School was full up. Nichola drove him there each day, and I would join her in collecting him in the afternoon. We all missed him very much. Suddenly the days seemed very dull. I missed his little chatter and all the lovely walks, so I would look forward to the weekends.

One day I was sitting by the fire when I had a mental picture of my friend June Fox, who lives at Oldham, Lancashire, and I heard her say, "Well, I don't know what I am going to do", and I knew that she was really upset. So I rang her and said, "Why don't you know what to do?" She said, "My Dad is not too good, and my Mum is looking after him, and I was worried as I was not feeling very well myself. But how did you know what I said?" So I told her my story, and I said I would send my prayers for them all, especially for June's nerves.

Also another such incident. I picked up my sister-in-law, Gillian, and her husband talking, and in the afternoon there was a knock at the door and standing there was Gillian and Frank. They had been staying at Bournemouth with Moira's daughter, Pauline, and had decided to visit us on the way back to Liverpool. Gillian was very poorly as she was suffering with cancer and she had lost a lot of weight. I recited my story to them, and they were very surprised at what I knew.

Also an incident involving Harry. I could hear in the background talking, children's voices, loud rumbling and flashes of light. In the evening Harry rang to say that he was visiting his daughter and grandchildren in Sussex. I said, "Is that where you are! I picked you up today, but what were all those noises and flashes of light? Were you taking photographs with a flash camera?" He laughed and said, "No. It was thundering and lightening here today so that is what you must have seen and heard."

One evening Arnold and I were talking by the fire when I felt a big shadow passing over me, blotting out the light, and I said to Arnold, "Someone is with us and listening to our conversation", to which Arnold laughed, and then the 'phone began to ring. It was my niece Ann from Liverpool, and she said, "I was with you a moment ago and I heard all your conversation. You were talking about Nichola." I said, "You are right. I was narrating a story to Arnold about when Nichola and I were shopping in Bristol and the traffic was very bad near the Bristol Royal Infirmary, when a driver in an empty ambulance tried to pass all the cars which, of course, was an impossible feat. But, when the lights turned to green, he pushed his way through, and, as he passed, he gave us a two-fingered sign, which shocked Nichola so much that she said, `Fancy doing that, Mum! And we are all dressed up!', which made me see the funny side of it all, and we both ended up laughing."

Ann said, "I rang you straight away to confirm that I had heard you." Of course Ann is now married and has two children, both boys, her married name being Cannock. She is also very psychic, and I am sure we have met before in a previous life.

We had a phone call from Harry to say that Sukie had passed away and we were all very upset as she was such a lovely dog, and we knew that Harry would miss her on his long journeys.

One afternoon, Arnold and I were sitting outside in the sunshine and I said, "I am going to try a little experiment. I am going to call Harry mentally, and see if he can pick me up." I relaxed and called Harry three times, and then I just sat thinking about the sea and the beach at Moelfre.

At six o'clock in the evening Harry rang us saying, "I had a funny experience today. I was walking along the beach, and I heard you, Joyce, call me three times. I thought I was dreaming, and then I looked round and there you were, wearing a yellow dress, and, as I watched, you disappeared behind the rocks." "Yes," I said, "I did call you this afternoon, and I am so glad that you saw and heard me."

A little while after that incident, Arnold and I were sat in the front room reading the Sunday newspapers, and I heard Arnold say, "Whatever is that?" I was too scared to look round after looking at Arnold's face, so I said, "What is it?" He said, "Behind and all around you there is a golden light." It stayed around me all the evening, and even was around me in the dining room later. I felt a great presence, and, as I glanced towards Arnold in the kitchen, his whole body began to change. In fact his eyes had already turned blue. And silly me! After listening to other people's stories not to get too involved with psychic phenomena, I turned away and so spoilt what was being shown to me. Afterwards I realised how silly I was as nothing can harm me. Everything I have experienced has always been carefully shown to me, and now I must wait patiently again for that enlightening experience.

CHAPTER 34

Harry came back again, but this time no Sukie. We did miss her going out in the car. Arnold always sat with her in the back seat and they were firm friends. In fact, when we returned in the evening, Sukie always tried to sit on Arnold's knee, pushing herself backwards, just leaving two front legs on the floor which looked so funny as she was such a big dog.

One evening I was sat on the floor looking for a pen in one of the sideboard drawers. Arnold was talking to Harry when I sat back and looked across to Harry as they joined me in their conversation and, although it was Harry I was looking at, he had changed. I saw him as The Christ with such a gentle smile on his face looking down at me, holding a staff in his hand and Sukie looking like the sheep we see portrayed around the`Jesus pictures' - in other words the picture of Jesus as the shepherd with his flock.

And a few nights later, on retiring to bed, Arnold and I called goodnight to Harry and he popped his head round the door to answer, his hair all ruffled, and this time it came to me so clearly, `The Young Christ', and I saw him about sixteen years of age. I retired to bed full of the glory that I had seen.

And as though I was given the answer, the next day, as I looked at Harry wonderingly, I had such a shock at what I saw, for it was the suffering face of our dear Saviour, Jesus Christ, as he must have looked while hanging on the cross which I can only really express in poem form which I have added below.

The Suffering Face of our Dear Saviour Jesus

Oh dear Jesus, your face of suffering I have seen
For our salvation to redeem.
Your face so tired, with all the strain,
Eyes heavy-lidded, racked with pain,
Blood on your face and matted hair,
From the crown of thorns they planted there.
The right side of your face, swollen and bruised,
As if like a punch bag you had been used.
Your face like an old man, lined and grey,
Oh what an ugly, terrible day

When one so pure and good in heart
Was from this world made to depart.
The pain you bore was with humble pride

As on the cross you were crucified,
With nails in your hands and feet alike.
Oh dear Jesus, what a terrible sight,
Your head lolling on your chest, too weak to hold up high,
The Saviour of this world on Calvary did die.
The picture will forever stay, and in my mind will grow,
Of one who gave His life for us, the highest for the low.

And so one day we will meet again, and then my arms will reach out to Him, Jesus,
But until then my work is here, to help Him to help us.
So with these words, in poem form, I paint for you the scene
Of the man who suffered just for us, our salvation to redeem.
So try to follow in His footsteps, as He taught us to do,
Then you will find a complete new world has opened up for you.
For, as He said, my body is the bread, my blood the wine,
What greater love can you define?

It was now time for Harry to leave again and, as Arnold and I watched him drive away, we missed the familiar face of Sukie looking out of the back window, which she always did until the car drove out of sight, leaving us feeling very sad.

Lots of times on my astral travels I find myself passing by places of interest such as the American presidents' faces carved in the rocks in Colorado. Also the tall statue of Jesus overlooking the bay in Rio de Janeiro which I marvelled at. I also find myself healing on my astral travels, and the poem below is a description of one of them.

Astral Travel

I find myself with my friend Harry and daughter
Nichola outside a cottage small,
But they seemed not to notice me at all.
It was late at night and I found to my surprise
On looking up a beautiful lady suspended from
the skies.
She was resplendent in a beautiful gown and
matching bonnet
With jewels like stars gleaming bright upon it.
I called my friend Harry and daughter Nichola to
see
The beautiful lady looking down on me.

The sky was suddenly full of stars which came
closer and closer to me.
As I was gently lifted up I called my friend
urgently, Harry! Harry!
But they did not hear me call his name
As they went on talking just the same.
I went up through the array of stars into the
great beyond
Just like the fairy in a play when she waves her
magic wand.

And then an urchin child I saw, cowering against a garden wall.
With feet deformed, she looked a sorry sight,
But looking straight into my eyes she said, you are alright.
And with great compassion I lay my hand upon her head,
"I bless you child for God", I said.
The tears fell down her grubby cheeks,
My emotion was so great I could not speak.
Taking her right foot in my hand
I bid it straighten at my command.
And with the left I did the same,
Bidding it to be well again.
And when I came to, on my bed,
For the urchin child my cheeks were wet from the tears that I had shed.

Also, I have met people who have passed from this plane, including my own Mum, and spoken to them. Also, below is another astral poem which I have experienced.

Astral Travel

Once more on an astral I did go,
But with a passenger in tow,
For, as I looked below my right,
A baby head was snuggled tight.
And, although not sure where I had to go,
I felt a tenderness and glow
That one so small had chosen me
To find the place of eternity,

As if to give reassurance and still all the woe
On a journey we must all eventually go.
And, with these words and loving aid,
I said, "My little one, I am not afraid."
And then my destination was erased from me
As not just yet the paradise I must see.
But, as I awoke upon my bed,
All I could see was that little head,
And a love so great swept over me,
Leaving me weak, and my eyes not to see,
But wishing that now was the time I could say,
"God has at last accepted His pupil to show His children the way."

I have also on occasion taken Arnold up to Moelfre on an astral which I have done many times myself, passing over the Menai Bridge which connects North Wales to Anglesey.

For quite a long time Nichola had been having a dream about a beautiful big house. She even described in detail all the rooms, a staircase and a lovely chandelier which hung in one of the rooms. She also described the gardens, which were in tiers, and she wondered what it was all about. I said, "Time will tell. You must be having it for a reason."

Then one day Nichola, Neil and I went to visit my mother's grave. We went a different route for a change of scenery, when Nichola saw the house she had seen in her dreams. It was situated on rising ground at Little Sodbury, and it was called Sodbury Manor.

We drove down the long drive to have a closer look, and perhaps to ask if we could look around the house and gardens as it was sometimes opened to the public. But there was no one at home, so Nichola said, "I will just have a peep through the windows", and there she saw the room in her dreams with the chandelier hanging in the centre. She then had a look at the garden, which also was the same as in her dream.

We left the Manor reluctantly, deciding to call again at a later date when it was open to the public. We felt a great impulse to call at a little church about a mile away, and inside on the wall there was a plaque of the death of a Baron de Tuile who had lived at Little Sodbury Manor, and who was related to an ancestor of the Duke of Beaufort's family.

Nichola had already said that she felt that there was a connection with the Beaufort family, but she did not know how. She knew she felt very sad as she stood in the church, and a kind of prickly feeling came over her, but after a while we left and continued on our way to my mother's grave at Hawkesbury cemetery.

The next time we went to the church, a few weeks later, Arnold and Neil came with us. After we had passed the Manor House, a little way down the road was another little old church called St Adeline. Arnold said, "Let us go and have a look inside this one."

As soon as we got to the gate Nichola just froze. "Mum," she said, "I just can't go any further." She was covered in goose pimples and her face was very white. I took hold of her arm and said, "It's alright. I am with you. Don't be afraid".

We reached the church door where outside was a stone plaque and on reading it we found it described how the stone had been removed from Sodbury Manor where William Tyndale used to preach. Also in the church he had served as a church warden. As soon as Nichola entered the church she went from cold to heat. She called me to the centre of the room where there was an old stove, unlit because it was the middle of summer.

For her the heat was terrific, but I felt just a prickly heat on my legs. She felt so strange that she sat down in one of the pews and sent up a few prayers. Then she called to Arnold to lift up her long hair to see if there was anything on her neck as it felt as though it was on fire. On looking we were astonished to see on each side of her neck two sets of finger prints showing blood red, as though someone had stood behind her and placed their hands tight around her neck.

We then realised that something we did not understand had happened. Obviously something of a psychic nature.

After about half an hour, Nichola was still very hot and her face was extremely flushed. Then, as we left and stood again by the William Tyndale plaque, I said, "Just a minute. William Tyndale translated the Bible. I do not think it is anything to do with Baron de Tuile. I think it is William Tyndale. I will see if there is a book in the church about him." There was just one book on the table, describing how he had lived at the Manor House and had had a chapel at the back. He had been hounded by the Church and ended up in a dungeon in the Castle of Vilvorde, the state prison of the Low Countries, where he had suffered immense cold and perpetual catarrh, much increased by the cell. He had remained in the dungeon for sixteen months. There was a mockery of a trial and he defended himself. There is no doubt of his heresy from the articles alleged against him, and on Friday, October 6th, 1536, near the castle, he was strangled at the stake and burned to ashes, and his last words were, "Lord open the King of England's eyes."

So Nichola had experienced all these things which he had suffered from, immense cold to extreme heat, even to the strangulation marks on her neck.

When we arrived home, my niece Ann, a dentist from Liverpool, rang me and asked me what we had been doing that day as she said it would mean such a lot to us in the future. As I have said before, Ann is very psychic. She could even describe William Tyndale in detail before I told her the story, which confirmed my own feelings.

A few weeks later, Nichola felt a great urge to return to the little church, so Neil and I went with her. It was a very misty day, and as we drove along Nichola said, "Someone will be there waiting today, Mum", and, as we turned the corner, sure enough we saw a tall figure standing by the open gate, and as we drew nearer it just merged into the background.

The church door was open, also the door of a little room at the back where, on looking in, we saw on the wall an oil painting of the Castle of Vilvorde, the dungeon where William Tyndale had been held. Nichola wrote in the church book to commemorate our visit. We all said a prayer, and this time all was peaceful. In fact we left the church feeling very tearful.

We returned once more to Sodbury Manor at a later date, hoping it would be open to the public, but the lady of the Manor told us that at the moment it was not so, but she very kindly allowed us in to look around the Manor.

Nichola was able to describe in accurate detail each room before we entered it. The lady living there said that many strange happenings had taken place there over the years.

We lingered a little while trying to imagine what it must have looked like all those years ago when William Tyndale sat in his little study, and then seated around the big table talking to abbots, deans, archdeacons and great beneficed men, and the daily clergy of the neighbourhood.

And then, as we reluctantly were leaving the Manor, Nichola's cross, which she was wearing on a chain round her neck, dropped to the ground at her feet, and yet the links on the chain and the cross were not broken, leaving us once again with many questions in our minds.

Since that time Nichola has had no repetition of her dreams, and she feels at peace within herself.

Added below is a poem that I have written which contains a message for mankind.

The Love of Our Saviour
(His Life He gave for Us)

The Bible is a heritage that has been handed down,
With stories of our Saviour, the pages do abound,
When on this earth He too did walk among His fellowmen
To prove to us that Love and Truth was God's own special gem.
The parables, He taught them that we our souls could save
The horrors that He suffered so that with glory our paths could be paved.

A lonesome figure in a crowd, and yet one to be seen

THERE IS A REASON

For all its calm and tranquillity, a pillar of strength on whom to lean.
To touch the hem of His garment was release for someone's pain,
To feel the touch of His hand was a Love for all to gain.
For to believe our Saviour, and listen to His words
Would make us all so happy, and sorrow a thing unheard.

The miracles He showed them were just to make them see
That if they would all listen, they too could help humanity.
As love for each other He tried to show them as He walked by Galilee
Calling to His disciples to do the same as He.
To some He gave the gift of healing, to others of prophecy
And some to teach the words of Love to all whose thoughts were free.

He only had a little time to try to make them see
That Loving, Giving and Sharing was all He wanted their lives to be.
And when His enemies came to take Him, to His disciples He said,
"Please teach what I have taught you so that my people will be led,
And find their way into God's House to a life of eternity
Where pain, sorrow and fear is no more an entity."

And, when they hung Him on the cross, He pleaded for their sin
Saying, "Oh God forgive them, and all their kith and kin."
And so our dear Lord departed. He gave his life for us,
And so I say dear children, "We must believe, we must,
As time is getting very short to know what must be done,
As time has proved to us that only Love can make us one.

Just believe that God is waiting to see His children free,
And of all the Love He is waiting for so patiently.
For all the killing and the hate must surely pass away,
For soon we will be coming to that great judgement day.
So listen to His disciples who teach the words of Love
Then you will have found your way to that Garden of Eden, Above.

CHAPTER 35

It is now January 26th, 1979, a date I will never forget, it being very cold and the roads covered with lots of black ice. Neil was fed up staying in, and I said to Nichola, "Wrap him up nice and warm and Arnold and I will take him up the road for a little walk. The trees were white and frozen, with a dull mist hanging over them, and the road was very slippery and dangerous. We had a job to stay upright. We found it better to walk on the grass verge which crunched underneath our shoes. In fact everything looked like a winter wonderland. Neil enjoyed it when he slipped on the ice, thinking it all great fun as boys do.

We had to cross the road to travel down to Lower Almondsbury, thinking it would not be quite so cold in the shelter of the woods, when halfway over the road Neil and I fell on some black ice and landed badly. My first thought was for Neil and his bad right arm which I had been holding.

In fact, subconsciously I had lifted and kept his arm off the road, cushioning it with my left arm so that I felt the full impact of the fall on it. We lay for a while stunned, and then Arnold helped to lift us up, and I felt a great need to hurry home as I felt so shook up. We took Neil back to Nichola's, explaining what had happened. She was very worried, and Neil was very quiet and upset over the fall.

Arnold and I left for home around 4.30 pm. I felt very strange in myself. About 5.30 pm I said to Arnold, "I think you had better call the doctor as I don't feel right." In fact I was shaking, and I could hardly get my breath. I was more or less gasping. Arnold rang the doctor, explaining what had happened and how I was, who replied, "Come and see me in the morning surgery hours."

What a night I had! I sat by the fire thinking I was going to die. I had like an asthma attack like Dawn gets periodically. The next morning I dragged myself around to get myself dressed to see the doctor. How I did it, I don't know. I was in an awful state.

When I arrived at the surgery it was nearly empty, being a Saturday morning. The doctor called my name, and I walked in to see him, telling him what had happened all over again. He listened and then listened to my heart which I was worried about because my breathing was so bad. After a quick check-up he said, "Your heart is as sound as a bell." He gave me a prescription for some medicine for my nerves, telling me that after an examination he could find nothing broken. I returned home feeling terrible, not wanting to eat or drink and feeling very giddy, and all the time feeling anxious about Neil and Nichola and not being with them.

I began to realise just how much the fall had disturbed me. When I hit the ice I must have fallen on a sharp edge as I could hardly sit on my bottom, and where I had thrown out my left leg to save myself all the aches and pains were a misery. It had also disturbed all my previous accident spots, such as back, shoulders, neck, head and ribs. I then realised I had a frozen shoulder which was agony. I could not dress properly, and I could only use my right arm to comb my hair so I had to take Brufen for the pain. The days passed by very slowly and I became a recluse, just sitting and watching Arnold doing all the things I used to do and helping me to wash and dress. The doctor put me on Valium, five milligrams three times a day, to relax me.

I just sat like a cabbage, watching everything going on around me like in a dream. Arnold would have to help me during the night to go to the toilet as I was so giddy and frightened that I would fall. In fact in the end Arnold bought a rubber sheet for the bed as I could not always make it to the toilet. I would lay awake most of the night, and the pain in my arm and shoulder would travel right up the left side of my face and head. I had a continual headache and all I did was cry. I began to wonder what was happening to me as I had always been so busy, going out in the fresh air, and now here I was like in a prison and longing to escape. I also missed Neil and Nichola, and yet they couldn't visit me because I was so poorly, and visitors I could not stand. I would cry because of the circumstances I was in, wanting to see them yet not being able to converse with them. I would stand at the window looking out and wondering what they would all be doing, and then sit back in my chair and cry again. In fact I just could not speak. It became such an effort that even to Arnold I just said `yes' or `no'. I had no interest in anything except to fret over what I could not do and feeling very poorly, having no strength whatever and an absolute nervous exhaustion.

Arnold was very worried about me and he was talking to Miss Vera Cripps, who had a grocery shop in the village, all about it. She very kindly offered to come and see me. She had already done a lot of healing for people. I was very worried about having a visitor, but in the end I said "Alright." Vera arrived one afternoon and she soon put me at my ease. She gave me a healing for my nerves which was relaxing. She stayed just a little while so that I would not get too tired.

She came each week, and just to see her walk down the path gave me a feeling of hope.

Jenny and Harry called in one day on their way back home after visiting their daughter in Sussex, but I did not want to talk. In fact I cried most of the time. Harry gave me a healing before they left, but it was a very sad occasion.

Another strange thing was that I was afraid to lift or carry anything. As soon as I did I would have a nerve eruption which would upset me for hours afterwards. Even reaching or opening doors had the same effect, so in the end I did not try anything, hoping each day my strength would return.

The days, weeks and months passed by with me feeling very ill all the time, and Arnold, thinking it would help, suggested I had a little car ride to give me a change of atmosphere. That first day was terrible. I didn't like to leave the house as I did not want anyone to see me. I wore dark glasses and Arnold brought the car right outside the gate so that I would not have to walk far or talk to anyone. That first ride was awful. I thought everyone was going to crash into us, and Arnold had to go so slow as speed I could not stand. We found a little lane where there was no traffic and we had a little walk. I felt about one hundred years old hanging on to Arnold's arm, but I do remember seeing some primroses growing on the banks, and it reminded me of when I was a child and I used to pick them for my Mum. So once again the tears began to fall for myself, my departed Mum, Neil, Nichola and everything I had loved to do for them, but now I was so weak I could not help anyone, not even myself. I know I was a big trial for Arnold who really was wonderful to look after me in our own home.

If the phone rang I was too scared to answer it, or if anyone knocked on the door. I even did not play my records any more. I was in my own little wilderness.

The doctor changed my Valium from five milligrams three times a day to two milligrams three times a day as I felt so confused.

One day, on passing Almondsbury, I knew I had to call and see Nichola and Neil as I knew that being without them was as bad as being with them to the extent that I could not converse with them. That first day was terrible when I passed by the window and saw their faces looking out and the joy at seeing me again and to know that I could not put my arms around them, for that was another thing I could not do was to hold them tight, or for anyone to hold me. So it was just a kiss on the cheek for us all. My body was so wracked with pain and nervous energy that I did not want to be touched. I could not wear anything tight so I ended up looking like a scruff bag - not me at all.

Nichola said, "Never mind, Mum, you will get better, and I would rather you visit us than walk the lanes with Dad, even if you do not want to talk you can sit and listen to us all and have a walk around the garden." Neil was very upset that I could not go walking with him down the lanes, and laugh and joke with him like I used to do.

Everybody had lots of advice to give to Arnold about what I should and shouldn't do. What they did not realise was that I was not the type of person to give in, always being active, but even I knew that until the nerves subsided I was enslaved.

I did decide to try and get out of bed myself as I could see it was getting too much for Arnold looking after me day and night. So instead of waking him up I rolled out of bed, pushing myself up with my right arm. It was quite an effort as from the fall all my left side felt as though every muscle in my body had been torn. But after doing this a few times I had an awful pain in my back and I felt as though I had pulled a disc out with the effort. The thought of going into hospital to have it seen to was too much for my nerves. I knew I could not go with all those people milling about. Then Vera suggested that I go to see a friend of hers who lived in Maidenhead, near London - a Mrs Eleanor Robertson, who was an osteopath. She also did acupuncture and was very psychic and was someone who I could converse with. Luckily Arnold, who was now retired, said, "Vera and I will take care of you on the journey."

What a long journey! The road seemed to go on forever with me feeling very nervous. In fact my heart was beating rapidly and I thought both Vera and Arnold could hear it as it seemed so loud.

Every mile we went I thought about my little room at home, wishing that I was there, as to me it had become a haven.

When we had reached Eleanor's house I felt worn out. She welcomed me and made me feel at ease, talking to me all the time, asking me how I felt and what had happened, preparing her acupuncture needles at the same time.

At first I didn't like the feel of the needles, and then I felt my body relaxing as they began to work. After that she felt all down my back and said, "Yes, you have pulled out a disc. That is why you have such pain in your back, and having nerves made it worse for you. We will soon put that right. Just relax. As she straightened my back I felt a sharp pain and I shouted out. "It's alright," she said, "It's all over, but you must come to see me again in about three weeks' time as I am so busy that is the only time I have free, but go carefully and everything will be alright." As I began to dress she told me a lot of things about myself, and she also gave me a message from the other side, from someone I had known very well, proving to me how psychic she was. I instantly knew I was in good hands.

The journey back home was not quite so bad as the acupuncture had relaxed me, but I was very pleased to reach home. Of course all the tensions of having the back attended to had upset my nerves again, and the pain was excruciating. Disprins were not strong enough to help me so I went to my doctor and told him about the pain in my back for which he gave me pain killers, but by the time I went back to see Eleanor my body had swollen up like a balloon, and my legs were so big and painful that I could hardly walk.

"Whatever has happened to you?" she said, "The pain-killers must disagree with you." She tested my disc saying it was still in place, and gave me some more acupuncture for my nerves and pain. I would not have to visit again, but I would still have to go carefully.

The doctor gave me some water pills to help my water problem which didn't help my weight at all. My legs were very red and painful and the ankles so swollen that I could not do up my shoes properly. In fact none of my clothes fitted properly. Nichola had to dash around looking for bigger sizes for me.

I had pills for diarrhoea, pills for pain, pills for constipation, pills for circulation and pills for sleeping. You name it, I had it over the months, and also I was slightly anaemic. Also I was still taking Valium for my nerves, so you can imagine how I felt. Each day was a misery, and I thought it would never end as I still struggled down to see Nichola and Neil, walking down Over Lane in the sunshine, rain and snow, and hardly keeping my feet in the strong wind blowing up the hill from the River Severn. I was so determined to go.

It was very difficult for me to sit in the car properly. I just climbed in the front seat, hoping no one would see me wearing dark glasses as I felt so upset being as I was, so useless.

CHAPTER 36

Neil had now changed his school as the one he was going to closed down, and as Nichola did not want him to travel too far away she sent him to a private school at Compton Greenfield, taking him each day by car. He looked very smart in his uniform.

My sisters Dorothy and Bess came to see me with their husbands, but I became so upset not being able to converse with them, and when they left I was always in floods of tears, and for a few days very unhappy. So I had to say to them, "Please wait until I feel better before you return."

Vera still came round to see me and to give me healing. She also put me on the healing list of a friend of hers, a Mrs Simpson who lived at Slough, Berkshire, and who had had a lot of healing successes.

The months passed slowly by, each day just about the same, and then we had some sad news. Arnold's sister Gillian had passed away, but it was really a happy release for her as she was in so much pain with cancer, God bless her. We could not go to the funeral, but our prayers were with the family.

Neil lost Bright Eyes, his rabbit. She had to be put to sleep owing to a growth she had. Nichola bought another rabbit for him, black and white, which he called Patches. Then one day I said to Nichola, "You are going to buy a puppy, and it will be a Labrador." "Oh no," she said, "I have not thought about buying a dog". But I was right. She did, and she called him Ruffles.

Ruffles used to sit underneath my chair in the garden and follow me round and round on my little walks. In fact where I walked each day I had made a path over the lawn and right round the vegetable garden. We would talk to Patches with Ruffles pushing his nose against the wire, trying to reach her, and Patches tormenting him by running up and down and round her hutch.

I would pick the fruit from the gooseberry bushes and the raspberry bushes, eating them as I went along, and so would Ruffles. You would see him behind me, gripping the fruit with his teeth carefully to avoid the thorns, and when that fruit had gone he would sit and eat an apple with Arnold underneath the trees, with Arnold cutting him off slices which he loved. In fact Ruffles loved anything he could eat.

Ruffles did not like sudden noises, and one day Nichola was trying to take some photographs in the garden of us all, but when Ruffles heard the click of the camera he rushed at Nichola to see what she had in her hand, and they both ended up in the gooseberry bushes.

I had now left off my Valium, taking off one at a time as I was so worried about being an addict. It was not easy, and I felt terrible, but I persevered. I also left off most of my other tablets. I was now only on pain-killers and water tablets. My weight was still about the same. The specialist said my legs were swollen due to my veins, so I carried on, hoping one day soon it would all end.

I was very lucky to have son-in-laws to help with the garden. Arnold had never liked gardening, and with me so poorly he didn't have time to keep it tidy. So Michael, Dawn's husband, came and cut down all the weeds, and what a job it was! Looking out of the window it looked like a jungle. It was very hard work, and Colin came and put down grass seed to make gardening easier. So Arnold bought a light electric mowing machine which made the work a lot easier for him.

I was very glad that Nichola had been a hairdresser as she always kept my hair nice, giving me perms when needed, doing all our washing and running about. And then there was Vera who always remembered our birthdays with cards, presents and birthday sponge, also presents at Christmas time. She was a real friend, bless her. Dawn always came when she could, or when I could stand company, bringing me presents and flowers.

CHAPTER 37

Neil had now moved to a bigger school at Filton, and he went every day by bus. He was now eleven years of age. One day, on leaving Nichola's to go home, we saw Neil walking down the hill loaded up with his school books and his coat hanging on his arm. Nichola, who was with us, had not expected him home so early, and so she dashed over the road to help him, but as I watched I knew something was wrong with Neil. It was the way he walked. He seemed to have such an effort to walk, and then it came to me - his muscles.

I said quickly to Nichola, Neil has something wrong with him. You had better see the doctor. She looked very upset and she said, "Are you trying to say there is something wrong with his blood?" "No," I said, "It is his muscles."

Nichola took Neil to see the doctor who sent her to see a specialist. She did not tell me for a while about it, saying she had not heard, but I knew something was wrong. The laughter had gone from the house. Then one day she said to me, "Mum, I have some bad news for you. I can't keep it to myself any longer, and you will soon find out anyway." I said, "It's Neil, isn't it?" "Yes," she said, "He has muscular dystrophy."

I must admit, although I knew it was his muscles, this I had not expected, and it was a great shock. We both threw our arms around each other and cried. We were heartbroken, and so were Colin and Arnold. I cried most of my tears at night when I was alone in bed so as not to be too upset in the daytime as we all needed lots of courage, and most of all Neil, who now only had a wheelchair to look forward to.

It was a very sad period. On top of it all I became very poorly and started to be very sick each day for quite a time. I had had an awful pain underneath my right breast which travelled round my ribs, almost making me double up. As usual everyone said it was just my nerves, having just heard bad news. But one night it became so bad, and I was being sick such a lot, that Arnold called the doctor who said it was either appendicitis or gallstones, so you can imagine how I felt as I got ready to go into hospital. The ambulance arrived and took me into Southmead where I had an X-ray which proved it was gallstones. So I had to stay in hospital and Arnold left to return home. I felt so very alone, which did not help my nerves, but knowing that at last I would be getting rid of the pain, and that I was in the right place, helped.

It was a big thing for me. All the hustle and bustle of people, nurses and doctors, hurrying about and visiting days, were an effort to put up with after being so long away from the public.

The nurses tested me for heart, blood pressure, just about everything, and my body was prepared ready for the operation. And then I was taken with three other women in wheelchairs for a last X-ray as now they would be able to see the trouble more clearly.

I thought we would be going to a special room just for the patients, but I was very surprised and upset to find myself taken to the Outpatients to sit and wait for my X-ray, and to find myself sitting with outside patients, all dressed up and me just in my nightdress with not even my hair combed properly. I thought to myself, "Oh dear, what a sight I must look! I do hope no one comes in who knows me."

Of course things were made worse in the hospital as there was a strike on at the time, so everything was not as it should be. My operation was the following Friday when it was discovered I had sixteen small gallstones. When I came round I felt like a trussed up chicken. If the surgeon had cut any more there would have been two halves of me and to move was agony. Anyway, it was over, and now I wanted to return home.

All the family came to see me, also Vera, but I was not much company as my nerves came back in force after the operation, leaving me exhausted. I was in hospital about ten days in all. Arnold came to fetch me home and he was very thrilled to have me back as he had found the house very lonely without me. I had to spend more time in bed again, being so weak, and then the nurse called to take the stitches out - thank goodness! So perhaps now it would soon get better.

It took a long time again before I could visit Nichola and Neil, and there I was once again leaning on Arnold's arm as I felt so weak. That first day walking down the hill and up Nichola's steep path was agony, but it was worth it. I was out again, but I must admit I felt very shaky.

Neil was finding it an effort to walk. In fact he had to have a taxi to take him to school, and for Nichola and all of us it was a very upsetting time to see the struggle he had, but he was a very brave little boy and struggle he did.

Nichola was very anxious that he should enjoy as much of his walking days as he could. She asked the Almondsbury Motorway Police Force if he could have a ride in their police Rover car, which they very kindly agreed to, and they picked him and Nichola up and took them over the Severn Bridge and back, and then they gave them both a tour of their control room. Michael drove Nichola and Neil to Bristol Airport as British Airways had organised a flight for him and Nichola in a Trident aircraft, and they flew over Badminton and on the way back they circled over Rolls Royce three times, which Arnold and I watched from our back garden. What they possibly could do for them they did.

Neil's wheelchair had arrived, and Neil was really glad to sit in it for long walks as he was now getting very tired from walking and getting far too many falls from his weak muscles.

Mr and Mrs John Alley of the Bowl Inn organised a fund to send Neil and Nichola to Disney Land, USA. Even Colin and his friends did a sponsored cycle ride to Gloucester and back, and Mr Ken Batchelor, a friend of Dawn, and Michael organised a disco to raise funds for him.

Nichola and Neil were driven to Heathrow by Mr Alley's father and Colin where they caught a flight to Orlando, and they stayed at the Hilton Hotel near the Disney Village, where they stayed for one week enjoying all the Disneyland amusements. And then they flew to Miami, staying at the Cenesta Hotel for another week. It really was a most enjoyable holiday for them both.

When they returned home Colin and John and Pat from the Bowl met them at the airport and took them out to dinner, and when they were nearly home a police Range Rover escorted them back to the Bowl Inn where all the flags were out, giving them a warm welcome home.

It was a most wonderful experience for them both, but it took another fortnight to get over the jet lag and to get use to our weather again as they found America very hot.

CHAPTER 38

Neil had to give up going to the Filton School as now he could not walk at all, so he had to wait for a place in a disability school with special facilities.

Nichola had to bring Neil's bed downstairs to sleep as she could no longer carry him up the stairs. I would sit and talk to him, play cards or read books and papers. It was a very long day for him, and Nichola always tried to take him and Ruffles for a walk each day - what a walk, pushing a heavy wheelchair up all those hills, and then at night to try and keep awake to exercise the boy's legs for cramp sometimes. Nichola just felt too tired even to sleep, giving her awful headaches and a bad back and neck from lifting Neil.

And then, as though that wasn't enough, one day she went down to get into the car to go shopping and found that the Council workmen were digging up the road near her car. "What on earth are you doing?" she said. "Where will I put my car?" They told her that someone had reported the cars parked on the side of the hill and it was a danger for the traffic.

But it had been used for car parking for years. Even back in the old days people left their horses and carts there so as to gain access to the cottages nearby. The Council was going to dig it up and put a new pavement with a high kerb so that no one could park there. So what about the poor people who had nowhere else to park? Also the road there had been very wide, but with a new pavement it would be a danger to even leave the car for a few minutes and, of course, that would not be allowed on the road at night. So what could Nichola do? Not even to have her car near the cottage to take Neil out was a calamity.

For the time being she parked her car halfway up the hill where there was a pull-in for the lorries. Quite a wide space it was, and then she wrote to various people to try and regain her parking space. About a week later, on going to take her car to put in the pull-in, she found a rock garden had sprung up overnight. Roses had been planted, and boulders scattered here and there. She came home in tears. "What am I going to do," she said. "I need my car space." Arnold went along to the Police Station at Almondsbury and they sent a policeman to see what it was all about.

He told her that it was not private land and she was doing no harm. "Take out the roses," he said,

"And put your car in", which he helped her to do. "You and Neil will be alright now," he said. But how wrong he was! The next day there was a big sign there, THIS IS PRIVATE PROPERTY, so once again we fetched the Police who said, "Take it out. It is not private property." So we did. But there was still a lot of aggression about it with people throwing down garden rubbish and dead leaves around the car. As though Nichola didn't have enough trouble, she would walk up the hill, pushing Neil with her heart in her mouth, wondering what would happen next.

Nichola went to lots of meetings, but she didn't seem to get very far, so she rang Bob Crampton on "What's your Problem", and he came out with his camera crew to see what it was all about, and he got her story on the TV, also getting in touch with Council people to help her and her son. I am sure it was through him that Nichola won a parking space that was put in for her halfway up the hill with DISABLED written on it. How thrilled she was to have no more worry. Now Neil would not get so wet and cold in the rain and strong winds as it was nearer the cottage than the pull-in.

I must say now I was very proud of my daughter Nichola for what she had done for her disabled son against all odds. She fought and won. But if there had only been love from everyone there would have been no need to fight for a just cause. So I have added a poem describing what love is all about.

Love

Love is for the aged, the lonely and the meek.
Love is for the young ones and the partners that they seek.
Love is for the mental, the crippled and the blind.
Love is for the weak in spirit and the courage that they find.
Love is for all nations and the goodly lives they live.
Love is free and wonderful and makes you want to give.
Love is for the animals, the flowers, the birds and the bees.
Love is for the rivers, the oceans and the seas.
Love is for the desert, the mountains and the plain.
Love is for each other, to heal and sooth our pain.
Love is for the simple things that bring us all together.
Love is all life, all wisdom, so all things we must treasure.
Love is the secret that has been handed down
So that one day we may all be seated, with the man that wore a thorny crown.

Mr Keith Hodges, who owned the Garden Centre at Almondsbury arrived at Nichola's cottage one morning with an Acorn computer, given to Neil by the Westbury Round Table, which gave him a lot of pleasure.

One day I was feeling very low and nervous, and fed up wearing my old and very large clothes as I still could not wear anything tight, and Neil, sitting in his wheelchair trying to do some drawing, upset me as it was such an effort for him. Everything he dropped, one of us had to pick up for him, which was very frustrating for him. And when I put my coat on to leave for home my heart was very sad, as now he could not wave me off from the garden and watch me out of sight. I knew that when I left he would still be in the same position all the evening and the next day.

I bent and kissed him, saying, "I will be back again tomorrow, my love," but looking into his eyes I could see the shimmer of tears which I also could not hide and, just as I passed by the window waving my hand, a voice called out, "Go carefully, my Rose, take care." I am afraid with these words coming from one so young I was sobbing by the time I reached the car, then when I reached home I wrote this poem in honour of my grandson Neil.

My Little Rosebud

My Charlie Chaplin trousers,
My Charlie Chaplin stick,
My red unfurled umbrella,
My mind that does not brightly tick,
My shoes a navy colour,
My coat a greenish hue,
My face so sad and woeful,
My thoughts so sad and blue,

My tummy big and swollen,
My legs a trifle weak,
Sometimes I find it frustrating,
Sometimes I cannot speak.
I sit and watch my grandson Neil
As in his wheelchair he struggles with his play,
And then it is time for me to leave.
I must go on my way.
But as I leave and say goodbye
He lifts his face so lovingly.
I kiss him, oh so gently,
As he sits patiently.
And as I walk away he calls
"Go carefully my rose, take care."
And with these words
My humility is hard to bear.
And so, my little rosebud,
I thank you for your care,
For it has made my burden a lot easier to bear.

The months passed by with each day becoming harder for Nichola to manage. Neil had now started at Courtland School, Knowle, South Bristol, a school for the disabled with special facilities, still going by taxi. It was a long day for him. He had to get up at seven as it took such a long time to dress and have his breakfast, and if he had had a sleepless night through cramp or feeling sick it really was a worry for Nichola as all day she would worry, knowing he would be feeling very tired after such a night. To me it did not make sense that such children should have to rush in this way when all they really needed was time, love and understanding.

Also Nichola found the cottage too small with a bed downstairs which nearly filled the lounge, and the steep hill to take Neil for a walk just wore her out. So she just had to look for another house. So she put the cottage which she had loved up for sale, for Neil came first.

People began to arrive to look around, and I am sure many made it a weekend tour, just for somewhere to go. What a trial it was, trying to sell something you loved, and yet knowing most of the people were not interested in buying! In the end a Mr and Mrs Stephens were interested in buying, so now Nichola had to find a suitable house or bungalow for Neil.

Every house she looked at I was sure it wasn't the right one. I felt that she had to buy a house on the main A38 road, Patchway near AZTEC, and in the end she did just that, where all the amenities were at hand, with plenty of room for parking her car which was an added luxury.

She was very sad at leaving her cottage at Almondsbury, but her new home had all the space she needed.

CHAPTER 39

It was a nice big house, with a large lounge and dining room together, large kitchen, hall and a room at the front of the house which Nichola made into a bedroom for Neil. Upstairs there were two large bedrooms and a large bathroom. There was also a garage and a small garden, back and front. It was a big change from Almondsbury, to wheel Neil on the flat road and to be able just to walk to all the shops. Nichola did not feel so isolated. Also a big bonus for her was that she had a telephone, so if ever she needed help she always knew Arnold and I were on the end of the line, or the doctor for Neil. So all in all everything was made a lot easier.

And then the work began. Neil had to have a lift put in so that he could move to a bedroom upstairs. Nichola once again had a bed in the lounge while the bedroom Neil was using downstairs was used for the lift, and what a job and a mess it was! Banging all day, and the dust got everywhere. In fact when the wall was knocked down in the bathroom we thought it was going to come through the lounge ceiling. Nichola had a new door put on in the bathroom, radiators moved, and all her carpets were covered with dust sheets. She had a room opened that was an attic so that the lift came up from the downstairs bedroom into a space which was made into a small room, and then Neil could reach the bathroom in comfort. Then she had a hoist fitted to the bathroom ceiling which travelled into the back bedroom and above Neil's bed so that he could have a bath and be hoisted up and taken through the new bathroom door which had a flap at the top for the hoist to pass through. What a big complicated job it was!

Then Nichola had a ramp built up to the front door for Neil's wheelchair, and a ramp built at the back so that Neil could go through the french windows and on to the lawn. Then she had to have an air vent put in the bathroom for health's sake. She was very glad when it was all over, but it did make a big difference and I must admit the lift was wonderful.

Neil was now thirteen years of age, the year being 1986. He now went to school by coach, instead of a taxi, picking up lots of other children on the way. I said to Nichola, "I hate to say this, but you are going to get a lot of trouble with your water pipes again." "Oh no, Mum! Not again!" she said. "Oh well, we must wait and see", I said.

One evening Nichola had a telephone call from a Mr Peter Liddington, who lived at Yate, asking Nichola if Neil had an electric wheelchair, and she said, "No, he hasn't". "Well," he said, "I raise funds for muscular dystrophy and I have an electric wheelchair here and you can have it for your son Neil. We are having a Pig Roast evening at the Farmhouse Pub, Yate, and if you would all like to attend we will present Neil with the chair.

Nichola did not tell Neil about it as she wanted it to be a surprise. Well, it was that alright! When it was given to Neil, and he was transferred to it from his push wheelchair, he just pressed the button and he was off yelling, " Yahoo! Dabby Doo!", and in fast gear went round the car park, his face alight with joy. In fact the man who presented it to Neil said, "It was all worth it just to see his face!" And when Neil arrived home with it he was so thrilled to tell me that now he had a vehicle of his own and his Mum would not have to push him for walks ever again.

Arnold tried to take me for a walk as Neil and Nichola wanted me to join them, but halfway up the road I just had to stand still and Arnold had to fetch the car to take me back. I didn't have the strength to keep walking. Nichola and Neil went on without me, but when she came back after her walk she said, "You are coming out tomorrow, and I am going to push you in the wheelchair which I have done many times for Neil, and you won't be any heavier." I said, "No, it is too much for you." Neil also wanted me to go. "Come on Joyce," he said, "I would love you to come with us."

So the next day I was ready, a little apprehensive as I knew that Nichola had an added burden, but she was so thrilled to think she was helping her Mum.

We had a walk round the AZTEC Business Park. It was lovely. All the little paths were made with bricks, something like the yellow brick road to me, going on forever, the lovely shrubs with roses and the perfume was very heady. There were two lakes, one each side of the road, with lots of ducks swimming around, and a waterfall on each one which sprayed and danced on the water, sparkling in the sunshine with Neil saying, "Look at this Joyce!" and, "Look at that Joyce!", so thrilled to show me all the things he had seen every day.

The big buildings and car parks for the workers were wonderful, a lot different from how they used to be - more like hotels with all the glass windows and big doors. Neil in his electric chair came alongside me and, holding my hand said, "Let us sing that song we used to sing when we went for walks." And there we were, Nichola pushing me, Neil and I holding hands singing, "We haven't got a barrel of money, but we'll travel along singing a song side by side." We must have looked a funny sight walking along, but to us it was pure heaven once again, all walking together and enjoying all the little things in life. It was something I had been thinking about for a long time, just to be out in the free fresh air and to be a part of the family again. I have added a poem which expresses all that I felt.

Through the Eyes of a Child

I never saw the grass so green, the sky so big and blue,
I never saw the trees so tall, except through the eyes of you.
The rivers with their sparkling joy, the flowers with their luscious hue,
I never saw the gifts of God, except through the eyes of you.

The birds that sing in the morning, each note so bright and clear
The butterflies in the sunshine, where all their beauty doth appear,
The animals in the woodlands, so timid and yet so bold,
Each day I am now waiting for some new wonder to unfold.

For, as a child to whom all things are great and new,
I have seen the wonders of God through the eyes of you.
And as you grow to reach my age, I only hope you too will see
The glories through the eyes of a child, that you once showed to me.

For as we all grow older, our eyes are blind to see
The wonders all around us that are so good and free.
And as we become entangled in a life of shame and greed,
Instead of flowers the Gardener finds His harvest full of weeds.

So through the eyes of a child I am looking, and what I see is joy
The sunshine warm and glowing, the wind my hair to toy,
The raindrops fresh and cleansing, the snow and ice so gay,
Through the eyes of a child I am saying, Oh thank you God for
this day.

Colin left home, which was a distressing time, but Nichola kept herself busy, painting and decorating the house so as not to think. Neil was a great help in comforting his Mum.

Nichola also had a high fence put round the garden so that Ruffles could not roam near the main road as it was so dangerous with the fast traffic.

Neil had his bedroom walls covered with his pop star pictures, also his lift which made it look very comfortable and gay. His real enjoyment were his records, and I would sit with him and listen to all the pop songs on his record player. In fact when I returned home I would be singing his songs as I knew all the words. Also we would help each other if we dropped anything. I would pick it up off the floor with a helping hand for the disabled, and Neil would lean over and take it from me, both of us understanding each other.

Dorothy's two daughters, Christine and Pauline, organised a disco at Hillesley with most of the inhabitants of the village joining in. Mr Spencer, a farmer, very kindly gave them permission to use one of his big barns. Nichola and Neil were invited as funds were being raised to buy Neil a video. It was a jolly good evening, and Neil enjoyed the music which was provided by Michael who is a disc jockey. Neil was thrilled with the video because now he was able to watch and buy his own tapes if there was not much to watch on television.

About this time I felt a strong feeling that I should start leaving off my dark glasses. The strong thought came again and again, "Look at the light. See the sunshine. Take off your dark glasses. You are only fooling yourself." In the end I did, and I began to talk to people again, not a lot but slowly. I felt as though I was slowly returning to life, and I did not need to hide behind dark glasses.

Mary Jewitt, a friend of Nichola's, organised a trip for Neil on a fire engine. The fireman, Paul Morgan, was a friend of Mary and he was a fireman for the Kingswood Fire Brigade, Bristol. He let Neil use the fire hose and ring the fire bell, which was a great thrill. Also he gave him a fireman's helmet which Neil keeps in his bedroom.

Nichola and Colin were now divorced. It was very sad, but that is life. We are learning lessons all the time, and only we ourselves can sort them out.

CHAPTER 40

I was right about Nichola's water pipes. First she had to have a new ball cock in the main tank as she had a constant overflow, then the water was coming up through the front lawn and the path from a broken pipe. Also the down pipe leading from the guttering to the drain had to be renewed.

Then Nichola had a leak underneath the kitchen sink and she had to have all new pipes. Then the cistern in the bathroom sprang a leak with a big crack forming down the front of it. She had to have it all renewed and then the pipe underneath the bathroom basin began to leak, so, all in all, all the water pipes were renewed, leaving Nichola with some enormous bills. She said to me, "If ever I move again, please don't mention water pipes!"

Vera had to give up coming to see me as she had an ulcer between her toes and it made walking very painful. I missed our little talks, but I knew that she would still include me in her healing prayers, and there was always the telephone if I wanted some advice. A friend of Vera's, Eunice Lovell, kept us all supplied regularly with freshly baked cakes and tarts.

Nichola wanted to give up smoking and she said, "Mum, do you think you could help me." I said, "Well, you have to really mean it - no half measures." "Alright", she said, "I really mean it." So I sent up some strong prayers for help for Nichola, to help her to give up smoking. About a week later, on going down to see her, she said, "Mum, I never want to smoke again. I had a very vivid dream last night," and she told me all about it, which I cannot divulge in my story as it is personal, but from that day she has not had a cigarette, and neither does she want one, so I can only surmise that my prayers helped her.

We were having some lovely walks now, and one of our favourite ones was walking down Woodlands Lane, and about one mile down we would turn down another lane which led to some picturesque cottages on a green with a pond on which there swam two geese and three ducks. We would take them some bread and I would pick some long grassy green sticky plants which, when I was a child, we called goose grass. The geese loved it, and they would strip the stems and enjoy their snack, and the ducks would watch and do the same. I am sure the geese were their guardians as they would follow the ducks and look after them wherever they went.

It was very pleasant just sitting and looking at the cool fresh water, and letting our minds relax. It reminded me of when I lived at Withymore and of my own geese, and I knew from experience what good pets they were. We would have liked to have lingered there all day, but we knew we still had to walk back, or rather, as I said before, Nichola would push me most of the way.

We would also travel down Patchway Common as it still looked like the lanes we knew and loved so well. Sometimes we would see a young fox cross the road that would stand and watch us for a moment and then go on its way. Also on a clear day we would see and hear the skylarks singing high up in the clear blue sky.

We would stand and listen, and Neil would ask me questions all about them. It was a real nature walk for us all as we all enjoyed the same things.

Neil had now learnt to swim on his back at school, graduating from armbands to swimming three lengths of the pool without them, and getting a certificate for it for which he was very proud. He did not really enjoy school. His joy was walking with us and playing his records. He knew all the pop stars and the names of all their records. Also he was very good at quizzes on the television and sometimes surprised us with his knowledge.

I would stand and wait for his coach to return from school each day, and I always knew by the look on his face if he had had a good day. If not, we would all try to make his evening happy.

About this time we lost Patches, the rabbit, and we were all very upset as she was such a loveable pet, and for a long time we missed feeding and talking to her.

One day we decided to have a walk back towards Almondsbury along the A38 road. We had just reached the top of Over Lane, near where Nichola used to live, when we realised Neil had stopped. We went back for him, and there he was, the electric chair facing down across the hill and the tears streaming down his cheeks. "Oh my love, what is it I said?", and he said, "I was just remembering when I used to walk with you and Nichola across the grass and down the woodland slopes where we fed Lucy the goat, and pick wild primroses, and you would chase me, playing little games." Well, what could we say? We could not change anything, only try to soften the pain with loving words. So I said to him, "I know how you feel. I am the same my love, wanting to run and walk all our old walks again, but we will one day." Nichola was too upset to talk so Neil and I walked slowly together talking over old times and trying to cheer each other up. But it was a struggle for us both and we both were very sad. But on the way back we talked about this and that, and it would be hard to say who cheered who up.

I received a letter from Harry who I knew had been feeling very poorly, and who, like me, did not want any visitors, feeling too ill to cope with any as he was suffering with emphysema, so both Harry and I could only send out our healing thoughts to each other. It was now a very long time since I had seen Harry as I just could not talk to anyone. My sisters had been to see me again, and I was just beginning to converse with them.

Neil had now left school and was so glad not to have to get up so early in the morning, and enjoyed shopping with his Mum, who took him everywhere she went. Each day, if it was not too cold, you would see the three of us and Ruffles taking our daily walk as it made such a difference to Neil's day to go out at least once a day.

Each day there were a lot of helicopters passing over the house and Neil said, "I would love to go up in one". So Nichola went up to Arlington Park, AZTEC West, and saw the receptionist, and asked if there was any chance for Neil to have a flight, explaining the reason why.

The young lady very kindly said she would find out if it was possible, and she would ring Nichola to let her know. About a week later she rang Nichola and said, "One of the pilots would be only too pleased to take Nichola and Neil up for a flight."

It was a lovely sunny day when they went. The pilot lifted Neil into the helicopter and up they went, circling over Almondsbury, Patchway and travelling a little way up the M4 motorway and over Nichola's house a few times so that I could watch them, wishing I was with them. When they returned home Neil was full of excitement about the flight, but Nichola had been a little afraid, and she was glad to be on firm ground, but she said she would do it all again for Neil.

One night Arnold and I returned home and our neighbours, Mr and Mrs Daniels, were waiting for us outside the house. I felt there was something wrong before they spoke. "We waited for you to come back," they said, "As we did not want you to be too worried, but someone has broken into the house behind us to steal, and they have been disturbed, and so, to get away, they have broken through our back hedge and yours, and then smashed your side gate to pieces." And what a mess! It didn't do much for my nerves either. I had an awful night, shaking with the thought of someone perhaps breaking into my house. We also had the worry of having the gate renewed, and filling up the hole in the hedge. So below I have added a poem to emphasise the terrible suffering that is caused by these people.

The Intruder

Stealthy footsteps in the night
Causing fear and needless plight,
Destroying, stealing, come what may.

Who are these people that on us prey?

Our limousines are searched for loot,
Our one spare tyre is stolen from boot.
Radios, handbags, coats and food,
Nothing is safe from the restless dude.

For the old folks who are sick at heart,
Their fear of strangers they do impart,
And youngsters too afraid to play
In case they too are stolen away.

No more to leave a handy key
For friend to join you for some tea,
As thieves will break into your home
And leave it bare, just like a bone.

What they can't steal and take away
They break and destroy, for which we pay.
No thought for someone's priceless gifts
As with greedy hands they lustfully sift.

Our clothes are stolen from the line,
A special dress for which we pine,
And undies taken by the score.
Who are these people we abhor?

For not to know your friend from foe
Is hard to believe it could be so,
For friends and neighbours we really need
To stamp out this kind of rotten seed.

For if allowed to grow and spread
Our living days will be a life of dread,

As others too will surely lead
If we cannot stamp out this awful greed.

I was now helping Arnold to do little jobs in the house such as dusting and washing up, and helping to make the beds, but I had to keep resting in between. I now had to strengthen all my muscles after sitting for so long, and it was a long, painful struggle. I was now only on Paracetamols which I only took if the pain was too hard to bear, and a water pill each morning as my legs and body were still swelling up a little.

The weather had turned very stormy, and one night, when we arrived home, our fence on both sides had been broken down and the tiles on the roof and our two chimney pots had blown off. Windy weather always made my nerves worse, worrying about what might happen.

But we were very lucky. The Council repaired the roof, and our neighbours on either side, Mr Daniels and Mr Hussey, very kindly repaired the fence for us, and Mr Knapp made us a new side gate, so, all in all, our neighbours rallied round, helping us in our time of need.

CHAPTER 41

Out of the blue one morning I had a telephone call from Harry as they had just had the phone installed. What a pleasant surprise after such a long time! It was as though it was only yesterday we had all been laughing together. So, of course, I rang Jenny as often as possible to find out how Harry was. The last time I rang he was very poorly and Jenny said he was still in bed and not able to come to the phone. About a week later the son-in-law rang to say Harry had passed away, the date being the 23rd of April, 1990, just one day before his 78th birthday. It was a very sad time for us all, and he was buried in the parish church at Llanallgo cemetery.

I am very sad to lose the friend who showed me the Way, but I was also sure that he will be watching my progress in the future, and I can only hope he will be proud of his pupil, for, as he once said to me, "One day, Joyce, you are going to cry buckets of tears, but one morning you will wake up and it will be all gone, and you will feel like jumping over the moon." At that time I could not quite understand what he was talking about, but now I know he was telling me about what I had just been through, and, remembering what he said, I am now looking forward to that prophecy coming true.

As I was beginning to look around me. I saw such a lot of changes. For a start, Stoke Gifford, which had been a sleepy village, was now more like a town, with new houses everywhere and cars filling every available space, blocking roads and pathways. The traffic was very bad. All the politeness on the roads with the drivers had gone. In fact it was not a case of `after you' but `by hook or by crook I am going to be first'. In fact, Nichola, Neil, Ruffles and I were crossing the main A38 road to reach home, when some lads, driving dangerously fast, tried to knock us down, deliberately putting on speed to reach us before we could reach the pavement, and then, because they missed knocking us down, they all turned round to look at us, laughing and giving two-fingered signs. But, as I have said so many times, "How can you know what you don't know", meaning we all have to learn the hard way, and I am sure one day those lads will also wish they had not been so stupid. Like myself, I did not realise just what being ill meant until I too was really ill. It is not enough to say, "Oh poor little or old soul", and leave it at that. We all have to help in every way we can to lighten another's pain.

One sunny afternoon Neil said, "Shall we go and see the ducks and the geese on the pond? It will be nice and peaceful there." For a change we had not been there for a while as there was such a lot of building going on at Bradley Stoke, and the lorries made such a dust as they passed by, also leaving lumps of mud everywhere which was hard to clean off the wheels of the wheelchairs.

It was so hard to recognise Woodlands Lane. There were big buildings on one side, business premises, and new houses on the right hand side, but we pressed on, thinking about our little paradise. But what a shock we had! As we turned down towards the pond the road was filled with cars and lorries, and with big buildings on either side - business premises again. And when we reached the pond we found it was all fenced round, and work still going on around it.

We hurried to have a closer look, and there, looking very forlorn and lonely, was one white goose. As we called to it, the goose hurried over, making a loud honking noise, and walking backwards and forwards from a big tree to us. I am sure it was trying to tell us all about it. Also a dustbin had been left in the gap at the bottom of the tree so that there was nowhere for the goose to perhaps sleep at night. It was very agitated and I am not surprised, with all the banging going on and the pond itself looked very dirty, with rubbish floating on the top of it. We were talking to a gentleman who was standing nearby, and we told him how lovely it used to be, a little corner of old England, and he replied, "That is why we chose it to build on." But I cannot see the connection, for now it is ruined. It is now just another building complex. We said goodbye to our friend the goose, but we hated to leave it in that environment. If only we had a lovely big pond with other geese and ducks to put it on! I could only hope and pray that someone would do just that.

Nichola was now finding it extremely hard to lift Neil in and out of the car, as he had now grown into such a big young man, seventeen years of age, giving her many bad backs and straining her arms and neck. When she heard and saw in the paper that Almondsbury Council had just sold land for just over three million pounds she decided to write to them for help. So she wrote a letter and went to see one of the councillors. He said that they would reply in time as they had had so many requests for help. She told him that she needed a van with a lift so that she would still be able to take Neil with her everywhere. Up to now she has had no reply, so she is now visiting all the business premises that have sprung up and is asking them if they can help, giving them a Neil Appeal poster to pin up on their walls with a poem for help which she has written herself. As she said to me, "Mum, I will beg for my son because I love him."

It is now Christmas, 1990, and I am ending the year with a poem describing that love for one another is the key to open the door.

The Brotherhood of Man

Father and mother, sister and brother,
We all are a part of God's great plan,
So that we may all love and help one another
And do every kindness we can.

For our father is our friend, whether near or afar,
In great times of need and despair.
Our mother is our guiding star
That nothing can compare.

The home is a refuge against the storm
Where family love holds each one together,
Where tears, laughter and trust is born
And forgiveness is on the never never.

So love one another, whatever the odds,
Not stop to wonder what people will think.
Have faith and courage to serve our dear God,
So that from his own cup we may drink.

What I am trying to say is that the whole world is a home,
Where we must all live in complete harmony,
Loving and helping and being able to condone.
What a wonderful world it would be!

For love is the key to open the door
For all God's creation,
The blind, the deaf, the lame, the poor,
And all colours of every nation.

So let us all make a New Year's resolution,
And do all the things that we should,
Then all will be bathed in the warmth of the sun,
Not lost in the dark depths of the wood.

For all brothers we must surely be
Before we can our last journey take,
For without our branch from the family tree,
We shall surely be left at the gate.

For brotherly love is a wonderful thing
Where all joy and sorrow is shared,
And the Angels in Heaven will rejoice and sing,
For they will know that our sins have been
spared.

And God, who is Father to each single one,
Will bless all his children alike,
And when the great day of judgement comes,
What love! What joy! What might!

CHAPTER 42

It is now August 1991 and the time is slowly passing by each day with me doing a little more work trying to regain my strength and to help my husband Arnold with the chores as now he finds it very hard to get through each day owing to having very high blood pressure and being 77 years of age.

Neil is now eighteen and Nichola is still having to lift him into the car.

We all had a walk one afternoon to see our friend the goose. The pond is now nice and clean and the goose was very pleased to see us but the buildings surrounding the pond, although very elegant, not quite the right setting for our feathered friend. It should have been just lovely old oak and willow trees and plenty of space for all the wild animals to congregate. But with such a lot of noise going on I am afraid it will only be for the humans to look at while they are having a quiet snack and, as an afterthought, tossing the remains on to the pond for the goose to eat.

We felt very sad as we left as we know that change is not always for the best.

I have now made my own working appliances. I have added little washing-up mops to long canes which are very light for me to lift. So now I can reach all those awkward corners on the walls, doors and ceiling. Also I can wash floors and by adding small brushes I can do the stairs.

My floor mop I keep in the kitchen in a large margarine container which is also very light, but it does the job I wanted so at last I feel I am returning to the everyday world again.

In the garden I use my disabled helping-hand appliance to pick up all the bits and pieces after Arnold has been working hard, weeding and cutting the privet hedge. We often have a laugh together at our disabilities. It makes life easier to see the funny side of it all.

I still find it very hard sleeping at night and I stand many times looking out of my bedroom window and I wonder just how many other people are doing the same. The nights are very long. When you are ill you think the morning will never come but, like all things, time does not stand still, and when the first flickers of morning light shine through your window you know that once again you must plod on.

So I find myself dressing slowly, wondering just what the day will have in store for me.

I now find it easier to talk to people again except about myself - that I do not want to relive. I want to put it all behind me and look ahead and, as I was once told, it will be a very slow recovery and it certainly is only by thinking back over the years that I realise how slow. But I must have patience which is not easy when I want to do so much, but I know I am in God's hands, and it is when "He" says the time is right.

CHAPTER 43

Neil has had a few trips to Weston-Super-Mare, picking up his cousins Pauline, Christine and Jason from Hillesley. It makes a nice change for him, Jason being a young lad fifteen years of age, so of course they have a lot to talk about. Nichola does all the driving and loves the company.

Arnold and I wait patiently for them to return and not once have they forgotten us as a little present is always brought back and given to us so lovingly saying, "Perhaps next time you will both be with us". Also Nichola and Neil visit the local public houses where they have a lemonade or a pineapple to drink. It is the music and the company which he loves. Everyone chats to him - he has that happy way with him. He loves fashionable clothes and he has his hair cut in the latest style. I am very proud of the way he conducts himself.

Nichola is now having to think seriously about transport for Neil as she is now getting bad pains in her neck, back and arms and has to wear special pads on her legs, and also it hurts Neil every time he is lifted up. So with the money she has collected for him she has sent away for a special seat which can be moved in and out of the car by a mechanical apparatus which costs £700. So the next thing is she has to have a new car with the right size door so that Neil can sit comfortably without his head flat against the roof of the car. She now has a motability Ford Fiesta three door which means more leg room for him to go in and out. Not as good a transport as some of the disabled vans Nichola had been looking at but you can only have what you can afford. The seat has now arrived with much excitement for us all but now Nichola has to have the front seat, Neil's side, taken out and the new special seat fitted which costs more money. It took quite a time for Nichola to manage the seat as it needed a bit of manoeuvring until Neil was comfortable. Even now he has to sit very straight, and looking at him I know I would not like to travel far in such a condition.

CHAPTER 44

Arnold is now having trouble with his eyes and he has to see a specialist, so now I must do the driving and after such a long time being just a passenger it was a big thing for me to do. We bought Nichola's Datsun which is a lovely car to drive and I found it very easy, but the first fortnight my heart was in my mouth and my legs were like jelly. But I persevered and told myself, "Come on Joyce! Don't be silly. It is just another obstacle for you to get through." So I carefully drove along the road doing all my hand signals and all the right things as I remembered before I was taken ill. But what a shock awaited me! The other drivers passed me like the wind even though there was a speed limit. Nobody cared - it was like a race track and nobody was polite.

No one seems to do the proper thing any more. Anything goes, even not caring if they smash their own cars. So I plodded along and if I had a rude sign I pretended I hadn't seen it.

After a while I also felt more at ease in the car. Even Arnold was full of praise as I know it must have been and still is very difficult for him to be a back seat driver. Nichola was very happy for me and proud that I was driving again. In fact one morning a knock came at the door and on opening it there was a lovely bunch of flowers for me sent by her and Neil. Written on the card was "To Nigel Mansell from Cinders" as she calls herself as she cannot go out a lot and enjoys herself, but like Cinders she has a heart of gold.

I had a trip to Thornbury with Nichola and Neil but I sat in the car while they both went shopping and sitting there I decided that it was time to visit my sisters at last. So when next day Nichola drove me to visit my sister Dorothy who lives at Falfield, what a day it was! I was very emotional and tearful but I managed to keep calm and I enjoyed being with Dorothy in her home once again.

Then I decided to visit my sister Bess who lives at Hawkesbury Upton. It was a lovely sunny day and Nichola on the way over took me along the lanes I knew as a child at Charfield. Bess was very thrilled to see us all. Arnold came with us and we all enjoyed our day out although it was filled with sad and happy memories.

Then I felt it was time to visit my mother's grave. I had thought about it so many times and then one morning while I was working I had a vivid picture of the Churchyard, so peaceful in the morning sunshine, so I knew that it was time for me to return. Nichola brought some lovely flowers for us to take and Nichola, Neil, Arnold and myself set off to visit the grave at Hawkesbury. It was a lovely day. The peace and quiet was like another world, not even an aircraft flying overhead.

We got out of the car and slowly entered the cemetery. It was difficult for Nichola to push the wheelchair but Arnold gave her a helping hand.

We found the grave easily as my sister Bess and her husband Steve had had a stone erected in memory of her. As I stood and looked at her name I felt very sad and my mind returned to a bygone day when we were all children. Nichola filled the jar we had taken with some water from the pipe just inside the lich gate. It was ice cold so we all had a drink as well.

Nichola put the flowers by the headstone and we all sent up a prayer. Then we sat under the trees on a wooden seat enjoying the peace and remembering.

Then we decided to visit my niece Pauline and her husband who lived in a cottage at Hillesley but unfortunately when we arrived they were not at home, but they had left a note on the door to say they would be back soon. Neil was very disappointed as he did not want to return straight home, so I said, "Shall we go down and visit Shirley?", my other niece who lives at the bottom of the village. "Oh yes please!" said Neil, "I will then see Ray", Ray being Shirley's husband whom Neil had met before and he liked him very much.

So we walked through the village, past the little house where we used to live. A lot of new houses had been built since making the main street look much smaller than I remembered.

Nichola knocked on Shirley's door. She also had a lovely cottage and came out to see who it was and she was very pleased to see me after such a long time. Ray helped Nichola manoeuvre the wheelchair through the door. They made us very welcome and gave us sandwiches and some hot cups of tea which I found very refreshing as it was such a hot day.

Shirley thought I looked just the same and she fetched her sister Yvonne who lived next door to come and see me.

Ray played some of his own tapes for us to listen to. I never knew he could sing so well. It made our day. He told me he sang a lot for charity. We stayed for quite a while talking about the past and my Mum. I had a hard job not to break down. Everyone understood and I loved them for it. When it was time to leave Shirley and Ray said, "Please come again". We called back on Pauline and Bryn, her husband, and chatted for a while. I was feeling very tired by then so we decided to return home.

CHAPTER 45

Arnold is now having a bit of trouble with his eyes and he finds it very difficult to work in the garden. I wanted to plant some flowers at the bottom of the garden but I knew it was too much for him so I said, "Never mind. We will just leave it love as long as the weeds are out".

One day Nichola said, "I will take your car Mum and get your petrol for you. I won't be long". But as the evening progressed I thought, "Oh dear! She is a long time. I hope she has not had a car crash, and just as I was looking out of the door she returned saying, "Sorry I am late but I met someone I knew." Anyway on our way home I said to Arnold, "I know where she has been. She has bought us some flower plants and put them in our garden to save us the trouble, knowing that deep down I wanted them so that I could look at the flowers through the back window".

As soon as we arrived home we both looked out of the window and, sure enough, there was a lovely glow of different coloured flowers peeping at us from the hedge. We thought what a lovely surprise and she did it out of her love for us, not wanting thanks, as she had such great pleasure herself just pleasing us. Once again it is what you do for others that matters, and from the heart. So all we have to do now is to keep the garden free of weeds.

The next time out we all had a long car ride with me showing Nichola, Neil and Arnold all the places I had lived and known. Not a lot of change in the country places, and it was lovely travelling all the country lanes with the road just wide enough for one car with passing places and the trees making a wonderful green roof overhead, especially at Upper Kilcot.

There I said to Nichola, "We must return through Inglestone Common, my beloved Inglestone Common". We passed through Hillesley through the lane to the Common gate, and as we passed through my heart was beating rapidly remembering when I used to swing on it and catch the pennies thrown to me by passing tourists as I held the gate open for them.

We passed the cottage at Orange End where I had lived with my sister Bess for a while. It looked just the same except someone had given it a new coat of paint. Down across the plain and between the woods I had played in as a child, and where I had watched the squirrels at play in the tree tops on my way to school at Wickwar when I had lived at Kilcot.

Looking through the trees I remembered the times I had propped my bicycle against the gate leading into the woods to pick the honeysuckle which climbed the tall branches to take home so that the perfume would linger a little longer.

Down past the cottage I had lived in as a child, slowly passing by to take in all the peace that surrounded it and my eyes hungrily devouring every detail, not wanting to talk as it might spoil the memory.

Down past the cottage where my sister Milly had lived, and where for a short time Mum and I returned to.

Then on to my sister Win's cottage, and I thought, "Oh dear! If only we could go back as it was, but of course that would be impossible. We all have to journey on. It is what we learn and take with us that matters. Past the farm where I fetched the milk and then on to the public house, The Fox and Hounds, but it was not a public house any more. It was now owned privately and had been enlarged with a big sign on the gate calling it The Fox with a picture of a fox on it. A sad change for us all.

The bushes on the common seemed to be growing nearer to the road than I remembered as they used to be cut regularly to stop them from spreading.

Then past the late Mrs Carter's house, my brother-in-law Alf's mother, lying well off the road, and in my mind's eye I could see her standing at the gate with her long hair flowing in the breeze. And then we were through the second gate leaving the Common behind us and a large part of me.

CHAPTER 46

Arnold has now been to see the specialist but I am afraid it is not good news as the retina is worn through old age making it impossible to see to read, write or to do any close work. A big shock for Arnold as now he can only see shapes and his eyesight is very misty.

But still we must soldier on and remember that miracles do happen.

July 13th, 1992. A very sad day. We lost Ruffles. He had a tumour on the brain and he was in great pain. The last few months he had become very agitated, barking and crying a lot. At first we thought that he was just being a baby, wanting to follow us all about as children do. He wanted to be stroked and loved all the time and he took to rubbing his head with his paws or rubbing his head on the ground.

The telephone rang about 1.30 am and Nichola told us that she had been sitting up with him trying to comfort him and would we go down and help as she felt so exhausted and she would need the rest to help Neil.

We dressed and drove down, and found them all very upset. We sent Nichola to bed to have a rest. I lay on her bed downstairs and Arnold sat up with Ruffles all night. About 6 a.m. Arnold came in to see me, worn out, saying Ruffles had been restless all night not knowing what to do.

Nichola got dressed and rang the vet about 9.30 am for an appointment. She left the house with Ruffles on a lead and some biscuits in her pocket as she knew he did not like going to the vet. It was pouring with rain and they looked a pathetic pair walking down the road.

I waited and waited at the window for them to return. I then saw her walking slowly back alone. I knew then it was sadness for us all. She carried his chain and collar in a paper bag. His collar he hated to be without it at any time. She said, "Oh Mum, he is gone", tears pouring down her cheeks. "What shall we do without him?". He was ten and a half years of age.

We all loved him very much. He was part of the family. Whatever we did he was always there ready for whatever was going on. We always called him Ruff the Tuff, and he was, right to the end a character in his own right.

The days are going to be very sad and lonely for a long time as a little of us all went with him, leaving a great ache in our hearts and knowing that the days ahead were going to be very sad as we take Neil for the all the walks that Ruffles always loved and we all will be remembering. But we all know through our faith that he is only a footstep away and his pain is no more. With that we must be thankful and in our love for each other find consolation.

Ruffles, Our Labrador

A little pup of six weeks old
You came and stole our hearts,
So full of life and love so great
You did to us impart.
The garden steps you could not climb
Your little legs, they would not reach
So we would lift and pick you up
Until you yourself could reach.

You followed us wherever we went,
So inquisitive and eager,
Your little nose snuffing amongst the bushes
Just like an eager beaver.
Each little thing was something new
For you to find and chase
To run and play with
Or to eat and taste.

You grew so tall and very strong
And we all agreed you were so aptly named

In fact we all were very careful
When you joined us in our friendly games.
Your eyes would shine, your tail would wag
Just like a child entrancing,
Your legs so strong and very long
Jumping up and prancing.

You greeted us each day we came,
You ran to us and barked a welcome.
A bone we brought for you to chew,
So big you could not carry,
But with all your strength you would drag it
away
And growl if we did tarry,
Enjoying every little bite and chew,
It surely made your day.

You loved to go for walks with Nichola and
Neil.
Jumping up and down beside the wheelchair
Looking into all the rubbish bins you passed
To see if there was any chewable fare.
You padded along just glad to be there
With Neil touching you and calling your name
And a loving kiss you gave to them
Treating them both the same.

You never did like very loud bangs
And firework night was a nightmare
And all the cars passing with their noisy horns
You would turn round and stare
As if you were thinking the same as us,
"If only there was peace and quiet
Instead of all this noise and fuss,

With traffic, leaving behind a trail of dust".

You sat with Arnold underneath the apple trees
When the apples were all ripe
And would share each little piece
And enjoy every little bite.
And when the gooseberries and raspberries were ready for to pick
You would follow in our footsteps
And when we were not looking
You yourself the fruit would pick.

You loved to race across the fields
The horses for to chase
But when they turned to follow you
To home you ran in haste.
Then you would turn and bark at them
Looking over the garden wall,
But you just did not frighten them
No, no, not at all.

Then came the day Nichola had to leave
Her cottage on the hill,
How very sad that day was
And many tears did spill.
But she needed much more room for Neil
And for the wheelchair the hill was much too steep
So her lovely views she had to leave.
Her cottage she could not keep.

The new house was much bigger
And nearer to the shops
And much easier for the wheelchair,

Not so many pants and stops.
But we all did miss the cottage
With the garden large and free,
No more to sit and reminisce underneath the apple trees.

Like Neil, Ruffles did not like the rain
For no walk would they have that day.
In fact one day I let him out
To run around the lawn and play
He took one step and felt the rain
Then he turned and gazed at me
And telepathically he said
"It's bloody raining again!"

As the days rolled by
Our friend Ruffles also grew in age
But as a puppy he remained
Doing all the little things
For which he was truly named.
We never would play any games
Unless he was included
And if by chance we fell asleep our dreams too he intruded.

One day he did not seem so well.
Nichola took him to see the vet
Who said to keep an eye on him
And if no better him to get.
As the days rolled by he would rub his head
As if in a lot of pain
In fact he would follow Nichola about
Just like a child when in pain.

And when one morning he became so ill
Not knowing what to do
We all did our best to comfort him
But of his pain we knew
We had to ring the vet again
Who said to bring him down
Of which Nichola did with a pain in her heart
Knowing what would be found.

I waited at the window for them back to return
And when I saw just one dear lonely form
My heart with pain did burn
And in her hand a paper bag
With a collar and his chain wrapped inside.
"He has gone now Mum" she cried
Her tears falling fast and free,
"If only I could bring him back, for all the
family".

He had a tumour on the brain,
His pain at times must have been hard to bear
But like a puppy he would play
And all our sweets would share.
The balloons he would chase across the room
Our tights with glee would tear
And if we tried to rescue them
He would run away and his eyes would say
"Catch me if you dare".

We miss him so. A family pet was he.
There is not one thing that we can do
Without a memory.
He was a character in every way,
A pal for Neil, his friend,

But in our hearts we will always know
We will meet him at the end.

CHAPTER 47

Neil now needs a new electric chair, a man's chair, as his is too small.

We got in touch with Mr Pete Liddingstone who does a lot for charity, and he arranged for an exchange chair for Neil which is much better.

Nichola is now finding that the swivel seat is causing her a lot of anxiety as some times the mechanism sticks and she has to struggle in the wind and rain to get it out. One day she could not, and she had to ask someone to help her. It became a worry not knowing if the seat was going to play up or not. It came to a climax one day when she and Neil went out for the day and she decided to wear her nice new long dress I had bought her for her birthday. Bending over to help Neil she caught the hem of her dress in the apparatus and she could not get it out. She was almost in tears with Neil very worried thinking they would never get home. In the end she had to tear her dress away which was ruined. "That's it", she said, "I am now going to try and get a van as I haven't got the strength any more for all this lifting and worry" as she still had to lift Neil from the car to his wheelchair.

But first of all Neil has a twenty first birthday to prepare for and Nichola wanted it to be something he would always remember. She booked the Waterside Wine Bar at Aztec West for the evening.

Dawn's husband Michael brought his own mobile disco. All our relations and friends came. It was a lovely evening with Neil helping Michael with the microphone making everyone laugh. There was plenty to eat and the room looked lovely with all the balloons in their different colours. Neil had lots of presents and Nichola gave him a gold signet ring of which he was very proud.

CHAPTER 48

Nichola decided to see the manager of Patchway cars to see if he could help her to buy a van. He was very sympathetic but he said it would cost about £7,700 to buy and convert a van for Neil's needs. As soon as she can collect enough money he will look for a suitable van.

So once again she is asking people if they can help with the cash. She wrote to the Observer newspaper who sent a reporter to take Neil's and her picture and he wrote all about their problem, hoping someone would read it and help them.

The first person to arrive was a Mr Mike Bow who already knew Nichola and Neil and who himself was suffering from Muscular Dystrophy of the spine. We sat and chatted for a while and as he left he pressed an envelope into Nichola's hand. "Wait until I leave before you open it", he said. We waved him off at the door and then

Nichola opened the envelope. "Oh Mum!", she said, "just look at this £200 for Neil to start his fund", which Mike had given from the kindness of his own heart although it meant a loss to him from his own pocket.

It gave Nichola a feeling of hope and strength to canvas again for Neil's van. She organised bungee jumps, discos and raffles. She would visit the public houses while Arnold and I would look after Neil. She had one gold coloured biscuit tin which she carried to put the money in. She called it her lucky tin as she always came back with it full and so heavy with coins she could hardly carry it and we would all sit round and count them.

It was a laugh in the pubs with the biscuit tin as anyone who had a dog with them thought there were biscuits inside and they would sit down beside her. She also found that the people in the public houses were very kind. In fact a lot of the young people would give twice if they saw Nichola in another public house saying, "We love to give to Neil. He is always so happy". She would return at night worn out from walking and talking as everyone wanted to hear her story. In fact she lost her voice in the end.

Neil said to his Mum, "I want to help to raise some money, but what can I do?". I know he said, "Mum, I will sell all my toys, tapes, clothes, anything I have grown out of, as now I am a young man and do not really need them". So

Nichola had a stall at a boot sale which raised £190. Neil was very thrilled to think he had helped.

A Mr Paul Starr did a walk to Weston-Super-Mare and back with his daughter Sadie who had asthma but she read about Neil in the paper and she wanted to help. In fact they raised £200, a wonderful gesture greatly appreciated. A friend of Nichola's from Almondsbury gave a further £200. So little by little the fund is growing.

In the middle of all the cash raising Moira, Arnold's sister, passed away. She had cancer of the womb and she had been very ill for some time. A very sad period with Arnold feeling very unhappy, leaving him with lots of childhood memories, the date being the fifth of February, 1995. She was cremated as was her wish, in Great Crosby, Liverpool, and her ashes were scattered over Longland Bay, Swansea, where she had many happy memories as a teenager.

CHAPTER 49

Nichola still busy raising money and wondering if she will have enough for the disabled van.

She went to the bank where she had opened an account in Neil's name to find out how much was there. She still needed about £800 so she had the swivel seat taken out of the car which cost her £30. She managed to sell it for £300 making a loss of over £400 when it was new, but although it was spotless it was second-hand. It was a joy to see the man's face who bought it as he just could not afford a new one for his wife so in the end we all help each other, sometimes winning sometimes losing.

She managed to raise the £30 again she had spent but she felt so weary and she sat down and cried. She still needed £500, but where, oh where, could she find it?

Arnold put his arms round her and said, "Don't give up now that you are right at the end. You are just tired. Don't give up hope".

Then out of the blue he said, "Have you been to the George and Dragon public house at Winterbourne?". "No", said Nichola, "I could never get into the park. It was always full up". Arnold said, "Try it". So Nichola once more got out her gold biscuit tin and off she went leaving us all saying a few prayers that she would be lucky.

Well in about an hour we heard her key in the front door. "Oh my gosh", was our first thought, was she alright?. She didn't say a word for what seemed an eternity. Then she threw down the biscuit tin and said, "Mum, Dad, Neil, I've made it!". We all sat and cried with joy.

Apparently there was a lady in the pub who did a lot for charities and she said to Nichola, "Have a word with the landlady. We are always helping and collecting in this pub for charities". So Nichola told the landlady her problem who listened to her story. Then she said, "If you come back tomorrow there will be a cheque for £500 for you". Well Nichola could not believe it just like that. She had the last money for the van. No more out every day begging for money. She had reached her goal.

The next day she fetched the cheque and everyone in the pub cheered her and she arrived home looking just like the fairy that sits on the top of the Christmas tree, full of joy and sparkle. The next day Nichola went to see the Manager of Patchway Cars to see if he could find her a van.

"We have one here", he said, "come and have a look at it." It was a Renault Traffic Prima, very good condition, only one year old. Nichola liked the look of it and decided to buy it. The manager said, "I will have to send it to Portsmouth for the conversion."

It had to have windows, reinforced floor, ramp, clamps, fire extinguisher, first aid box, strip lights, spot light at rear, and it would have to be felted inside for condensation. It would take a while to do. Nichola gave him £2,000 deposit. Now all we have to do is wait, but knowing that at last she has won.

CHAPTER 50

The converted van has just arrived and the garage hand took Nichola for a trial spin.

She was thrilled but very anxious as it was such a change from a small car. Anyway she did very well and we all got ready for a test run.

After the little car it was like sitting in a bus. Neil thought it was wonderful.

The ramp, such a change from the lifting, although Nichola still had to push the chair up, but for Neil it was much kinder for his weak muscles and he could look around at the other cars and people while before he could only look ahead.

We had a trip to Weston-Super-Mare with Arnold enjoying the long ride.

Neil likes to go in the arcades but for Arnold it is too noisy so we left him in a sheltered bus stop overlooking the sea smoking his pipe saying "We won't be long".

When we returned he was so thrilled. He had met a lady who knew Australia and she told him that a square had been named after Sir Sidney Kidman called "Kidman Square". What a coincidence! It made his day, something to think about. We all arrived home pleased with our day out with no worry or trouble. Even the weather was kind.

Everyday we would be out and about enjoying the freedom of our new van.

The motability car has been returned and, although it was a great help at the time, we were not sorry to see it go.

CHAPTER 51

One morning about six o'clock Arnold called me, very disturbed and upset he sounded. I hurried into the back bedroom where he slept. "Oh Joyce!", he cried, "Please stay with me". I held his hand and put my other hand on his forehead.

"What is it? Are you in pain?". He did not answer but let me know he had heard me. He gently squeezed my hand.

I stayed talking to him and then he sat nearly upright and started moving very strangely as if he was having a convulsion and then he lay very still and quiet.

I still was not sure that he had left me as I have never seen death before. I kissed him on the forehead, and I sent up a prayer for him, telling him to follow the light as I knew he must.

I then had to ring Nichola and I knew how upset she would be. For what seemed an eternity she did not answer, and then very tearful she said, "I will ring the doctor for you, and the family", as she knew that with my nerves I would not cope.

The doctor arrived and the ambulance, and although I knew what was happening I could not take it all in.

I answered all the questions in a dream. I just could not believe it was for real.

The family arrived all very upset.

They told me not to worry. They would do all the necessary.

I went back with Nichola and Neil, but I said I would be returning home that night.

Anyone who has lost someone they have loved will understand my grief. I was numb.

That night I prepared myself to go home, but then out of the blue I became very agitated and ill at ease and I said to Nichola, "Someone is very worried about me going home. I must not go".

"I am glad", she said, "You must stay with us Mum. I don't want you to go back on your own."

Arnold was given a post-mortem which revealed the cause of death was due to a coronary artery thrombo-embolus and a left arterial appendage thrombosis, the date being the fifth of May, 1995.

He was cremated at Westerleigh Crematorium near Bristol on the twelfth of May.

We had been married for fifty-two years and I know he will be watching over us as he was always worried about how we would manage without him.

CHAPTER 52

I decided to go and live with Nichola and Neil. I just did not want to stay where Arnold and I had made a home together.

Nichola fetched a few things in the van which was very upsetting for her to be in the house on her own. She filled her garage with most of it but a lot we got rid of as it was very worn and Nichola did not have the room for storage.

Roy, my nephew, sold the Datsun for me. He was a great help. Also my nephew Timothy helped him to move my bedroom furniture and arrange it at Nichola's house. It made me feel more at home with some of my own things around me.

I found it was very difficult at first to know that I had lost my husband and my home and that it was another chapter of my life that was over.

Neil was thrilled that I was living with them as now there was always someone to talk to when Nichola was busy as the three of us were great friends as well as family.

Mr and Mrs Daniels, my next door neighbours at Stoke Gifford, arrived one day with a garden seat which the people living near had collected enough money to buy as a memento, and now it is in the garden where we can see it every day and perhaps one day we will see Arnold sitting on it.

The days passed by and we were all very sad. We had lots of trips in the van to fill up our time.

Roy, my nephew, looks after the van for us. I do not know what we would do without him.

To All Who Contributed Towards My Husband's Garden Seat

**A BIG THANK YOU
AND A TRIBUTE OF MY OWN BELOW**

The Garden Seat

For him to come
And him to go
Although we do not see.
Among the flowers
In God's garden

THERE IS A REASON

The seat is a memory.

Our love is great
Our tears we share
But in our hearts we know
In each of our lives
When we just have to go.

He was one of life's gentlemen
Who, dare I say,
We do not often see,
But all who really knew him
I am sure they will agree.
And when we look upon the seat
Our thoughts and dreams are shared
Of one who was a loving husband,
A father and a grandfather
Who cared.

Joyce M Kidman

CHAPTER 53

Vera our friend passed away in the August three months after Arnold. She also was cremated at Westerleigh Crematorium. She had been suffering with a chest infection and she caught pneumonia. Her brother Charlie went to live with relatives near London. He and Vera had lived together for many years and as he was also an invalid he could not look after himself as he had difficulty in walking. We missed them both very much. They were both very sincere people with hearts of gold.

CHAPTER 54

Nichola, Neil and I had chest infections. In fact Nichola had bronchitis and she was very poorly. She could not lie down at night so she had to sit up with high pillows.

Neil had the physiotherapist out for his treatment as he could not get the mucus off his chest by himself. I felt so sorry for him as he had to have tubes down his throat and turning him different ways the physiotherapist would thump his back to release the mucus on his chest. It must have been agony for him as with his weak muscles he did not like us to hold him too tight.

By now Nichola was sleeping on the floor so that she could be close to Neil if he should call for help. It was a trying time for us all. We all felt so tired and ill. On the weekend the physiotherapist said that Neil must go into the hospital at Southmead for the treatment as there was no help for him at home on a weekend.

Well you can imagine our concern for him. The ambulance arrived, in came the stretcher with two paramedics. The poor little lad was so scared that they would drop him. He only trusted his Mum to lift him. When he was in the ambulance he called out to me, "Goodbye Joyce!" with such a shaky voice and I could feel the fear in him. Nichola went with him and I was left at home to wait and worry.

I spent a very lonely night without them. Our friend Beatrice Watkins looked after me making sure I was alright on my own.

The next day Nichola rang me to say she was returning home. There was no physiotherapist to look after Neil and she had spent the night in his wheelchair beside him not getting a wink of sleep. She was disgusted with the hospital and said she could look after him better at home.

She arrived home in a disabled taxi very upset but Neil was happy to be home in familiar surroundings and I was glad to see them. Of course there was the usual trouble, everybody blaming everyone else as to why there was no treatment available.

The treatment continued at home for a few days until Neil's chest was free. Nichola was worn out. She bought herself a camp bed so that she could sleep near Neil. It was very upsetting for me to see her lying so close to the floor as it was such an effort to keep getting up and down and she was losing so much weight. Also leaning over Neil's low bed to turn him was agony for her back and neck.

I decided that she must have a higher bed for Neil so I bought him one out of my savings which was much better. In fact it was so high that Nichola found it much easier for her to lift Neil up and down.

Nichola now has a nasty cough and it takes all her energy to look after Neil, but we must all struggle on.

CHAPTER 55

Dawn went into Frenchay Hospital. She had her left breast removed with cancer, very upsetting for her and she was so scared that it would spread to somewhere else in the body but as the months go by she has quelled her fears and tries not to dwell on the subject.

My sister Bess fell and broke her hip and she now has to use a Zimmer to walk with but being over eighty years of age it is a big thing and she gets very frustrated.

We then heard that Charlie had passed away. We were very sad but I know it was what he wanted. When he lost Arnold and Vera he said he wished he had gone too as there was nothing left for him except to watch the days go by, and his memories.

He gave Arnold a shaving Toby jug a few years ago as he then used an electric razor as it was easier for him.

It was a lovely ornament with one side of the man winking and the other side a very gentle wise smile on his face. I said to Charlie, "It is just like you", and he said, "I don't know whether to take that as a compliment or what". I said, "Please do, because it shows your gentleness within and your sense of humour."

We now have the shaving mug in a place of honour on the top of the cabinet in Nichola's bathroom and every day we all say, "Hello Charlie! God bless you."

CHAPTER 56

Neil has been poorly again. He now has bowel trouble. He has had this trouble for years but not so bad. In the end we had to have the nurse out to see him.

She said, "I am afraid I will have to give him an enema". Just the thought was enough as we all know what happens. We had to explain to Neil which was not easy.

We decided it must be at home because of his fear of hospitals. It was not an easy thing for us to do but with a bit of persuading and love Neil gave in.

The poor little lad was very good and the nurse very kind. When it was all over he said, "I don't want that ever again. It was not a very nice feeling."

Nichola said we must try something else for Neil to eat so that the problem will never arise again.

So now he is on cereal with bran and raisins for breakfast. He has plenty of vegetables to eat which so far has been a success. So we are keeping our fingers crossed.

CHAPTER 57

Michael left Dawn on the twenty-eighth of December 1996. It was a very unhappy period so soon after Christmas, but these things happen and there is nothing we can do about them. We all have our own lives to live and if we make mistakes we must live with them.

Arnold's sister Pauline passed away on the 3rd of April, 1997. She had been very poorly for a long time with asthma and also cancer. She then had a stroke which took her from us, a happy release for her but very sad for the family. She was buried in Rutherglen, Glasgow, Scotland, in the family grave with her father and grandfather.

CHAPTER 58

While out shopping someone ran into the back of the van. We were waiting at the roundabout at Pear Tree Road, Bradley Stoke, when such a loud bang sounded behind us. A car travelling at speed had run into us. It sounded like a bomb. Neil was very scared and Nichola very upset. She jumped out and spoke to the driver who tried to blame us, and all the time they were exchanging addresses the passengers in his car were calling out to hurry up or they would miss their train.

Nichola did all the right things but her nerves were in shreds.

She had an awful job trying to do the necessary as she could not find out where he really lived. He seemed to have two homes and two cars.

It was sorted out in the end but we were without the van for a week as the whole back door had to be replaced.

We have a sign on the back of the van for other drivers to leave a space, but no-one takes any notice, in fact it seems to anger them as though we have no right to be on the road at all. They do not make allowances for invalid vans or cars.

CHAPTER 59

Andrew, my grandson, got married in Connecticut, America, to an American girl. Only Dawn went to the wedding as we could not get there and the date being the seventeenth of August, 1997.

CHAPTER 60

Neil was finding the electric chair a problem as with his weak muscles and the controls so far in front of him that he had a long way to reach and to keep his hand on the switch was too tiring for him.

Also he developed a fear of going up the ramp into the van. He preferred his ordinary wheelchair with Nichola pushing it in case he fell.

Roy my nephew suggested that we had a winch fitted to the van as that would also save Nichola's back.

So Nichola got in touch with Mr Pete Liddington and asked him if anyone wanted a new electric chair and with his charity funds could he manage to let her have the money for a new winch. It was a loss on Nichola's part again as the electric chair was worth £5,000 and the winch would only be about £770.

But we knew that some poor child would appreciate the electric chair as it was one of the latest models and it had been given to us.

Mr Liddington said, "I will see what I can do".

A few days later the phone rang. "I have found an owner for the wheelchair who is thrilled to bits. It will also save my charity cash as the winch is cheaper to buy and fit.

So Nichola wrote to the other conversion people at Portsmouth who did her van and asked them if they would put a winch in the van for her.

She had a reply a few days later. They would fit a winch with pleasure for her but it would take about two days to do and to fetch and return the van would cost another £100 making it £870 altogether.

We told Mr Liddington who said, "Don't worry. You helped me so I will help you. I will take the van to Portsmouth, stay the night with relations of mine and return it the next day". We could hardly believe our luck and he did it for nothing as it was just the £770 from the charity fund.

When he brought it back he showed us how to use it, even going up the ramp himself. It was a marvellous job and all Nichola had to do was to guide the chair onto the ramp. A metal bar was then attached to the chair and a belt was attached to the bar and all I had to do was to press the electric button and Neil would sail up the ramp into the van.

He was thrilled to bits. It took Nichola and I a while to get it right as we were very anxious in case we made a mistake. We just had to remember to have the chair just right on the ramp and for me to gather up all the slack on the belt so that Neil would not hurt his neck as he started to go down.

It was a pleasure to go out shopping. No standing around getting wet through and plenty of room to manoeuvre the chair.

So we were all very thrilled with our latest addition to the van.

CHAPTER 61

One night we had just got Neil into bed when the electric went off. We had to do everything by torch and a candle. Our worry was how long it would last and praying it would return by the morning for his lift to take him downstairs and for the hoist which lifts him in and out of the bed onto his wheelchair.

The morning came. No electric. Apparently there was a big fault to be repaired when we enquired and they would not say how long it would be.

To Neil the thought of staying upstairs all day was depressing so Nichola said, "I wonder if the fire brigade at Patchway will help". So she rang them and they said, "With pleasure. We will be with you in about half an hour".

The thought of the fire brigade coming made Neil smile. Four firemen arrived to carry him down the stairs. It was an effort as they could not use his wheelchair and they had to lift him from the bed onto a large white basket chair which, of course, was foreign to Neil and not very comfortable.

He was very scared as they carried him down the steep stairs which, of course, he had not done before. It took the firemen quite a time as they were afraid of hurting him.

They were very good to him, cracking jokes to make him laugh. "Any time they" said, "don't be afraid to call us if you need help."

When they had gone Nichola said, "Next time we will wait for the electric to come on as it wasn't worth all the hassle for Neil as he was really scared being out of the wheelchair". There was not the same support in an ordinary chair. But we all live and learn the hard way, don't we? And just as we had finished it all the electric came on so it was just another trial for us all.

CHAPTER 62

We had lots of trips in the van. Our favourite direction was towards the Cotswolds. We would visit Badminton where the Queen stays when the horse trials begin.

We loved going down very narrow lanes with passing places, just enough room for us to get through with woods and fields on either side of us we would pretend we were walking them as that was what we really wanted.

Nichola and I are as much a prisoner as Neil as without him we could not enjoy ourselves so we all make the best of it.

We make it our holidays, with sandwiches and orange juice and all we have for music is the sound of the birds in the trees and the sound of the pheasants as they call to each other. It is paradise for a while and it gives us strength to carry on for another day.

CHAPTER 63

Since Nichola has had the bronchitis she has developed pains across her chest and all the time she is either coughing or clearing her throat. In fact it has become a worry and after having Neil ill with flu and sitting up all night with him exercising his legs and turning him every five minutes she decided to go and see the doctor.

He sent her to Southmead Hospital for an X-ray. We were all very worried about the outcome but in our hearts we knew that we would not carry on as we were not knowing.

The hospital told her to visit the doctor in seven to ten days time. To us it was like seven to ten years waiting.

She called back at the surgery for the results. Neil and I waited outside in the van and believe me it was a long wait.

When she came out she said, "I have a damaged lung which is causing the pain", and she now has a mild form of asthma which is keeping her awake at night as she cannot really lie flat. So he gave her a prescription for a Salbutamol aerosol inhalation BP which she has to use each night before she goes to bed and also he gave Neil some new pills to help him with the pain in his leg. "Try this for two weeks", he said, "and then come back and see me."

When she told me I cried because all that week we were waiting for the X-ray results I thought that it might be cancer. I knew that what she has is bad enough but the thought of cancer like dear Dawn was too much to take.

We have been sitting up every night with Neil and now he is getting better we must try and get our rest.

The doctor advised her to see an osteopath to make sure she had not done any damage to her back. He said that there was a good one who worked from his surgery, not too expensive and he was very good.

Nichola decided to make an appointment as the one she used to go to in Gloucester Road was very expensive and the parking was awful.

Filton was nearer and the parking a little better and it was not so far away from home.

When she met the osteopath she was very impressed and after one treatment she felt a bit better but she has to go again so that he can keep a check on her.

CHAPTER 64

Neil wanted to go to Weston again so on the next best day, although it was very cold, we wrapped up and set off. We went the old road, not the motorway, and it was a lovely trip for us all. We took our sandwiches and a drink which we have as soon as we parked the van.

Then we made our way through the market where it was nice and warm and full of Christmas fare. Then we took Neil to the amusement arcade where the music was blaring out and filling him with excitement.

We found a machine which he could reach with the help of Nichola and her handbag so that his arm was lifted up. To see the light in his eyes as he played was wonderful to see.

We stayed until he became tired of pressing the buttons and then as it was so cold we decided to have a look round the shops as before we had not done so as we had always walked along the seafront looking at the sea.

We found Marks & Spencers. In we went and looked at all the lovely clothes and latest fashions.

We carried on walking through into the Sovereign Centre of which we had not heard about before.

It was a wonderful sight to us. A big Christmas tree the height of the ceiling and covered with lights and colourful trimmings met our gaze. Neil was numb with the glory of it all.

There were shops all around us and seats for people to rest awhile. It was like a fairyland, all the bustle and colour and, best of all, you could do all your own shopping under cover with clean disabled toilets and a restaurant. To us it was like a dream come true.

Then we heard music as though there was a band arriving. We followed the people who all seemed in a hurry to see something and we found them all looking up at the wall and to our amazement the music was coming from the clock chiming the hour.

The clock had panels which slid open to reveal musicians, about eight in all. There was a man on a trumpet, a violin, guitar, cymbals, trombone, tuba, saxophone and a flute.

As the music played the man with the cymbals raised his cap automatically, which was too much for Neil. He laughed until the tears ran down his cheeks. Everyone watching enjoyed the spectacle and a lot were taking photographs. It was as though we were all children once again. A great joy shone out of everyone, the old and the young, and then, when the music stopped and the panels closed shut one by one, you would not have known they were there if you had just passed by and the clock had not chimed the hour.

I could imagine it was a great meeting place as there were a lot of people standing around and old folk resting on the seats out of the cold.

There were see-through lifts that reached the top floors. Neil just sat and watched everything. In fact for once he had nothing to say. He was entranced.

We sat for a while watching all the people passing by, loving every minute of it. Then we decided we must leave to escape all the heavy traffic on the way home.

We left reluctantly but knowing that we would be back.

CHAPTER 65

It is now Christmas 1997. The cards are all around the room. The tree is covered with lights and imitation snow. It is just the three of us and as we sit and open our presents we remember the past and the loved ones we have lost.

It is a time for the little ones who have been waiting for weeks to see what Santa has brought them.

Neil loved his tapes, clothes and video presents.

Nichola bought me a book about Diana, Princess of Wales, as she knew how sad I was about her death, to be killed so young and to have to leave her lovely boys whom she adored.

We will miss her very much. She only stayed a short while amongst us but she showed us the way to God through her great love for everyone.

She also had to suffer to find herself but she did, and she became a great person.

The love she gave out was returned to her, and we will miss her very much, but it was her time to go. She came to show us the way, to help and to love one another no matter what afflictions we might have. She was born a Lady, she became a Princess and she died a Saint, a lesson to us all, and so she became what she always wanted, our Queen of Hearts.

CHAPTER 66

It is now January 1998, a very wet and windy start with lots of rain which Neil hates as he thinks he might have to stay in.

He has felt a little better on his new pills but of course there are still a lot of aches and pains, and cramp in his legs and the damp weather is not helping.

Nichola now has osteo-arthritis in her back and pain in her knees, hands and all her joints. She now worries that she will lose her strength and not be able to help Neil. She is having treatment from her new osteopath which is helping to keep her going. Once a month she goes to him.

Mr and Mrs Godkin who live three doors away have lent Nichola some holiday videos so that Neil can watch them if he can't go out. In fact we are all enjoying them as they show us places we have never seen, lovely long cruises and tours where they are given guided tours of each city they visit. And then in the evenings they are given a live show where they have dinner and dancing.

We pretend we are there and Neil sings to the music and he says, "One day Joyce and Nichola we will be there". So far we have visited Turkey, Syria and Jordan. Train journey to China and Russia. Tour and River Cruise China, up the Yangtze River - what a long river! Arabia etc (Yemen). Cruise Aqaba, Jordan - Safaga, Egypt. Cruise Irrawaddy River, Burma and Singapore. Cruise Bangkok, Thailand. Cruise Russian Rivers, St Petersburg, Petrozavodsk, Kishi, Goritzi, Hglic, Moscow.

They are all places you do not see on the TV holiday programmes and it was a great insight to know how other countries and people live. But all in all we are all the same, except for our clothes and the language barrier. Also there are still very rich people and very poor people everywhere.

CHAPTER 67

Yesterday Nichola had her three elm trees at the back cut down. They have been gradually dying for a few years. All the leaves had gone and the trees were looking very bare. Also there was a danger of them falling in the high winds and causing damage to the houses behind us.

It was very sad to hear the sound of the chain saw as it cut through the trunks and to see the branches falling into the ditch which was full of water that the elm trees had drunk from for years.

We will miss all the birds coming to see us. They would sit in the trees and swoop down to the bird table which was always full of tit bits for them. In fact they would line up and take it in turns to have their fill.

There were robins, wrens, crows, thrushes, blackbirds, blue-tits, wagtails, magpies, pigeons and some little birds we did not even know the names of.

At night we would hear the nightingale singing, and see the occasional squirrel trying to steal the nuts from the little bird container on the shed. So we will miss all our wild life friends, but we hope they will still visit us and have their morning wash in the bird bath. To see them at such close quarters is wonderful.

It is very bare without the trees and we were all very sad to see them go.

CHAPTER 68

Today the 28th of February is Neil's birthday. He is 25 years old. He had lots of cards and money from friends and family. We made it a happy day with birthday sponge and music from Neil's CDs and tapes.

Dawn came to visit us and to show us Andrew's wedding photographs.

They were lovely except on each one Dawn was crying. I think what she then realised was that she had lost a son as well as a husband as Andrew would be living in America and she still was worried in case her cancer returned.

We tried to cheer her up but only time can do that and good health and every day fears to cope with.

CHAPTER 69

Mr Godkin our neighbour gave Neil a figurine of a Buddha and told him to rub his tummy and to say a prayer. Neil held it all day in his hand and when I looked up he would be talking to it. That night when he went to bed he still had the Buddha tight in his hand and the next morning when I went into his bedroom to say good morning he said "I have said a prayer Joyce and I hope it will come true."

I said, "What did you wish for love?" and he said, "That I will be able to walk soon and that Joyce will not be so tired, and for Nichola's strength to look after us both".

I kissed him and said, "I do hope with all my heart that your prayer will be answered".

Then Neil said, "What can I call him?" Just Buddha did not seem enough. So not knowing much about it I rang our friend Beatrice as I knew that she would help us.

She looked it all up for us and gave us this little story.

Buddha "Enlightened One"

This is the name given to Prince Gautama Siddhaartha, born in Nepal in 563 BC and died in 483 BC.

At the age of 29 he left a life of luxury to escape from the material burdens of existence. After six years of austerity he realised that asceticism like overindulgence was futile and chose the middle way of meditation.

He had an experience under a bodhi tree near Buddh Gaya in Bihar in India and from then till the end of his life travelled round North India teaching.

The Buddha's teaching consisted of the four Noble Truths:

1. The existence of suffering
2. Suffering has a cause
3. Suffering can be ended
4. Suffering can be ended by following the noble eightfold path:

    Right views
    Right intention
    Right speech
    Right action

Right livelihood
Right effort
Right mindfulness
Right concentration eventually arriving at Nirvana.

She said it was difficult to give Buddha a nickname in the same way as it would be if one tried to give Jesus a nickname. He founded one of the world's great religions several hundred years before Christianity started. Certainly it is one of the most spiritual, gentle and compassionate, and concentrates on "being" rather than dogma.

So she said, "If you don't want to call him Buddha, how about Gautama?". So Gautama it is for Neil. He thinks that's great.

I also on writing this story realise how much like Gautama I am in my thinking, doing and living.

We do not need all the trimmings that we think are essential. Just being kind, gentle, loving and helping one another then we too will find Nirvana.

CHAPTER 70

Neil needed a new carpet for his bedroom as the one he had had become very worn with the use of the wheelchair and while servicing the hoist which lifts Neil into bed the workman had dropped pieces of hot metal from the soldering iron and burnt a few holes in it.

Nichola looked around for a carpet suitable for a wheelchair which she found in a nearby shop. The man told her it would be just right for wheelchair use and very durable.

She chose a deep blue which looks lovely and makes the room look much bigger.

She also needed new curtains as her old ones which were red with a white stripe were also wearing and the colours did not go with the new carpet.

So she had some made which were very pretty with pink roses and mauve and lilac flowers on a white background. Neil's window is very wide but not very deep so she had to have the curtains made to fit.

I must say what with the walls a pale shade of pink with pictures and ornaments of pink and blue the whole room was a picture. It is as if the garden has entered the room with one whole wall a picture of colour and the carpet a great finish the colour of bluebells.

Neil was delighted. He said how peaceful it all looked with his bed all white with pink cushions scattered at the top and in the two white basket chairs alongside. In fact we all agreed it was a bedroom to be proud of.

We also found that the colour scheme was very soothing and the bed so very inviting. As Neil said, "Just like a film star's".

CHAPTER 71

Dawn has just lost a very dear gentleman friend she has known for many years. He died of lung and kidney cancer after being ill for a long time, the date being the 12th of May, 1998.

She is very upset. So many things have happened to her of late. One minute she is surrounded by loved ones and the next she is alone, not even being able to get a job as she has been assessed unfit to work owing to her asthma. With her son in America and her daughter in Israel she finds life very hard to cope with.

Nichola has helped her in the garden, even putting up a line post as Dawn's was rusty and leaning over, trying to give her an interest in life again. She now has flowers and a neat lawn at the back so that she can relax and enjoy the sunshine.

She comes to us once a week, staying the night and going for a country ride in the van, enjoying all the old places she once knew, but even that does not help as there are also sad memories, so now there are four of us each trying to help the others through our sorrows.

CHAPTER 72

We have a new visitor to our garden, a hedgehog who comes twice a day and even walks right up to the window. In fact one day, when it was raining, we were most surprised to see the hedgehog shaking itself just like a dog when it has been in a pool of water, or when given a bath and shaking off the excess water. It looked really funny.

Also we had never seen a hedgehog before with its body stretched out full length. It really raced down the lawn. Something must have attracted its attention. Then we saw a magpie with a long slow worm in its beak. We did not like that, but as nature intended there was nothing we could do.

Also we watched a magpie sitting on the fence very still and we could not understand why. We had never seen one sitting so still and intently looking up at the tree behind our neighbour's garden. Then we heard such a noise from a pair of blackbirds trying to drive it away. Our neighbours informed us that magpies will take little baby birds to eat if given the chance. Well we have lived in the country all our lives and yet we did not know that, and we did not like it. You can learn something new everyday.

We did not lose our birds after the trees were cut down. In fact we seem to have gained more with the parents bringing their babies to feed showing no fear of us whatsoever.

We had a picnic on Horton Common one day and to our surprise we were joined by a baby black rabbit. It showed no fear whatsoever and it sat by the van eating the heads off the clover. Of course we were worried that someone might take it home and put it in a rabbit hutch in the garden. We did not like that idea, but we decided to leave it where it was as it had plenty of food and a nice high hedge for shelter and freedom.

We returned home worrying about it, wondering how it came to be there so the next time we went through the Common we looked to see if our friend was there and to our delight and joy there it was sitting by the field gate without a care in the world eating all the clover heads. We drove on knowing that the little black rabbit would look after itself.

CHAPTER 73

One morning Nichola noticed a parcel outside the door, and she was very surprised to see that it was addressed to me. "Oh Mum", she said, "someone has sent you a present". I said, "Don't be silly. I don't know of anyone who would have sent me one".

We all gathered round to open the parcel. It was packed so well and I was afraid of spoiling whatever was inside. Imagine our surprise to find a beautiful deep blue tankard inside with the handle shaped like a ship's rope and on one side the picture of an old fisherman, with Yarmouth Stores written underneath and the year 1898 Centenary. On the back was a picture of two fishermen with a basketful of fish and dressed as they would have been a hundred years ago. Inside was a certificate to certify that the tankard is number 90 of a strictly limited edition of only 150 especially designed and handcrafted in 1998 by Great Yarmouth Potteries to commemorate the hundredth anniversary of the Yarmouth Stores.

I felt very proud to receive such a special tankard and I will treasure it always, but just a little sad to think that it was I who had received it and not my husband who I know would have been very thrilled to have received it. He had told me so many stories of Great Yarmouth. I only wished I had listened more intently. His grandfather, Mr Milburn, was very involved in the fishing industry, and he had many shares in the Great Yarmouth Stores. Unfortunately through his death and of his family the shares were split up so that now there are only a few left in the family, me being one of the lucky ones. I might add that just before it arrived I had a picture come close to me while I was in bed - an old face with a large curly beard and a fisherman's hat on his head. I stared for a few minutes and then it went away leaving me wondering what it meant, but of course I know now it was the face of the old fisherman on the tankard and I was being prepared for my present. How wonderful to be so involved and to have such a gift of knowing in advance of what is about to happen. It makes me feel very special.

CHAPTER 74

Dawn is now officially divorced and after 34 years of marriage is finding it so lonely, but she still has a roof over her head and she must now look forward to a new life.

CHAPTER 75

Nichola had to buy Neil some new trousers. Unfortunately she has to buy four pairs together as she has to choose plenty of them as he sometimes uses two pairs a day and in the wet weather it is a problem washing and getting them dry.

We find Tesco's clothes department at Yate very reasonable as sports shops are very expensive. They have to be the right length, the right material and no zip fasteners. Also they need to have plenty of depth from the waist to the crutch as when he uses his portable 'John', urinal bottle, it is easy for Nichola to stretch out the trouser for use. That is when sometimes there is a problem and the trousers get a soaking, but Nichola says, "Don't worry Neil, we have another pair at home".

Then comes the problem after buying the trousers, which I might add are the latest fashion with plenty of buttons and stripes, like all the other lads as Neil is a fashion follower. We go to see a friend of Nichola's, a lady who Nichola knew years ago when she was a hairdresser and who was a dressmaker. Nichola has always kept in touch with her. Her name being Miss Macginnes, a very nice lady who told us she would always help Neil with his clothes if anything needed altering so it has been a great help to us all through the years. So Miss Macginnes takes out the stitched-in elastic round the waist as it is always too tight for Neil. Then she sends them back to Nichola and I buy a new elastic to put in which will be more comfortable and easy to stretch.

Then we have to try each pair for the right size round his waist with safety pins attached for the right width.

What a job Neil has to lie on the bed and Nichola has to turn him over and over until the trousers are just right, by which time we are all worn out.

Then I have to join the ends and stitch them together but leaving enough elastic in case of altering them again in the future. Anyway, when he is dressed ready to go out in them and says, "Thank you for my trousers Nichola and thank you Joycey for sewing them", well it has all been worth it knowing that he is one of the lads.

Writing this I can see out of the window and although it is raining, all the flowers in the garden give a lovely glow and as it was prophesied a long time ago that we would not know one season from another. I can believe it as we have Spring, Summer, Autumn flowers and winter berries all growing together making a lovely splash of colour.

CHAPTER 76

It is now November 1998 and the saddest time of our lives. We have lost the love of our life as our darling Neil passed over to the other side on the 18th of November. He just bent his head and passed over peaceably just like the poem of the rose on the bereavement cards. Nichola had just gone to the shops and Neil had asked her to buy a CD for him of Phil Collins. She had no sooner left when Neil just bent his head and passed over to the other side.

I was devastated and did not know what to do except to put my arms around him and tell him I loved him. You just cannot believe what has happened. He had been suffering with a chest infection and it had turned into bronchial pneumonia.

We all had chest infections but Neil found it very painful as he could not cough to release the phlegm and so he had no strength to fight the infection and so the good Lord took his son who had suffered so much in all his 25 years back into his arms where he will be made whole again.

Nichola rang to tell Ann, her cousin in Liverpool, to say what had happened. Ann said, "Neil has left you a present Nichola and I am sure you will find comfort from it".

We realised it was the CD she had just bought as all the tunes Neil and she loved were on it including "Two hearts beat as one" and that is what they felt for each other and they always will until they meet again.

Neil was cremated at the crematorium at Westerleigh, the same place as Grandpa.

The minister was the Reverend Basil Rogers and Mr Derek Tyler was in charge of the funeral arrangements. They were both very kind and feeling and made the day easier to bear.

Neil had decided beforehand what tunes he wanted played at his funeral. Three of his favourites were "Amazing Grace", "Wind beneath my wings" and the "Lord of the Dance" from the Michael Platley tap dancing show.

It was very sad to hear the music and to know that in the future Neil would not be singing it with us as we did when the tunes were played at home and to hear him say, "That's not right Joycey" as I always sang the wrong words.

Colin, Neil's dad was very upset and held our hands while the tears flowed. There were lots of flowers, friends and loving relations, and money tributes for the Muscular Dystrophy group to help someone else like Neil.

The family followed us back home but it was like being in a dream for us as we just could not believe what had happened. No Neil to welcome us back like he always did. As soon as we opened the front door we would shout out, "Alright Neil?" and he would answer, "Alright Nick and Joycey! I missed you", and there would be kisses all round. Now there was a great silence as we walked in and it will always be so in the future for us. A great loss.

Neil told us a little while ago, "I will be walking in 1999. Someone told me". Of course we both said, "You will," as we always gave him hope. But now we know it was true as he will be walking on the other side and what a joy it will be for him.

Dawn has been staying with us and she has been a great help with all the letters and forms we had to write. She had also come to love Neil very much and she was, like us, feeling his loss.

Mr Derek Tyler brought Neil's ashes to the house and Nichola, Dawn and I took them and scattered them at a favourite place of his where there were trees on a hill top and an open space where you could see for miles and never again would he be a prisoner but as free as the birds with the wind beneath his wings.

CHAPTER 77

It was a very sad Christmas for us all. We could not enjoy the festivities as Neil always loved the Christmas tree and presents. We did everything in a dream, even laying out his presents which we had already bought knowing that he would not want us to be unhappy. He always tried to cheer us up when we were sad so we try to live as he would want us to.

We have often watched the animal programmes on the television and we used to feel so sorry for the ones that were put in cages and taken to a different country to live so that they would have a better chance of survival. Well Nichola and I feel like those animals - the cage door is open but there is nowhere to go, and like the animals we hang about inside our cage until we too have the courage to venture outside.

CHAPTER 78

POEMS

To Be Thankful

The smell of clover, the hum of bees
The grass newly cut, the sweet smelling breeze,
To take a walk through the fields and have time to stray
Relaxing and thinking of an earlier day.
Of when we were young with the world at our feet,
Everything exciting, our happiness unique.
But now, a little older with sorrows to bare,
We know what joy there is for someone to care.
So just now and then think for a while
About a sister or brother who are too down-hearted to smile.
And just give a willing hand to help them along the way.
Then you can thank God for this glorious day.

--oOo--

Think Positive

When you are surrounded by troubles and fear,
Think positive and they will all disappear,
For life is a book we must all learn to read
And not let the fears and anxiety feed.
To surrender to thoughts that are not positive
Will only result in our own negative.
For if we are to maintain our own discipline,
We must exclude useless thoughts and nonsensical whims.
We must all learn to suffer our troubles and pain
If, like our Dear Saviour, our own souls to gain.
For as soon as you realise you're just here to prove
That as a true Christian all obstacles you can move.
For fear is a drug from which all kinds of forces grow,
And you will be lost, for your courage will go.
Be not like the blind man, the deaf man, the lame,
Or you will lose your chance of soul to claim.
And when you have passed all of your tests
You will know it was all for the best.
For God is Love, but we must all show
That to find perfection we must good seeds sow,
So that we may be picked by His Own Precious Hand,
And forever live in that peaceful, promised land.

--oOo--

The Totality

Our willing deeds, both great and small,
Are seen by God who loves us all.
We cannot hide our plans from Him
As all our thoughts come from within.
And we all know that in reality
We are a part of the totality.
So the many facets that we bear
Will be a burden for all to share.
And God in his wisdom knows it must be
That through love and suffering we find humility.

--oOo--

God's Garden

Lovely flowers and perfect views,
So lovely that it makes the news.
The woodland slope and winding lane,
The little church with weather vane.
The spire so tall and graceful, reaching to the sky,
A landmark to the ever faithful, a beauty to the eye.

The cemetery looks so lonely with tombstones old and grey,
But here and there a new one, with flowers bright and gay.
The church bells ring out, they're calling you - you can hear them from afar,
And you remember the old days, when it was the horse and cart, no petrol fumes to mar.
But all things must change to develop our inner minds,
And to accept the course of history and to help and save mankind.

For with each change and era, problems there are bound to be,
And so we must remember each home must have charity.
So it is not enough to win first prize for a village that is beautiful and clean,
But for ourselves, our thoughts, our generosity to lean.
For with the coming winter the flowers will fade and die,

The leaves all brown and withered in the streets will coldly lie.

But the people will all still be here, their problems still intact,
So let a little of your work be to help them along the track.
It is good to have a garden, with flowers so bright and gay,
But please, all do remember, life is a garden where God's children work and play.
And to hear the sound of laughter of children playing games
Is far better than a village where just beauty is its aim.

To sit behind the window and watch the world go by
Is not enough to help your neighbour to see, and talk and sigh.
So live, and let live, in all you do and say,
Let your heart be an open garden where no-one has to pay.
For remember, loved ones, when it is our time to go,
You will look back and say, "Oh dear, I wish I had let go".

"And helped a little more to save another's fears,
Instead of turning a blind eye and a deafening ear."
For as we judge ourselves, we will be ashamed to say,

"Oh dear Father, do forgive me, the sin is mine I pray."
So open up your hearts and, like the flowers gay,
Give of your own true light and colour to illuminate the day.
And as <u>HE</u> sees your love and kindness, your reward will be
A special place in God's own garden for all eternity.

--oOo--

Forgiveness

Oh world so full of beauty, yet so much pain,
Our fears, our loves, no hope can remain.
Amongst our midst such rampart foe
Causing such strife and meaningless woe.

Each new day brings another sad thought.
We've forgotten our God whose love we were taught,
And instead are bent on breaking His word
Which, of course, will surely not go by unheard.

So please, before it is too late,
Show each other your love instead of hate,
As each day brings us nearer to God's Own Home
Where never again will you want to roam.

So go down on your knees, and ask Him to forgive
The meaningless life you are trying to live,
And like a true Father, who always knows best,
He will give you a smile and bid your heart rest.

And you will be filled with a Heavenly peace
As like a mortgage on a new lease.
And God will be pleased, His child has returned
With the knowledge, his old life will be truly spurned.

--oOo--

Eventide in the New Forest

The glorious green of velvet plush,
The serene calm of evening hush.
The shadows dark and strangely still,
Where thoughts and fancies roam at will.
The gentle murmur of the stream
Where all God's creatures drink and preen.
The water, like transparent glass,
Watching the seasons as they pass.
The trees, a background for your charms,
Where branches reach like loving arms.
And the dappled sunlight gives a glow
That drives away our fears and woe.
The memory will forever fill
My heart with longing for peace so still.

--oOo--

Blended

Washing blowing on a line,
Shirts a frolic, arms entwined.
Little dresses, fashion wise,
Dancing under clear blue skies,
Playing, hugging, gay and bright,
Enough to gladden any sight,
Except, of course, if you are blind
And do not want to use your mind.
Then you will miss what God intended
That all His colours should be blended.

--oOo--

The Lonely

Furtive face at window peep,
Behind the lace so fine,
At world so full of people
Yet not one to confide.
And as we stand and watch all day,
But never join the throng,
Yet hoping that a smile our way
Will make the day a song.
And, as we wait, our time to pass,
And pray to God above
Will lead us to that restful place
Where everything is love.

--oOo--

The Bluebell Wood

Oh what a hue in the woodland glade!
A carpet of blue has just been laid,
The pile so thick and luscious too
That to walk on it would spoil the view.

The trees a cover for your head.
No ray of sunshine leaves a tread
As cool the bluebells like to be,
A message of peace and tranquillity.

Even the birds dare not alight
As in the trees they sing their delight
Of beauty, just to see and praise,
Which, if untouched, will last for days.

So please, if you just happen to see
A carpet of blue that nature has given free,
Just look and pass by and don't pick a flower
As bluebells were meant for us just to admire.

For when they are picked their beauty will pass,
Their fragile appearance will droop and not last,
But under the trees, where all nature is one,
Just one single glance will bring out the sun

--oOo--

Nature Gone Berserk

I stand and look across the bay
At the sea in all its mad array,
Big rollers crashing to the shore
Covering the rocks we used to explore.

The roaring wind shouting them on,
Pushing and pulling with a mournful song,
The raindrops falling to join the swell,
Discovering the secrets that therein dwell.

A tumultuous sound, so great and strong,
And yet so mournful, like an unhappy throng
Bewailing their sorrow so great and small
That the sunshine is wasted and not seen at all.

The wind then goes rushing across the fields
Breaking and tearing all the things that won't yield,
Causing such damage and needless fear,
Shrieking and laughing for all to hear

All nature's elements joining the fray,
Lasting all night and most of the day,
Making life miserable for the whole human race
As if testing our strength and general distaste.

So Storm, please be still, so that we may see
That wonderful peace and perfect harmony
Where our minds can devour such beautiful thoughts
Not the pain and suffering your tumult has wrought.

The Broken Home

My Mum has gone, no more to see,
No arms to love and cuddle me.
The home is cold and silence strange
After so much fun and games.

The people ask, "Where is your Mum?"
I only think, "What have I done?
If only I could get in touch
And ask her why she left so much."

No pleasant smell of oven baking,
No Mum to call me on awakening,
And as I struggle through the day
My tears are not so far away.

The days pass into months and years,
And with it goes my love and fears.
To see you now would be such pain,
And we neither would have much to gain,

As like a stranger you would seem
As from a child I have grown to be
So independent, no more to lean.
But, oh dear Mother, why did you leave me?

--oOo--

The Mistress, The Sheepdog and The Poodle

The one so big, the one so small, such faithful friends are they
As, with delight, they run and jump and frolic while at play.
The motherly attention the poodle gets for free
Would make any little orphan child wish that it were he.

The poodle has her face all washed and sits with suppressed glee
As the sheepdog with her big wet tongue just licks her lovingly.
What confidence does love bring to all who find its treasure,
For to an animal, the same as we, nothing else can measure.

And then, when they have played enough, their mistress they will seek
For in their love as one, they know, she loves the humble and meek.
So with these three, you find what God has shown,
That to be like the Mistress, the Sheepdog and the Poodle our sins we must atone.

--oOo--

Solitude

So proud, erect, oh wondrous tree!
Golden foliage, such a scene,
Standing lone for all to see.
Give, oh give, your strength to me!

Heart of oak and frame unique,
Oh, if you could only speak!
But just to gaze with thought and awe
Has given me a love for all.

I know how lonely you must feel
With wind and rain to lash your heel,
But when the sun begins to beam
You, in all your glory, gleam.

--oOo--

Lament

Are we to lose our country scene,
public walks and village green
to hear the rumble of the train
and shrieking roar of aeroplane?
The motorway forever winds
round and round and thus entwines
until we feel just like a top
spinning mind and dizzy mop.
No more to wander aimlessly,
looking at the scenery
rushing up and down the street
meeting policeman on his beat
Buses rushing to and fro,
helicopters flying low,
soon no more a quiet scene
only in a far off dream.
So with regret we lose our peace
as noise and progress will increase
Our little village, like a core,
the centre of the traffic roar.

--oOo--

The Beachcomber

What a wealth of knowledge there is to find
When a beach is freed by the outgoing tide.
Little shells, big shells, stones of all sizes,
The beachcomber's glory, a handful of prizes.

Stones made smooth by the power of the sea
As the waves beat against them powerfully,
And the sun to bleach them, making them clean,
With the sand as a soft bed where their glory doth gleam.

The beachcomber stops and looks at each one,
Wondering if some day he will find a rare one,
Perhaps not realising the knowledge there is to find
In one simple stone although not a rare kind.

For each stone has a store of knowledge if only we will look and see
Instead of just throwing them back into the sea,
Making a splash to see how the ripples will fall,
And yet missing the secrets that lay open for all.

For each line is a pattern made by the elements of time
With sometimes a fossil engraved in the lime.
If only we knew what the ages could say
We would all be professors and wealth be our stay.
And then perhaps the secrets of the future would unfold

And we would be masters of knowledge, a
priceless gem to behold.

--oOo--

A Child's Memories

As a little child I can remember days of sun-blest gold
When time seemed not to matter, and there were no speeding cars to fill the road,
Playing outside the front door, too young to roam far away,
Walking amongst the chickens, and to hear the sounds of the hens as they lay,
Or as they strut around pecking at this and that,
And lifting a head sideways, a watchful eye on the family cat.

And in the distance the chime of the church bell, with its lazy ding dong,
Reminding all worshippers to hurry along.
With my little pinafore to save my Sunday dress,
Short hair and a fringe was my only head-dress.
I remember my mother, standing just outside the front door,
Beautiful in a velvet dress with a lace collar, when I was only four.

And then came black-berrying time when with baskets filled to the brim,
Faces flushed and bodies tired, aching in every limb.
My mother and sisters would return, pleased at the thought of the money they would gain,
And the old range fire would be lit, the big black kettle on the burning coals would be lain,
The cups and saucers quickly found, the spoons a lovely tinkling sound,

And then, when the tea was brewed, the taste was joy profound.
But all too soon my joy was short-lived as we moved to another home.
The people were all new to me and so I stood alone.
No little friend to talk to or share my little games,
And so I found my solace in inventing ones with names.
My sister's dog and I became as one as we roamed the fields,
Just a little mongrel dog who to all my commands would yield.

Black and white he was in colour, and Tiger was his name.
To me he was my pal, good enough for any hall of fame.
But once again my joy was ended, for on returning home one day,
I found my little friend had died, and on the floor he lay.
For he had played a game without me, chasing rats beneath the shed,
And one had caught him by the throat, and now my friend was dead.

So once again I was alone, my loss was hard to bear.
Never again to call my Tiger, our little games to share.
It is very hard when one is young, their sorrow to express,

And so we hide our grief and pretend we could not care less.
Our parents try to soften the blow by offering a bribe,
But at the same time knowing no solace can we find.

--oOo--

Dreams

I remember the day my dreams came true
When chosen for fairy at the village school.
My lovely dress of silver white
And wand with star so very bright.

I learnt my lines. My hopes were high
That on the day myself would fly
Up in the clouds, as fairies do,
And audience think me very true.
But alas, alack, it was not to be.
My dress and wand were taken from me,
And given instead a suit of red
With bugle and jester's hat on head.
My disappointment knew no bounds,
My dress I gave without a sound.
My heart was sad, my tears were near
As my dreams slowly disappeared.

And on the day I crept on stage
With bugle call. It seemed an age,
And, at the shouts of children small,
I thought, "Oh dear, I was a bore."
But suddenly, on looking down,
I saw small faces, black and brown,
Standing, clapping, just for me -
A jester, not a grand fairy.
And now, on looking back, I know
That it is not the dress you show
But of yourself you give such fun
To make life brighter for someone.

--oOo--

The Death of a Lobster

Oh Lobster, pitiful to see,
As death devours your mind,
Your eyes, so dark and full of pain,
Oh please forgive my kind.
You look so lonely lying there
For everyone to see,
Yet strangely proud. We can't compare
As you wait your destiny.

The people watching, standing near
Like Punch and Judy show.
Their children touch you without fear,
They are too young to know.
To them you are just another toy
Whose spring has broken down,
So into sea they jump for joy,
Their mind on pleasure bound.

But parents, knowing of life's pain,
Should really feel a pride
That, like a hero, you attain
The courage of mankind.

--oOo--

My Cat Smudge

He sits on chair with kingly grace,
Black of coat and smudge on face,
Waiting to be loved and seen
To know that he is still supreme.

With eyes so green and fathoms deep,
He gazes straight at you
As if he knew another world
Where love and friendship grew.

You stroke his head. His body lifts
As if to greet your love.
The purrs he gives, you know it well
Yet rise to greet this love.

He sleeps all day and plays at night
His loved ones to despair,
Just as the dawn begins to light
His lordship starts to care.

He snuggles in beside your bed
With nose a little high,
And looks so gentle, like a babe,
You stroke instead of sigh.

And then, as you begin to doze,
He hears a sound so low,
And out of bed, without a noise,
He creeps and looks for foe.

You open window. Out he goes
From roof to garden wall.

Why do you do it? Goodness knows,
Except he is your love, your all.

--oOo--

The Wondering Eyes of a Mother-To-Be

Peeping from a shawl of lace,
A little baby angel face.
Puckered lips, just ripe to kiss,
Bright blue eyes, so full of bliss.
Shall I really have a babe so dear?
My heart is full of wonder, and yet of fear,
That one so precious can be born to me,
A hungry, loving mother-to-be.
But, as I look and feel a movement small,
I know, one day soon, I will listen to my own child's call.

--oOo--

In Search of Sun

Our holiday has just begun
And so begins our search for sun,
Rising early to peep outside
To see if any clouds abide,
Wondering which way to take
In case a storm will quickly break.
And so with food and deck chairs stacked
And into boot with swimsuits packed.
We make our way down to the beach
Our little spot we quickly reach
And into swimsuits we swiftly change
And into sea but not long range.
Just gently wading just to feel
The lapping waves against our heel
Then back to deck chair for a rest
Hoping that we look our best.

Reading, sleeping, or just to dream
Sheer heaven, as sun begins to beam
Warming bodies, oh so white!
Painting them golden. What a sight!
And, as we each receive our tan,
We admit that life is good for man,
And just to rest and think of peace
We leave our worries on a lease.

Back to caravan we go.
Can't sleep all night for sudden glow,
Bodies burning from too much sun,
Our mirror tells us, "Too well done."
Our search for sun has sure succeeded.
If only our parents we had heeded

THERE IS A REASON

That every day the sun will shine
If love and friendship will entwine.

--oOo--

Snowden

Each time I pass I do not see
Your head is still a mystery
Like a timid bride who seeks to hide
Behind her veil so fine and wide.
A damp white mist surrounds your charms
The sun peeps through and thus disarms
The thought that you do not appear
To mind if we then stop to cheer.
The climbers, in their coloured suits
With packs on backs and big strong boots,
Look just like clowns in a circus top
Except, of course, they do not mock
As with intent they try to climb
Your tempting height, their minds sublime
For just to conquer is their aim
And not your beauty to attain.

So, next time I pass, I hope to find
That just this once you will be kind,
That I may see your glory high,
Your body reaching for the sky.

--oOo--

Unison

Flowers in abundance grow
In beds so neatly raised
Colours to set your heart aglow
And mixed up like a maze.
Yellow, white, black, brown and gold,
So pleasing to the eye
With petals soft and perfume bold
Gazing at the sky.
Their message very loud and clear
To all who want to see
That if man sows the seed of love
Our life we hold so dear
Will be a better kind of place
With friendship instead of fear.
And so I wish with all my might
That like the flowers gay
All colours of the world unite
To make a grand array.

--oOo--

God Is Everywhere

You will find Him in the moonlight,
You will find Him in the stars,
You will find Him in the sunlight
Gleaming from afar.
You will find Him in the garden among the flowers gay,
You will find Him in your homes, helping you to make your way.
You will find Him in the river and the stream agurgle with hope,
You will find Him in the forest, the woodland and the slope.
You will find Him in the market place among the humble and the meek,
You will find Him when the days are grey if you will only seek.
For God is everywhere. You only have to see,
And, when you say your prayers at night, please say, "Oh God bless me."
And when the time has come and we will meet Him, face to face,
I only hope we will not be a child of His disgrace.

--oOo--

Togetherness

Love is where the heart is, no matter where we roam,
As love is such a strong bond it calls to all it owns,
Whether it is just a day or a year the longing to return is so great
For love is such a strong bond, no time for fighting or hate.
The teasing and the happiness are linked and felt as by one,
The little struggles and the heartaches melt as though by the sun.
And so indeed my loved ones, what you have found is great.
No need to envy others wealth when you have found a way through the gate.
As we each have a loved one to call our own, so keep yourself clean and free
And you will be glad that you waited as true love is for eternity.
For to share our little blessings is a gift to all who seek
And when you have found your other self then you will feel so humble, yet a joy unique
As both are one in all that we do, the pleasure and the pain,
As God has made this beautiful gift that only true lovers can claim.

--oOo--

Beautiful Rose

Beautiful rose made by a beautiful thought,
Your perfume lingering and pleasing,
As a bud your petals so soft and beautifully curled
That the temptation to pick is so teasing.
Like a baby in all its nudity waiting for the final hour to face the outside world.
So, as one looks and adores one of God's beautiful creations,
Remember the baby looking on a new life and hoping for the same admiration.
For like the rose we are all made by a beautiful thought
So you see every day a new miracle is wrought.
Different colours but with the same chance to glow
So that we give pleasure to each other as we blossom and grow.
So, if like the rose, you want to be picked, give the best of yourself that you can
And when you are in that special show let your beauty spread out like a fan.
For it is no use pretending to our creator as He knows just what we are like,
So remember the rose when life seems to be dark, and then you will see the light.

--oOo--

"The Master's Masterpiece"
The Ever Changing Picture

Patches of grey amidst patches of blue,
Feathery streaks as the clouds wander through.
Colours so hard to copy and frame,
Only a mind to absorb and a voice to exclaim.
For the one who painted with such a flourish and care,
Not one single person can ever compare.
As with each new day a new picture is hung
From the early morning dew, to the setting sun,
A picture that hangs in God's house for all the world to see,

Not hidden in some locked room for all eternity
For one person alone to gloat over and praise,
But a picture for all to gladden our days.
So no need to queue outside a picture gallery,
Just glance around you and what beauty you will see,
A picture that doesn't just hang on a wall
But a living glory that changes and stays still, not at all,
For, as through the day the changes are wrought,
The colours will change as a new picture is sought.
With the sun peeping through, sending a warmth on its rays,
Making one forget the blues and the greys.

And then once again, in the evening glow,
A radiance of colours that slowly will go,
Leaving a background of black velvet decorated with stars

Like diamonds, in a show case, but with no need of bars.
What beauty we see every day of our lives
If only we will look and see with our eyes.
So do not fret that like your neighbour you have no masterpiece to hang,
Just step outside your door and open your eyes as wide as you can,

For the Master who painted His pictures for free
Is hoping His children will notice and see
That although He is our Father, The Great Spirit of All,
His pictures are a message, and a lesson for all.
That one does not need money for Heavenly Things,
But just eyes that are open, and a heart that just sings.

Cobwebs

Cobwebs in the corners
Cobwebs on the stairs
Cobwebs hanging from the ceiling to catch you unawares.
Cobwebs hanging from the roses
Cobwebs hanging from the trees
Cobwebs floating in the sunshine persuaded by the gentle breeze.
Big ones, small ones, like gossamer wings
Enchanting, but serving a purpose to catch little things.
Like the cobwebs of our mind ever searching there to find.
And to grasp the truth and knowledge that can into a bundle bind.
So if like the cobwebs you find yourself floating like in a dream
Remember that you can be as beautiful if only your beauty can be seen.
And to reach out to all mankind with a smile and a helping hand
And you will be glad that like the cobwebs your service was at hand.

--oOo--

The Storm

The clouds are gathering, the storm is near,
Gather in your children but be of good cheer.
And when the storm breaks you will be glad you
are home
With people you love, instead of alone.

Across the dark sky code messages fly
With lightening flashes, some low and some high,
Thunder-like drums of a three piece band
And rain to cover the whole of the land.

And, while we cower because of the din,
A little afraid for ourselves and our kin,
We realise that storms, that bring us together,
Can't be too bad, so don't curse the weather.

And, while we watch with eyes full of wonder,
We realise a power that must live up yonder,
Someone who sends us a storm just to test,
Hoping His children will soon do the rest.
So don't be afraid as God will be near,
Watching to see if His love will appear
As we all help each other our fears to dispel
And God will be pleased and bid the storm quell.

--oOo--

The Church Spire

The church spire reaching to the sky no flag to state who reigns there
Everyone knows God is always at home and waiting for His children to return there
But if you arrive and find the church door is locked just stand for a while in the porch
Then you will discover the blinding light that has been missing from the torch
For like the battery that is damp we each forget to show each other the way
But when a battery is recharged with friendship and love then it will be like night turned into day.
For it is only through reaching the bottom of the well that a light is what we need
So that we may climb to the top and reach out to our God, then our journey will succeed
For God is LOVE, and He wants His children to be free
So if you pass His house just drop in for a while, lonely you will not be
For he will be waiting to receive your love and give to you His blessing
For He is one that cannot be fooled, you cannot keep Him guessing.
So if the church spire doth beckon to you when on a mission bent
Just stop for a while and remember His love and you will be glad that you went.

--oOo--

The Surfers

Atlantic rollers sweep inshore
With surfers having fun galore
Each one waiting for his cue
And then on wave will ride right through.
Like ballerinas in a show
Their balance true as they sweep low,
Their tiny boards so thin and frail
Like little yachts, without a sail.
Again, and again, the show is repeated
With spectators enjoying the undefeated,
But many are the shouts and falls
But lots of fun is had by all.

--oOo--

The End of Summer

The summer has gone, the days are getting cold
The flowers are nipped as the frosts are getting bold.
No more to wander down leafy lane
With time to spare are thoughts to gain.

The trees asway with gentle winds
A soft murmur of music from creaky limbs
As if they too are sad to feel
The sudden change against their heel.
The golden leaves begin to fall
Like confetti at a fancy ball,
Their beauty plain for all to see
As on the grass they gently ski.

The smoke is drifting from chimney pots
A sign for sure to change our frocks.
But what a treat for us to see
A Glowing fire and welcome tea.

And as we sit and feel at rest
We know that change is for the best,
For to enjoy life's treats and thrills,
We must have change to meet life's spills

--oOo--

The Old Folks' Lament

Am I to be alone and free,
No one to love and care,
When what I want is company
And friendship that is rare?

I sleep all night and dream all day
Of days of long ago
When I was young and fit and gay,
But now my movements slow.

The paint is peeling like my heart
As time drifts slowly by,
And garden weeds where insects dart
Are tall as corn and rye.

There is no weekend any more,
Each day is just the same,
Especially if you are poor
No special treat your aim.

Where are the friends I knew so well
Who always played with me
Until I was so old and frail
And now I do not see?

So hear my prayers, oh God divine,
Not let me linger so,
And take me in your arms sublime
For I am glad to go.

--oOo--

Test Flight

Tiny speck up in the blue
Do I look so small to you?
As you wend your way up high
Through the clouds, up in the sky,
Leaving trails of smoke behind
As if inviting me to climb.
As I watch you disappear
First to play, and then to leer,
Hide and seek, among the clouds
Without a wave without a sound,
As you dip your silver wings
Making signs, and shapes, and things.

You make your message very clear
As clouds you sail without a fear,
To show us that we must not shun
The things in life that must be done
Your wings spread out across the sky
Look just like arms to pacify.

--oOo--

Little Boy

Little boy trying to walk like mum
Little face glowing like the morning sun.
Little eyes shining like the evening star
Little legs trying but cannot go far.
Little body swinging to and fro
If only he could go, go, go,
But for one little boy, oh what joy
When mummy tells him, "What a clever little boy!"

--oOo--

Pure Love

Two lips that meet and feel as one
Two hearts that beat together,
Two arms that hold with love so pure
Two hearts just like a feather.
So God's love enfolds each one of us
So we can become as one.
No cold, no dark, no place to fear,
As we bathe in the warmth of the sun.
Then our bodies will heal, and all the world will be
peace
As we each have a love for each other,
So no reproach, no regrets, no `I am sorry',
As a love that is pure is not folly.

--oOo--

Over Lane
Almondsbury

Over lane, and over fields, to where the river
Severn flows
Glistening in the morning sun, and in the evening
sunset glows.
To wander through the woodland glades
So cool, and tranquil, against the sun's rays.
Little paths invitingly climb
Daring all explorers to seek and find.
Hollow trees to line the way
A treasure for any child at play,
To hear the echo of their shouts of glee
Makes one wish that as a child we still could be.
To climb the hill you easily tire
But what a view of the old church spire!
There are welcome seats to sit and gaze
At all the glory on summer days.
The traffic can be but a minor flaw
If one can close their mind to it all.
For the beauty, and the peace is there
And brings such joy to all who care.
The cottages all neat and clean
All nestle close like a fairy book scene.
The people all friendly with ready smiles
Who still have time to talk awhile.
What more could one wish for in this time and
pace,
But a Shangri-la that we all can grace.

--oOo--

The Blackbirds

The blackbirds are nesting in the garden again
Each year they return my joy is the same
Each doing their share, but enjoying the task,
Watching me at the window as they fly past.

They seem to know I am their friend
And let me see what they intend
A cosy nest, the perfect home,
Where little babes are safe to roam.

Then for a while I do not see
As birds are sitting patiently
Waiting for their eggs to break
And of this world young birds partake.

And then one day with parent pride
Along my hedge five blackbirds stride
With Mum, and Dad keeping a watchful eye
On little babes, who try to fly.

The day is near for them to go
I shall be sad, I will miss them so
But will look forward to next year
When my friends the blackbirds will reappear.

--oOo--

The Elements of Nature

Another dry day, no wind to cool the air,
A merciless sun blazing down, your eyes cannot stand the glare.
The flowers have lost their sparkle as with thirst they are devoured
If only for a little while with rain drops they could be showered!

The earth is cracking, so there are no grubs for the birds to find
The roads are dry and dusty, and on your shoes wet tar you find.
The elm trees wretched in their nakedness make one feel so sad and blue
And, as we look, we know that soon some more trees will die and spoil the lovely view.

The leaves are already falling as Mother tree tries to shed her load
And as I look up at the sun I feel I want to scold.
For what would we do without the trees in their glorious array
What would we do without the flowers?
They make us feel so gay.

The green and pleasant land we knew is parched for the want of rain
And crops are wasting in the fields, so the barns in the winter will have no grain.
The sun is what we have always prayed for as of rain we have our share

But what a welcome change to have something more than a tan to compare.

So once again we have been made to understand the hard way, life's lessons to learn
Realising that without the rain, the hot sun would just scorch everything and burn.
So we must be contented with what nature has in store
For the one who knows all the answers will also settle the score.

--oOo--

A Country Cottage

I do not need a mansion
To feel contentment and peace.
I do not need a Rolls Royce
Or stables I can lease.
No yacht to cruise the world in
But just a country cottage full of love is my great aim.

To hear the sound of children's voices
The singing of the birds.
To relax and think is what my choice is
Not the needless use of words.
As our stay is such a short one
On this little world of ours
So all I want is a garden that is full of lovely flowers.

To see the blossoms as they grow
To watch the seasons pass.
And the gentle sweep of the grass.
My wish is full of humble plea
For I know God will be there
Waiting to welcome His own dear child, because, for the simple things, He cares.

--oOo--

Beyond the Garden Wall

When life seems drab and full of pain
I know a place where peace doth reign
And so I climb the garden wall.

As I step down the other side I feel a new release
For God I know is waiting there to fill my heart
with peace
And in the shadows of the stately trees I feel so
weak and small
But suddenly from the birds and bees, I hear
God's loving call.

I walk on a carpet lush with colours gay
Purple and blue, yellow and mauve, with green as
an underlay.
I see the summer house where lovers used to meet
And then to walk the twisting paths their
happiness complete.

And as I walk a presence I can feel
As if someone from long ago behind me stealthily
steal
For in my heart I know that someone like me
must have memories to recall
For like me now, long long ago, they too climbed
over the garden wall.

--oOo--

The Morning Chorus

The early morning hush prevails
No noisy crowds on nature trails.
The air so still, no wind disturbs
The perfume of the woodland herbs.

And then the maestro's voice is heard
The thrilling notes of a lone blackbird
To welcome in the new great day
And chase the fears of night away.

Like a violin with golden strings
Each note so different as the blackbird sings.
The beautiful sound one cannot compare
As with all nature its joy to share.

And then as if a sign intent
A chorus on the air is rent
A show just fit for any Queen
If only the artist could be seen.

But just to hear is such a joy
No colourful plumage your eyes to employ
So that all its beauty you derive
Of something small, yet so alive.

The stage it is a woodland glade
No human form to spoil the parade
As with one accord our feathered friends
Upon the air their music send.

What little secret do you hold
At this early hour to be so bold?

THERE IS A REASON

When most of the world is fast asleep
Your daily ritual you do keep.

But whatever the reason, come what may,
Your singing is like a sunshine ray.
As I start the day with a song in my heart
My thanks to you I do impart.

--oOo--

My Neglected Garden

Looking from my window what do I see?
The weeds growing in my garden nearly as tall as me,
For no time have I had lately to tend my garden gay,
No time to rest my body as at night I wearily lay.

The gardens of my neighbours are all so neatly laid,
The lawns all freshly cut with flowers of the best grade,
The deck chairs in the sunshine, with tea and refreshments gay,
While I have just the time to hurry on my way.

But as I look I feel a joy, knowing that I have won
By giving of myself to help a lonely one,
For that is what God intended, that we help each other on the way,
So that, like the flowers, His children will show beauty every day.

--oOo--

The Old Willow Tree

At the junction you stand
With an air that is grand
The grandfather of all willow trees.
That for a moment we gaze,
Our eyes from the road raised
At such beauty that doesn't need fees.

Like a signpost you sway
To show us the way,
That will save mind and body alike.
The deep peace you give,
To help us long lives to live,
Is lost in the rush of the might.

Your one branch you bend
Like a knee you extend,
As if inviting us to sit for a while,
So that we may see
And know why you plea
As we watch all the traffic defile.

As if to erase
The rush and the pace
You stand like Old Father Time.
Your leaves fall like tears
As if knowing our fears
And for us you do truly pine.

But perhaps one day we will see
Your desperate plea
And know the love peace truly brings,
And return to the pleasure

That no gold can measure
Where time no longer wins.

--oOo--

Regretting

Do not waste your life regretting what you might have been
Do not let the days go by like a puppet in a scene.
Do not waste your tears and sorrow, for fear is what you gain,
But smile and be kind-hearted, and let love be your aim.
For tears are not for crying, but just like the morning dew
To damp the lashes from your eyes so that like a window you can look through.

To see the glories that doth abound
If only you will look around,
Instead of being a prisoner of one's own self and whim
Open up those glorious eyes and see thyself within,
And know that God is waiting there to clasp your cherished hand
And guide you to that loving place, that Glorious, Cherished Land.

--oOo--

Be Kind to Each Other

"Be kind to each other," we often say,
But how often do we say what we mean?
How deep are our feelings through each single day,
Through the good times and the lean?

If only we thought before each word was said
No hurt would ever be done.
No need for loved ones to be sorry they wed
If only their words were for fun.

Just wake up each morning, and think for a while.
What a lovely day it would be!
With everyone kind, instead of trying to rile,
And living in complete harmony.

Our days would be blessed with a Heavenly peace,
Our love would blossom and grow.
No wars, or sorrows, or someone to fleece
For what we reap, we must sow.

So take heed and remember what the caption says
And think before you speak,
As a word can bring sunshine into a day
And we will find the love we seek.

--oOo--

The One-Legged Blackbird

Oh blackbird! I admire your skill
As on one leg you balance still,
Your body taut against the wind,
Your head against your feathers pinned.
No one to give a helping hand
As on one leg you lonely stand.

If only I could talk to you
Your fears and sorrows I could sooth.
With your hopping gait you spell despair.
To lose a limb is hard to bear,
Your head just darting to and fro,
An easy prey for deadly foe.

And as I watch your ungainly tread,
The toss and turning of your head
Alert for any kind of change,
Your food itself must be short-ranged.
And as you sway to keep your stand
I feel I want to clap my hand.

But like a soldier you play your part
As for your food you quickly dart,
Your wings aflutter, your mind intent
As with your beak you quickly rent.
Your courage there for all to see,
A lesson in biology.

--oOo--

The Christmas Tree

Oh Christmas Tree! You look so gay,
As presents in profusion lay
Around your feet as though to cheer
A little tree that is so dear.

Each Christmas time you give a show,
With fairy lights and mistletoe
For little ones with eyes agleam,
And old folk by the fireside dream

Of days when they too were young,
Of Christmas carols that they have sung
For loved ones. No more to see or hear
A little smile, a little tear.

But courage we must always show,
Like the star upon your tree top glow,
For to see the light is all we need
For love and friendship to succeed.

So little tree, so bright and gay,
Thank you for our thoughts today,
When just to see your sparkling face
Our grief and suffering will erase.

--oOo--

A Day in the Mountains

Up in the mountains, away from the bustle,
Where only the wind blows to make the grass rustle.
The rocks stand out so dark and grey
With patches of colour from the sun's rays.

Resting on carpets of red, brown and gold,
With fir trees like sentinels guarding a hold.
The sheep quietly grazing as though still alone
Or if they do see, no fear then is shown.

The sound of miniature waterfalls
Breaking the silence and yet to thaw
The innermost quiet so great and still
That you are almost frightened the peace to kill.

To stand and breathe in the clear cold air,
Your arms outstretched to show you care
About such space and beauty wild
And, as yet, so undefiled.

The narrow roads invitingly wind,
Calling all travellers to seek and find
All the glories given to us for free
From our dear Saviour whom we cannot see.

But we feel His presence, so great and strong,
Our hearts are uplifted as though in song,
And in our prayers at night we say,
"Thank you, dear Father, for a lovely day."

--oOo--

Persuasion

Oh Tree of Knowledge! Talk to me,
Tell me all I cannot see.
As you wend your way up high,
Miles and miles up in the sky,
Your arms reach out to God above.
I know, you know, God is love.

I wish that I could climb your trunk
And people think it for a stunt
To make them see, just for a while,
The meaning of a kiss and smile.
As love is there for all to find,
No need to be a special kind.

Your leaves, so thick and moist and green,
Will give a show fit for a Queen.
The birds will light and start to sing
Of all the glories done by Him.
For they are much too pleased to know
Their God, our God, loves them so.

The March winds blow, you sway and sigh,
Your patience of our kind, oh my!
You can't believe that we can be
So woolly-headed not to see.
So in the summer, just for kicks,
You show your glory, luscious, rich.

The autumn comes with leaves aglow
And mountain streams forever flow
Where animals and birds will meet
To talk about our God unique.

THERE IS A REASON

You listen with a mother's pride
And wish that we had nought to hide.

When winter comes you bow your head
For what you think is best unsaid,
But another time, another year,
You do your best to make them hear.
And if you lose another show
Your frozen tears on trunk will flow.

--oOo--

I have found `Him'

At last I have found `Him', dear Father of all,
And now my home is like a castle, and my heart as big as a stately hall.
While I am working I feel `His' presence by my side
And I know in my heart there is no sin from `Him' to hide.

And, when I go out walking, the birds and bees all sound and look anew.
The harsh storm of the morning, the sunny afternoon,
All is one and all to me since my `Father' I have found you.

I see the pain, the sorrow, that in this world, in ignorance bear
And my tears are great and many as with them their pain I
gladly share.
If only, like me, they too would find their goal,
Then they too would look around and find their own true soul.

But alas and alack, it seems to easy just to love and be as one,
And so, instead of offering a friendly cheek, they turn the other one,
And turn away from deeds all good and free
Because, dear `Father', they do not yet love thee.

Instead they go on hurting their own great family,

Tearing one another apart, causing pain and misery,
So that from their deeds their pain doth start and grow
Because through vanity they do not want to know.

So, dear sister and brother, I can only write what has happened to me,
But even then I cannot describe the peace and upliftment that my true heart can see
For `His' love is so wondrous, no one can explain the glow,
And so I say, dear one and all, be like `Christ' who gave, and in your garden good seeds grow.

Just start with little things, like feeling sorry for someone,
And then an extra smile for a face that looks so glum.
Then gradually it will come so easy as with your heart you feel a pride,
Then, like me, you too will have no sin to hide.

And `He' will see your goodness and send you a gift or two,
And you will feel `His' presence, a treasure just for you,
And you will know, my dear, the truth I tell,
That in your life of goodness there is no room for sin or hell.

--oOo--

Wonderful Wonderful Sun

What would happen if there was no sun,
No golden glow to brighten our lives,
No sudden warmth to fill our hearts?
Then we might as well be blind.
And yet what a dreadful thing to say
For, even when blind, the warmth our bodies feel
And, with a sudden beautiful thought,
We know God really loves mankind.

For He sends His great creation, a masterpiece of warmth,
Reaching into all cold corners
So that His love for us we can feel.
For His warmth is love, and the sun is trying to say,
"Enjoy me, one and all, and for each other be a sunshine ray."
And, when the clouds sweep across the sky,
It is only for a while,
And then the sun will come back again
To help you to climb that stile.
So reach out with loving arms, enjoy the warmth,
Draw from its power and know
That here is one great source of life
That helps our minds to grow.

--oOo--

Oh Mighty Ocean!

Oh mighty ocean, fathoms deep!
If only I could take a peep,
At all the secrets you withhold
And all the tales that could be told,
Of monsters lurking down below
Just waiting for a passing foe.
And on the evening sunset rays
A path of gleaming jewels display,
Each one winking like a star,
Blinding eyes that look afar,
Dreaming dreams that won't come true
But for a while you feel anew.

--oOo--

Snowstorm

I awake and find to my surprise
A world so white it blinds my eyes.
I stand and wonder why the change
And know that God has won again.
For he is Lord of all you see
But what he wants is harmony.
So just to show us what He means
He sends a day to make us see
That if life's balance is the same
We lose our chance of soul to claim.

--oOo--

Another Spring

As I go about my daily chores and wish my life to change,
I hear the birds in chorus sing and know my view to be short-ranged
For suddenly my heart beats a little faster as I feel the breath of spring,
And with the birds in chorus I too begin to sing.

I look into the distance. A clear mountain range I see,
And, although in body I am here, in my mind on the mountain I roam free.
I stand aloft and look around at the beauty that is clear,
And to breathe in the cool fresh air I feel no pain or fear.

For that is when I am close to Him who watches over me,
And as the Christ to the wilderness did go, I too go joyfully.
Especially when the spring is here and new hope is born for all,
Then like the birds and all things new I listen to His call.

For it is there, in every sound of spring, a message for mankind
If only we would stop and listen, a wealth of knowledge we would find,
And life would be so easy knowing that with all nature we are one,

Father, Mother, Sister, Brother, Daughter, Son.

Is it this spring He will return, the son of God who gave His life for us?
And, if He does, will he find that His words are just as dust?
For what a waste to suffer in vain if others do not see
That He is love, and all He wants is eternal life for all humanity.

So be like me and accept His love for you, and your life will richer be,
For, as He said in the Bible old, suffer little children to come unto me,
For as children we will always be until the truth is known,
Then, and only then, will we journey to that great Celestial Home.

--oOo--

Lonely Daffodil

Lonely daffodil, straight and tall,
A solitary figure on the garden wall,
Holding your golden trumpet with such pride,
Not for you your gift to hide.
The wind it pushes against your stem
Teasing and relentless, but like a true gem
You just bend a little to and fro
Like a haughty lady in a fashion show.
And, as we watch, we know we too
Are part of what you try to do,
Standing there so all alone,
A splash of colour against the stone.
With your golden glow and the strength you give,
You help us our lonely lives to live,
Showing our true colours wherever we happen to be,
Growing straight and tall for all eternity.

--oOo--

Let Go and Let God

When things seem more than you can bear
Just close your eyes and say a prayer
As god is waiting just to hear,
"Oh please help me, Father Dear!"

And as you accept His love for you
Your day will be as something new,
A radiance that is rare to find
With fresh new hope and peace of mind,

To know that someone really cares
If we ourselves our bodies tear.
For comfort in this world so mod,
Remember, Let Go and Let God.

For trust in Him is all we need
For our plan of friendship to succeed,
And when we say, "Oh please help me!"
We give ourselves implicitly.

--oOo--

Neglected Garden

Paths that once were weeded for grand ladies to gracefully tread,
Trails of honeysuckle just reaching overhead,
Magnolia blossoms reach out with arms of pride.
Not for them their true beauty to hide.

Little steps reaching up towards the summer house,
Now deserted except for the odd bird or field mouse.
No grand ladies seated there, except in my mind
I picture them
Enjoying the view, with long silken gowns and their hair embedded with a beautiful gem.

The moss covered steps leading down to the lily pool now covered with weeds.
No fishes swimming gently round or coyly hiding in the reeds,
And as the sun sweeps across the grassy bank my mind in a dream state goes,
Back to the days of plenty when the garden with pride did grow.

But now the weeds have taken over and you have to push your way
Through the bushes and grasses tall where the baby rabbits run and play.
And yet a beauty still remains. Each plant has its own sweet charm
Growing up amongst the thorns. It does not die for the want of man,

But goes on growing in a wilder state. No need for pruning or direction,
The sun and the rain is all it needs and the tall trees for protection,
Where underneath the branches the bluebells sway in the breeze
And the daffodils, with their gold trumpets, to pick them, they really do tease.

So, beautiful garden, your weeds I do not see,
Just the smell of your perfume and the hum of the bee,
The birds in the tree tops as they call to each other
And the sound of the little ones as they are fed by their mother.

The little seats, in a secluded spot where lovers used to sit
Gently kissing and holding hands, as the sun across their faces doth flit,
Perhaps not seeing the beauty around them, so in love and engrossed in each other.
Yet there will come a time when each will remember and, like a true lover,
Will wish once again the garden to tread and to feel the great peace that to them was once fed.

And so, beautiful garden, a lesson to me you have taught,
That you cannot stem such beautiful plants, such beauty can never be bought.

So, if we all struggle to reach the light, the brambles will have to give way,
And, like a true seed of God, you will blossom and grow, and you, in your turn, find your way.
So no need for your path to be tidy. Let the flowers in profusion lay,
And when "HE" returns to walk in His garden, what a glorious, glorious day!

--oOo--

Reflections

Reflections on the water of animals do I see,
And, as I stand still closer, a reflection there of me.
So near and yet so far, as I gaze so curiously
As the water gently flows and disturbs my fantasy.
Just like a dream that as you stretch to clasp
It fades away so quickly you don't have time to grasp.
So do not let the days go by without a goodly thought in view
Or you will find no true reflection waiting there for you.
For life is just for giving, and those whose gifts are free
Will one day reap a harvest of true Love and tranquillity.

--oOo--

Arboretum
A Botanical Garden Devoted to Trees

Trees of every description, trees of every hue,
Oak and ash, elm and pine, horse chestnut and yew.
Some from foreign parts where the weather is warm and fine,
Others from a cold place, all standing in a line.
Some tall, some small, wherein their beauty lies,
Each in its own splendour, a picture to the eyes.
For size does not really matter when you see such a grand array
As the tall trees are a background for the small ones lining the way.

How small one feels when walking beneath such stately boughs,
And you can see the tops of the pines reaching for the clouds.
For one can be alone with `God', our hearts to feel at peace,
And for awhile to be as one, and for ourselves a great release.
No sound to disturb the silence, except for an occasional breeze,
And then the branches will sway a little and a tinkle will come from the leaves,
Soothing in its whisper, a sound of peace and joy.
If only we would walk beneath the trees every day, no psychiatrist would we employ!

For just to relax and let one's self go for a while and forget the chores of the day
Is the finest healing a body can gain, without any pills or money to pay.
For it is within one's self we find our peace, if only we will look and obey,
And, like the trees in their glory, stand together, whether big or small, then we too will make a grand array.
For the trees are life-giving sources which we need to inhale and restore,
So you see what a lot they all give us, we cannot afford to ignore.
So if you cannot manage to visit the arboretum, just stand beneath a lovely old oak or elm,
And let your imagination run riot, and, like a ship, let the tree be your figurehead, to steer your way at the helm.

For the trees can teach us a lot as they stand so majestic and calm,
And, like a true mother, give you shelter, and in the wind a welcoming psalm.
Just lay your head on her trunk and you will feel like a child once again,
For you will find peace in her embrace and a great strength you will gain.

So let her be your figurehead, your ship in times of stress,
And she will guide and shelter you in the way that she knows best.
So plant your own tree to guide you so that you can watch it grow,

And then you will know of its blessings and the wonder of the seed that you sow.

--oOo--

Georgie My Budgie

Although you were so very small,
To you I gave my love, my all.
The day you came, too weak to stand,
I cushioned you against my hand.
The days rolled by, your strength you gained,
Your love of sleep began to wane,
And so with interest you would stare,
Your bell you rang as if to dare.

Each morning as my vacuum I start
A duet from you and me would impart,
Each trying to outdo the other,
Just like a child and his mother.

When in the evening my letters I write,
You fly around my pen. You bite,
Just teasing me like a child would,
Being naughty instead of good.
I taught you to say, "Hello Mummy."
My family thought you very funny,
A loving bird with mind so quick
You could do any kind of trick.
A whistle to outdo the rogue,
As through room I swept just like in Vogue,
As if you knew how to praise
A glamour girl in belt and stays.

"I love you Mummy," you would say.
To hear your words would make my day.
And to return from shopping spree
It was your "Hello Mummy" that greeted me.
Then came the day you were too ill
No chirpy bird to fly on sill.

THERE IS A REASON

Just sitting in your cage so blue
Not wanting anything to do. I lifted you out upon
my hand
You were too weak, you could not stand.
You snuggled up against my face
As if to give a last embrace.
And I know now it was goodbye
No more would you talk or fly.
No more would I call my own honey,
But I forgot to teach you "Goodbye Mummy".

--oOo--

To be a Bird

As a bird I would like to be
So I could fly from tree to tree
To watch the people passing by
With my ever watchful beady eye.
To listen to their footsteps as they walk the lonely lanes
All wrapped up with umbrellas low against the pouring rain.

No private sign to spoil my view
No human form to say, "How dare you!",
For I could go just where I please
The family cat for me to tease.
With a swaying gait, to walk the garden path
And near the rockery a pool to have my bath
And for me a garden treat when the housewife with her loving care
Has laid the bird table with luxuries to spare.

To tap my beak on a window pane
And if open to fly in and out again
To dip in the snow with the sun gleaming on it
To fly with the wind in playful frolic.
To be free, no ties, no strings, just dipping and wheeling,
From the hedgerows low, to the bright sky ceiling.

With wings spread out like a beautiful fan
Who could possibly want to be just a hu-man
Where signs and pictures always say

"PRIVATE, TRESPASSERS WILL BE PROSECUTED, CHILDREN MUST NOT PLAY"?
So to be able to fly alone and free
I would be a happy bird with all nature for company
And when I pass from this earth plane
To be as a bird is all I claim.

--oOo--

The Silent World

Little eyes that watch in earnest,
Lips that speak no sound,
Trying hard to get the gist
Of everything around.

Little hands expressing thought,
Expression so sincere,
Afraid of missing something bought
Because they do not hear.

Little present bought to please
For birthday treat in store,
With little friends and birthday tea.
Who could ask for more?

But as I watch and pray to God
Someday their treat will be,
To be as other children mod,
And shout with joy and glee.

To hear the sounds we take for granted,
The birds, the gurgling stream,
And know their hearts to be enchanted
Like in a fairy scene.

And so we thank our God above
For being as we are,
To speak and hear the words of love,
The greatest treat so far.

--oOo--

The Cuckoo

Why do I feel so sad when I hear your joyous
sound,
Bringing us good tidings of warm days that
abound?
Far away, and then so near,
Your haunting cry doth bring a tear.

Is it perhaps of a memory sweet
When your yearly visit was such a treat?
Or is it for a loved one who is no more
That stirs my heart when I hear your call?

Whatever the reason, I still like to hear
Your haunting cry bringing such cheer
As even an ache is good to feel
When we know it is for something real.

So Cuckoo, please keep up your trips
As little children with soft lips
Will imitate your distant call,
And one day, like me, will have memories to
recall.

--oOo--

Children Playing

Children playing, what a scene!
Mums and Dads, or so it seems.
Except for different words I hear
Then whose, is what, I greatly fear.

"Breakfast ready," calls the Mum
Pills on the table all girls have one
Just in case they make mistake
And for them a baby make.

Mum walking round with tummy high
Pretending to be with child, oh my!
What a game for little tots!
Surely we are silly clots.

As pride of parents will surely go
If we do not clean habits show
And teach our children to respect
The marriage vows instead of sex.

As in the end each one must pay
For wrongful deeds each single day
So think awhile dear children small
As life is given to test us all.

--oOo--

The Wild Snowdrop

At last the signs of spring are here
As little heads of white appear
Pushing through the soil so damp
Their glowing beauty like a lamp.
For they have come to lead the way
For God's; own rockery display.

Surrounded by their leaves so tall
Their droopy heads on chest doth fall
As if in prayer for their release
so that they in turn can give us peace.
For just to see their glowing face
Our grief and suffering will erase.

So thank you, Snowdrop, for your care,
And all the promise that you bear.
Our hearts are uplifted as though in song
Our day so gay, we skip along
As if freed from a prison cell
Our deeds and promises will excel.

--oOo--

Rain Rain Rain

The streets like Venice are afloat
No traffic can get through
If only we had little boats
With gondolier as crew.

Of what a difference to a day
Instead of moans and groans!
With people singing on their way
While cleaning out their homes.

With gaily painted sails ahoy
And messages so clear
To help the people to get by
And help reduce their fear.

For to be ready for life's storms
Is a battle partly won
Where helping hands and friendships form
And fear turned into fun.

And when at last the floods subside
And all is right again
Let us not our friendship slide
As there is much to gain.

--oOo--

The Glory That is God

To lose one's breath at the pure beauty that is God
To reach out with eager arms to enfold His love
To walk beneath the glorious trees and listen to His voice
To feel His presence all around you in the warmth and gentle kiss of the sun
And in the freshness of the morning dew as each new day begins
To see creatures wild all free as the air and the blackbird with gladness sings,
Brings tears of joy and an emotion that is new
And yet, oh no! this must be what `The Christ' tried to tell you
Of a love far beyond one's thinking, of giving and being as one,
Helping and serving, sharing our joy and our pain
And knowing that one day we each in our turn, a reward we will gain
And find our true selves with a love so strong and so great
That we will walk in His image. What a glorious fate
To know one's self and each other with no secrets to hide
And then with our Father and Maker we will always abide.
So do not tarry too long on the way
Look and listen, and start your journey today.

--oOo--

To Be Satisfied

Isn't life a bore! The same things day after day.
What would we like to do if we had our way?
To travel the world the marvellous sights to see,
To be a Prince or Princess in a fairy tale, is that what we would like to be?
To have lots of money and plenty of good things to eat,
To have lots of parties and famous people to meet,
To explore unknown parts and have a Sir, or Lady, added to our name,
To be covered in jewels like some silly game.
But, like all things, we each have a time limit to play,
And if we think about it, it could not be done any other way.
For to be good at our job it must be done again and again
So that perfection is what we will gain.
So just when you are thinking, "Oh not the same old job!",
Remember your worth and sing a song not a sob.
For if we all chased moonbeams and had no anchor to drop,
Life would become so boring and our dreams just a flop
As we all need inspiration and a mind that explores
To discover ourselves and become a just cause.

--oOo--

Life's Bank Account

When life has had its way with you and lessons you have learnt
Then you will be a different you when all the sin is burnt
And you have only been a little singed so that you could take account
Of What this life was meant for and gain your own discount.
Then you will know that your tears have been a credit,
Your balance duly signed,
For now the tears have washed away the dirt
And you are no longer blind.
You see the world in a different way, your step will be more sprightly,
Your laughter like a sunshine ray, your eyes gleaming so brightly.
Like searchlights searching dark-lit skies,
You too have searched and found your goal,
For now that you can stand alone
A cheque you can write to claim your soul.
For to know one's self and to have found the truth
Is a blessing truly gained,
For now you stand in God's own eyes
A picture gladly framed.

--oOo--

A Child's Fear

Whenever I see a firework display
My mind returns to a bygone day
When friends and relations were gathered to see
A beautiful bonfire with fireworks and tea.

But as I stood and looked around
I felt a fear, my heart did pound,
For no sister could I see with friends,
And no one knew or did pretend.

The night was dark and very cold.
A tramp who looked so very old
Was standing just outside the glow,
As if afraid that we were foe.

I felt that there was something wrong
By certain words amongst the throng,
And when the fire began to wane
I felt as though I were insane.

And then the tramp spoke just one word,
My name, of course, it was I heard.
I realised it was just for fun
My sister had dressed up to come.

But never will I forget the fear
At the thought of losing someone dear,
And never will I joke the same
To cause such misery and pain.

--oOo--

The Sailing Ship

Like a dainty lady on a lake of ice
With sails a billow as if to entice
The wanderer who seeks to find
That summer sun and peace of mind.

The water shimmering like ladies' frills
Surrounded by the distant hills
Beckoning all who want to roam
And leave behind their friends and home.

So just for a while we look and dream
Of ports and countries we have never seen
Of coloured folks in native dress
Where birds of Paradise still rest.

Where animals of different kinds
Still roam and are free, no cage to bind.
A perfect place for man and beast
To work and play, love and feast.

For in reality we know
On sailing ship we will not go
But with minds refreshed and thoughts so free
To home we return our loved ones to see,

Hoping that one day our dreams will come true
When all will be united and the sun will shine
through
For all to be free and loving so great
With no more suffering, killing or hate.

--oOo--

The Hunt (Part One)

The scarlet colours of the jackets gay
Jaunty caps at angle lay
Black boots shining, crops at hand,
Horses restless where they stand.

Ladies, haughty, seated proud,
Smiling, laughing, talking loud,
A glass of wine they do partake
Before they ride with fox as bait.

The huntsman with his horn so gay
Standing amidst the hounds at bay,
Shouting, calling each one by name
As restless they are for the game.

The crowd just watching, standing still,
The gay display their hearts to fill
Wishing that they too could be
A part of all the pageantry.

The time has come for them to start
And through the fields they quickly dart,
Hounds all eager for the chase
Runners trying to beat the pace.

Through the woods and vales they pry
The huntsman's horn like a battle cry,
Showman jumping hedge and stile
As on they ride for many a mile.

Then through the trees a creature bold

THERE IS A REASON

With tempting brush of burning gold,
A prize for anyone to claim
Who dares to put their soul to shame.

The hounds excited start to bay
Confusion spoils their grand array,
Each one rushing to be first
To satisfy their lust and thirst.

But the little fox has gone to ground
Into an old drain pipe he found
A disappointment for the chase
As all their antics must erase.

So the riders in a circle stand
A happy, laughing, little band,
Without a thought for a creature dear
Who now is hiding wrought with fear.

--oOo--

The Hunt (Part Two)

Then into the drain a dog is sent
To drive out the fox whose strength is spent
And when at last it does appear
The crowd just gives a lusty cheer.

But for the fox my heart doth bleed
As in a flash the hounds take heed
And without more ado
The living frame is torn in two.

And as the blood fell on the ground
The people in a circle found
No pity for its anguished pain
As golden prize they cut from frame.

And with the blooded brush a face they mar
That will forever leave a scar
For God to see and contemplate
Upon their punishment and fate.

For it is easy for a crowd to win
When their victim is such a little thing,
But it takes Love and Courage to do God's will
And to help all creatures, instead of kill.

--oOo--

The Thought of Being Afraid

When I was oh so very small
My fears were oh so great,
Of puppy dogs and garden walls,
And the swinging of the gate.

And then to school I lonely went,
My fears were sevenfold,
To play with other children bent
On making me their goad.

Each day would seem a lifetime
As I struggled to attain
The knowledge that would help mankind
A better world to claim.

And when my schooling days were through
Once more I stood alone
Afraid to start on something new
And leave my much loved home.

And then a friend gave me some hope
By quoting me a rhyme,
And now I know I was a dope
For such a long, long time.

Now life for me has just begun
As now I know the toll
That expecting trouble from someone
Made me a frightened soul.

And to all who have their fears inlaid
Let me a lesson give,

That it is only the thought of being afraid
That spoils the life we live.

--oOo--

My Neighbour

Peeping from my window what do I see?
A gift left by my neighbour, a generous soul is she
For, although she has a husband and a family of four,
There is always enough heart for helping just one more.
Spring, summer, autumn, winter, no difference does it make,
I know there is one good true friend my troubles I can take.

For true friendship is a lasting thing that goes on and on forever,
A bond that nothing in this whole wide world can sever.
I do not think she even knows how much her root of kindness sows,
For it is easy when one is rich to give
But when one is not what a lovely way to live.

Loving and sharing, each little thing we do
Will make each cloudy day not quite so glum and blue.
We do not need the sun to shine to feel all warm and gay,
Just a little friendly smile to gladden each new day.
So please remember, it does not cost a fee
To have, and to be a neighbour, just like the one next door to me.

--oOo--

A Family Scene

I watch with awe a family scene
With eyes so full of wonder
For Dad is bathing baby Jean
With squeals and roars like thunder.

Pretending ships to navigate
While tankers rest in shore
Oh, what a noise two people make
When having fun galore!

Then babe is taken out and dried
And powdered just like Mum
And Dad is filled with family pride
As round neck her arms are flung.

Little bottom smeared with cream
And napkin safe and firm
No need for babe to shout and scream
As from Dad she will quickly learn

That she must do as she is told
To be a better girl
And not to cry for toy to hold
When hair is brushed in curl.

And looking on I realise
How much that I have missed,
No Dad to teach me when, or how,
Or to be loved and kissed.

And so with envy I admire
Each home that has a Dad,

So when your needs are really dire
Of his great strength you're glad.

--oOo--

The Loch Ness Monster

Oh Nessie! Lower your slender head
And keep them in suspense
For when they know
That you are foe
There will be no recompense.

So keep your secret one more year
Until the fever dies
Then you can reach
Up to the beach
And see the clear blue skies.

For when they know just what you are
There will be no further rest
They will hunt you down
Till you are found
For they think they know best.

--oOo--

The Glorious, Glorious Spring

The winter has been so long this year,
The sun too coy to linger near,
The damp and fog a disheartening foe
That saps our energy and glow.
How long have I waited for spring to appear!
It seems like ages instead of a year.

But now the spring is here at last,
The sun a friend in which we bask.
The birds they sing with joyous intent
As they fly in pairs their minds on courtship bent.
Just to hear and see their antics gay
Has made it such a lovely day.

The lambs so newly born and frail
Following mum up hill and down dale,
Running, jumping, enjoying life to the full,
And, when tired and sleepy, to snuggle against mum's warm wool.
For life so newly born and weak
Mum is the love and shelter that they seek.

The snowdrops pushing through the soil,
So clean and fresh for all their toil
As they push through the soil of clay
Not one small leaf is bent or frayed
As with new life they lead the way
For all the springtime flowers display.

The fields all fresh with a luscious hue,
A carpet of green for the wild life to chew.

The streams a gurgle with hope and glee
Where the moorhens swim swiftly and furtively.
The trees no longer gaunt and bare
As mother nature shows her care.

Even the people start to smile
As the joy of spring makes them less guile.
Everywhere is new life and hope,
Thrilling, throbbing, joyous scope
As once again life is reborn
On this very glorious springtime morn.

So once again to us has been proved
That all our fears may be removed,
And a promise that was to us once made
That all our faith will be repaid
If only we will look and take heed
That we are all a part of God's own precious seed.

--oOo--

A Scientist's Love

Little eyes of cats you sew
So that the wonders of this world they will not know.
The movement of the long sweet grass
The little creatures that sweep pass.
The furry prey, to stalk and play,
To frolic in the new mown hay,
Their eyes alight on mischief bent
Or wide-eyed curiosity intent.
How can you say you love such charm?
When all you do is cause them harm.
To take away God's previous gift
Will surely be your biggest rift
From all the glories of mankind
For all the suffering you leave behind
As your kind of love is hard to understand
For all you want to do is brand.
And as you say their eyes like human's are,
How can you say their pain is not a par?
I say, you do not love at all
God's own sweet creatures who trust us all.

--oOo--

JOYCE M KIDMAN

The Hungry Seagull

From rock to sea your journey takes
Your easy flight no noise you make.
With wings spread out like Chinese fan
Your head bent low with eyes ascan,
Seeing every minute thing
From tiny fish to discarded tin.
You make a noise just like a sigh
As you descend nearer to spy.

You call to friends who soon appear
Who circle round and round to leer
At picnickers upon the cliff
Hoping for aperitif.
But when you get no tiny snack
You fly away with mournful quack
As if to show your strong distaste
Of beauty spoilt by human race.

Your cries of disapproval last
Until your tiny forms are past
As from a rock way out at sea
You sit and ponder patiently
And wonder where the fish have gone
That you should have to look anon
And cry for memories so sweet
When seas were clean with food to eat.

But now with sewerage there afloat
And oil patches from tankers float
The birds are doomed right from the start
As mind and soul this world they part.
I only hope it will not be too late

THERE IS A REASON

For something to be done to elevate
The beauty marred by human hands
And to be restored for future plans.

--oOo--

The Oblivious Mind

Little body, soft and warm,
No more the sky will you adorn,
No more to flutter here and there
With chirpy song to fill the air.
Your little frame, so small and still,
A trickle of blood the earth cracks fill.

My heart is sad to know the cost
Of a life so precious that is lost,
Of a daily song that is no more
Of which we all must pay the score.
Such needless killing, just for fun.
Oh God! Forgive this guilty one.

For as a child who does not know
How can his heart be touched with woe?
So all parents please a ruling make
That life is given not to take,
And if a rifle you must give
Then with your conscience you must live.

--oOo--

True Love

True love is like a snowflake, white and pure,
Exceeding all other powers of greatness, a gift for you to store
And keep within your heart letting other people share
When in your time of greatness to help them their pain to bear.
For then the snowflake will become a snowball of goodwill
And can be thrown to one and all so that from it the snowflakes spill.
So do not let them melt away. Gather them into your heart,
Then you in turn can build a snowball and from yourself impart.

--oOo--

Georgie My Budgie

To lose a pet is hard to bear, your heart is sad and mellow,
No more to play and jokingly say, "You are a clever little fellow".
No more to hear your chirpy sound, especially when the baby is asleep,
No more to say, "Hush! Hush! No noise!", as you yourself are asleep
And have gone to rest in God's own care where all your friends are waiting.
So now you can talk to your heart's content. I hope a good picture of me you are painting,
And when the day comes that we will meet again your friends will know I am she
Who loved and adored my beautiful pet, Georgie, my own little budgie.

--oOo--

True Love

She does not have a face of beauty to all the world at large,
She does not have a figure that to your account can charge.
Her legs are slim and swift like the deer as she hurries on her way,
But her eyes is where her beauty lies as she smiles and bids you good day.

To feel for others when they are in pain,
To give a shaft of sunlight as in the darkness they wane,
To give a helping hand when all seems so hopeless and lost,
Then, and only then, can you begin to count the cost.

For a heart that is full and overflowing for all of God's creation
That for herself she does not cry for gifts and admiration
When you have found a girl like this who does return your love
Then you will have found that heavenly gift your very own true love.

For you will know without a doubt no hurt will she induce.
Your days will be of sunshine, no need to make a truce
For your pain is her pain, your joy so gladly shared,

And, when her arms are tightly round you, you will be glad she cared.

--oOo--

Time

When time is short and there is so much to say
Do not waste a moment on useless words and play
As this life is such a short span so make the most of it
Do and be so generous that you will benefit.
For hurtful words and cruel deeds are just a waste of time
And when two people are apart a broken heart you'll find
So if you only have an hour out of every single day
Just be kind and you will find a peace while you're away
You only need a little time so make the most of it
Then happiness you both will find and all will benefit.

--oOo--

The Whispering Tree

Why are you whispering so softly dear tree?
Is it because you are thinking of me?
Trying my deepest thoughts not to disturb
As I sit in my chair with eyes that are blurred.

The rustle you make as the wind gentle blows
Is like a caress to soothe all my woes,
And, as I listen, I feel a great peace
As though you're a friend sent to me on a lease.

I wish I could hear all the things that you say
For I am sure you are trying to show me the way,
As with a gentle shake and a mournful cry
You are trying to say, "Don't cry, don't cry".

--oOo--

A Forest Scene

A shady glade, a forest stream,
A sturdy trunk on which to lean,
The glorious colours of the leaves
As the sun just filters through the trees.
A bank to sit and think awhile
Doth ease my pain, brings back my smile.
The peace is there for all to see
A place for God to visit me.
And so I thank you forest free
For all the joy you bring to me.

--oOo--

Little Friend

Little friend my prayers I say
To make life easier for you today.
And if you should feel any fear
Just close your eyes for God is near,
Watching and waiting through all your pain,
To see if you your faith will abstain.
For God is love to all mankind
But we ourselves must true finality find,
And when at last you do win through
Then god Himself to you will prove
And lift you in His arms to bless.
Then you will have found true happiness.

--oOo--

Coventry Cathedral

Your height and beauty doth impress
Your workmanship a dream
Where visitors will come to rest
And pray to God supreme.
All colours of the nations
Will meet and pray as one
And the God of all creation
Whose work is never done
Will hear their cries of sheer despair
And suffering so great
That he will give them peace of mind
And love instead of hate.
So full marks for your cathedral
Where god's children are as one
And the eyes of our dear Saviour
Will smile and say, "Well done!".

--oOo--

Smudge My Daughter's Cat

I took you in and gave you a home against my will and judgement
But through the years my love has grown and now I know what being one meant.
It took a long time to gain your trust, your antics drove me wild,
Your fear of everything unknown was just like a little child.
With patience, love and kindness I won your respect and love
And god who is Father of all things sent His blessing from above.
And like the furniture that you climbed you climbed into my heart,
No more to rush away from me and outside quickly dart.
The day you jumped upon my knee my heart was overflowing
And with such trust you looked at me with eyes so very knowing
But now my little one you are gone from me I miss those glorious eyes
So full of love and gratitude, so very worldly wise.
But as the days go by I know that we will meet again
As love of each other we both so willingly gave, our lasting life we will gain.

--oOo--

Swallow Falls

A beauty that surpasses all
A sound that is a deafening roar
A time to stand, to think, to dream,
A place so cool, no sun to gleam.

Like lace protruding from a loom
Ever falling from noon to noon
A pattern so intricate in design
Reminds one of a by-gone time.

And as we watch such strength and power
Such beauty doth our minds devour
As time stands still, just for a while,
Like the broken hand of an old sundial.

And as we leave with great regret
We feel like butterfly caught in net
As we struggle to regain our thoughts
To leave such peace that can't be bought.

And as we make our way back home
We realise it is good to roam
To know that in our race for power
Ourselves we lose inside our tower.

--oOo--

A Picture on a Wall

An avenue of trees, a lake so clear and blue,
A cornfield in the distance with such a golden hue.
The sky with just a shade of pink, a soft glowing touch so warm
With just an occasional soft white cloud the glory to adorn.
And although it is a picture that hangs upon a wall
In my dreams I walk the woodland path and feel the glory of it all,
The trees so tall and stately, their grandeur a pleasure to see,
And the lake just like a mirror where the shadows creep so stealthily.
So from my chair I have a view that fills me with delight
For the artist with his brush and skill has given me a clear insight.

--oOo--

A Mother's Prayer

Oh daughter, if thou were but young again
That I could love and soothe away your pain!
A sweet or two to stop your tears,
A mother's love to stem your fears.

But now you are a woman grown
No longer do you live at home,
Too big to lift and kiss away
The hurts that you receive each day.

Your eyes they look such sad appeal
I know exactly how you feel.
Your troubles to me you can confide
But you yourself must a solution find.

And so I pray to God above
That He will guide you with His love,
So that I may see a laughing face
To go with that loving heart I know you grace.

--oOo--

Glory Glory Halleluiah!

The glorious trees in their autumn parade
Aglow on the hilltops and in the glade
Shimmering dresses of red, brown, yellow and gold,
Their beauty reaching out for you to enfold.
The breeze like sweet music as it tinkles the leaves,
Sweeping them into bundles as they fall from the trees.

GLORY GLORY HALLELUIAH

The sun's golden rays shining through the branches so gay
God's torch of light to brighten the day
The warmth of it reaching a heart that is cold
And for a moment it melts as the heat takes a hold
And makes one realise that pain is not for ever
And so not for us our bodies to sever.

GLORY GLORY HALLELUIAH

And so on the hilltops God's mountain of peace
Just send out your thoughts for a moment's release.
Just be quiet and take in all the beauty around
From the sunlit blue sky to the lush green velvet ground.
Listen to the birds as they sing and rejoice
And you will find comfort and join in with fine voice

GLORY GLORY HALLELUIAH

For to include yourself with everything else around
A love that is spiritual you will have found
So your heart will beat faster you will become breathless with delight
Your arms will reach out to embrace all in sight.
Oh dear God, to have been blind for so many years!
Take me! Love me! And dry all my tears!

GLORY GLORY HALLELUIAH

--oOo--

How do you know
If you don't know.

--oOo--

It's not the light that shines without
It's the light that shines within.

--oOo--

It's not the evil you see in the world
It's the evil that you don't see.

--oOo--

It's not the good that you want God to see that matters

It's the good that he does see.

--oOo--

It's not what you say
It's what you don't say.

--oOo--

It's not what you show
It's what you don't show.

--oOo--

On the debris of our despair
Our characters are born.

--oOo--

All my poems are easy for everyone to read, so that when the time comes for us to leave this school of learning no one can say, "I did not understand". There are no difficult proverbs to decipher, just simple words in story and poem form. And for everything we experience there is a reason.

CHAPTER 79

THE END STORY

From Nichola

A year has passed without our Neil. We do not want to go on. We do not eat or sleep. I had a mole come on my lip, Mum said 'Go to the doctor's'. He said he did not think it was cancer, but he would write to the Hospital to have it removed. Christmas eve, a rash on my left leg and bottom appeared. The doctor arrived and said I had shingles. I was in bed for 6 weeks, the pain was horrendous. Dear Mum looked after me, I didn't speak, only to say thank you when she brought me tea. It must have been such worry for Mum.

One morning, a letter from the hospital came with the post. They would have it removed. So off we went. I drove us there, feeling very ill, but Mum was with me comforting me. We sat in the waiting room, when in walked a prisoner in handcuffs with two policemen. It was too much for my Mum, she started to laugh, which started me off. The prisoner joined in the laughter, he said he couldn't stop. We started to talk about Neil, the nurse called me in. We said goodbye to the young man. When we came out, we wanted the loo. In our hurry, went into the gents by mistake. A man in there told us we made his day, we rushed out quicker than we went in. We had a good laugh about it after.

Just then, the prisoner came out. He was getting into a taxi. He said look after each other, you both did all you could for Neil. Mum said God Bless you.

It was now February, Neil's birthday. We went back where we had laid Neil to rest. When we went there last time, it was so overgrown, we had to fight our way up the steps. As usual, my mum was right. It had all been cleared away. A sad day, we are lost without our Brave Heart, our special nickname for Neil.

We go out when we have to. When we are in, we want to be out, and vice versa. We are broken hearted but we must go on.

I was at the hairdresser's. I looked in the mirror. I saw Neil, Dad, Ruffles. They looked so happy. They changed into birds and flew away over fields. I didn't understand, then I remembered they used to go to that special field for walks.

A few nights later after, I turned in bed, Neil was laying beside me. I looked into his lovely face, it gave me a lot of comfort.

A few months later, Mum's friend June rang up from Oldham. She said: 'I have a young man with me. He's very excited. He's got a message for you. Thank you for making me so strong. It was easy to pass over for him. Tell them I'm wearing my red brocade waistcoat.' I knew it was my Neil as I recognised the waistcoat.

A few weeks later, June rang again. She said Neil was back, to tell us he was well and happy. He said to tell them: 'I'm now wearing a T-shirt, jeans and my white trainers.' We cried because he loved his T-shirts. He could not wear jeans because it was so uncomfortable in the wheelchair. The white trainers we had bought in Florida. He had to stop wearing them because his little feet were twisted inward. We were so glad to know that he was well and happy and able to wear the cloths he loved. He said someone told him he would walk in 1999. And so it came true. Neil gave us both enough love to last a lifetime. He was pure, gentle, kind and loving. He never had a bad bone in his body. He was our soul-mate. Now he was with our Lord, Grandpa and Ruffles.

We are now looking at houses. Our house is for sale, we would like to move to the country, back to our roots. We were not able to move, but looking passes the time. We went to look at a house in Bearlands, and Wotton-Under-Edge. We saw a nice house, but not quite what we wanted. As we were leaving, Mum pointed to a house. 'I would like that one, with a bow window.' As we drove home, perhaps we would not like to live on an estate. A few days later, I took our house off the market, but Mum said we could still look around.

One morning, as I came into her bedroom with a cup of tea, she told me she had a stroke. I called the doctor, who came straight away. He assured us she didn't suffer from a stroke, but suggested she should have tests at the hospital.

A few weeks later, I was combing my Mum's hair in her bedroom, when lightning struck me. It went through my body. My Mum grabbed my hand saying: 'I will take it from you.' It passed from me to Mum and out of the window. No-one else saw lightning that day. A very strange happening!

A few months have passed, she has not come down to breakfast. I called several times, no answer. I rushed upstairs. Mum could not speak, when she did it was very slurred. Her pretty face was twisted to one side. I gave Mum healing, then rang the doctor. By the time he arrived, her face was normal. Again, he didn't think she had a stroke. He didn't see her before the healing, but I was sure he would not believe me, so decided not to tell him about it. He went by what I said, and we took her to hospital for tests immediately. They kept her in for a week. A lot of in-patients were dying of a virus. I was so concerned for her that I took it on to myself to discharge her. The doctor then told me he thought she wouldn't have lasted long in hospital. Within a week, she looked a lot better. Hair done, painted nails and lots of love. The doctor was most impressed with her health. We went to hospital for more tests. At that time, I was told she only had two years to live. She had had multiple strokes and a heart attack.

My mother was a strong, kind and loving woman with a heart of gold. She always worried about the world, especially the little children. I always called her the mother of mothers. She was the best in the world to me. Mum took care of me as a baby and as a grown woman. It was now my turn to care for her. Mum tried to go on with everyday life, to make the most of every day. She couldn't talk very much anymore, but I was just glad to have her with me. I so miss her singing. She always sang whenever happy or sad. She tried to carry on, but she had lost so much. Her dear husband, and now her beloved Neil. We both had broken hearts.

My cousin Pauline rang to say she had not seen us for 2 years. It didn't seem that long, so we talked on the phone now and then. Mum can't be left on her own, in case she falls down the stairs. She would not know where I was, so I always had to take her with me wherever I was going. My friend and neighbour Yvonne does all our shopping for us.

It's Christmas again. Pauline rings to ask us round for Christmas diner. I said we would come if Mum was not too ill. We did go for diner, Mum had a nice day and ate everything, and even 2 helpings of apple pie and custard. We stayed until late afternoon and then made our way home. We have now started to go out in the car for something to do pass the time.

Before we look again, it's another Christmas. Mum is worse. I have to wash and dress her. She was always shy, but I said I would not look. I said: 'We all look the same. And I don't mind because I love you.' Dawn and Steve came to see us. Steve said: 'Don't you look beautiful Joyce!' And she did.

Then Mum had a very bad night. She was crying. She said she was feeling useless. I said: 'I still need you Mum. We will get through this.' That night I slept with her. I rang the doctor and he came straight out. Once again, he looked at my mum and said: 'You look lovely Joyce.' Mum said he was a lovely doctor, because he had a disable son himself. As he left, he turned round to me and said: 'I know you will take care of her.'

New Year's Eve. Mum is incapable of speech. She's not well. Her voice seemed a long way away. Eight o'clock, I said I would ring the doctor. Mum said: 'He can't help me. I'll be alright.' I carried her to the lift and put her into bed. I rang an ambulance, but she was not with me, she was fading fast. The ambulance arrived and rushed us to hospital, me holding her lovely hand. She hand beautiful hands and long lovely nails. I had been looking after them like she used to. When we were in A&E, the doctor said that she could hear me. I told her that I would love her forever. My dear mother passed away that night, midnight 31st December 2002 in Southmead hospital. As I came back into the room after they laid her out, she turned towards me as if to speak, I said: 'It's alright mum, I know you love me. I'll try to be strong like you.' All the bells rang out, and fireworks. When I looked up at the nurses and doctors, all were crying. The doctor said she went out with a bang. A fitting end for someone like my Mum. She was always a quiet person. There would be great joy when gets to the other side. She will then be whole again. And will see her husband, grandson and mother again. About 2pm, the nurse rang Pauline who said: 'Don't let her go home, she must come to me.'

So here I am in a taxi in the dark, driving on the motorway to Pauline's house. I can't remember the ride, nor getting there. I feel numb. I found out later that the hospital paid for the taxi. It was so kind of them. The doctors and nurses were wonderful.

A few months later, I haven't seen our toad yet this year. He's normally in the flowerpot by the door. Perhaps he's passed away too.

I have lost my Mum, my best friend. I cannot eat or sleep. Gone thin again, don't care. Six months have gone past, I have put the house back on the market. I'm looking at houses, there quite nice, but not for me.

I think I found a house. Then my cousin Ann rang from Liverpool. She said she can see a house on a hill, and at the back are fields going downwards, with beautiful views all round. A few weeks later, I go for a ride down to Bearland, feeling sad. I see a house for sale and ring to view. I fetch Pauline, we looked around and I fell in love with the house. I walked out onto the patio and sat there was a baby toad. I knew this was an omen to me to buy the house. I rang the estate agent straight away and put in an offer. I sold my house a few weeks later. My Mum came to me last night, she held out her arms to me. I rushed out of bed. I was so excited, but she was already gone. That was wonderful to me for Mum to come to me so soon after her passing.

The offer was taken on the house, so things were moving. All I had to do was pack.

Roy and Pauline came to put a floor where the lift had been. It took a few weeks for them to get it tidy again. What would I do without them? They are like brother and sister to me. Pauline would bring me flowers and diners on plate for the 3 of us. And when she didn't cook, Roy would go to the Fish & Chips shop. They make me laugh a lot and tease me for my constant talking. Pauline showed me how to make me a cup of tea the way they liked it! That was a laugh to them.

Last day in the house. So many memories. The Neighbours come to say goodbye and bring gifts for the new house. So off I go with my memories.

I arrived at the new house, Christine is waiting for me. It's raining hard, but Christine takes over, making tea, handing out biscuits. Alan, Christine's boyfriend, arrives to help. New neighbours came to welcome me the next day, gave me a card and a bottle of wine. Previous neighbours had left a card a bottle of wine, so very kind of them.

My new neighbours are wonderful, they help all they can, putting censor lights, 3 in total. They also put in a phone upstairs for me. They all help one-another here. I think I'm in heaven. The views from every window are breathtaking. A gate into the fields at the back of my house. I wish my loved ones could be here. But I know they are, they will never leave. We will meet again, never to part.

Then I remembered what Ann had said about this house, it was just how she had told me. Mum had chosen this house a long time ago. She also sent the toad so that I would remember the old toad was young again, like we all become when we pass over to God.

And the lessons that I have learnt, is to love and to look after each other, and to do God's work the way that it was planned. 'till we meet again, amen.

Printed in Poland
by Amazon Fulfillment
Poland Sp. z o.o., Wrocław

60231283R00304